TWENTY ADVERTISING CASE HISTORIES

Edited and introduced by

Simon Broadbent

HOLT, RINEHART AND WINSTON

LONDON . NEW YORK . SYDNEY . TORONTO

Holt, Rinehart and Winston Ltd: 1 St Anne's Road,
Eastbourne, East Sussex BN21 3UN

British Library Cataloguing in Publication Data

Twenty advertising case histories.
  1. Advertising—Case studies
  I. Broadbent, Simon
  659.1′0722   H5827

ISBN: 0-03-910543-1

Typeset, printed and bound in Great Britain by Butler & Tanner Ltd, Frome and London

Last digit is print no: 9 8 7 6 5 4 3 2

Contents

Preface

This book contains twenty case histories about advertising campaigns. They are chosen from the best papers submitted for the Institute of Practitioners in Advertising Advertising Effectiveness Awards, 1980 and 1982 and published in hardback under the titles *Advertising Works* and *Advertising Works 2* by Holt, Rinehart and Winston. The authors describe the decisions taken by the manufacturer and the advertising agency. These start at the business background and end with campaign evaluation. In the introduction I outline the typical steps taken in making decisions.

The collection should help teachers and students, including trainees in marketing and advertising companies, and those already doing the work who realize that they can learn from others. People taking courses in business studies, marketing and advertising will find the examples particularly useful. These include students in CAM courses (Communication Advertising and Marketing Education Foundation Limited).

Acknowledgements

I am grateful to the following whose comments and ideas have encouraged the publishers and the Institute of Practitioners in Advertising to produce this volume, and helped me to write the introduction.

Professor M. J. Baker, Dept of Marketing, University of Strathclyde

J. C. Clarke, Senior Lecturer in Marketing, The Polytechnic, Wolverhampton

K. Crosier, Lecturer, Dept of Marketing, University of Strathclyde

D. S. R. Foard, Director, West London Business School

G. J. Goodhardt, Sir John E. Cohen, Professor of Consumer Studies, The City University Business School

L. W. Hardy, Senior Lecturer – Marketing, Dept of Business and Administrative Studies, The Polytechnic of Wales (Politechnig Cymru)

N. A. Hart, Director, the CAM Foundation

R. W. Lawson, Lecturer, Division of Economic Studies, University of Sheffield

D. Thurley, Lecturer, Department of Business Studies, Middlesex Polytechnic

K. Simmonds, Professor of Marketing and International Business, London Business School

J. D. Waterworth, Professor of Marketing, University of Warwick

G. Wills, Principal, The Management Centre from Buckingham

Introduction

SOURCE OF THE CASE HISTORIES

In 1980 and again in 1982 the Institute of Practitioners in Advertising ran a competition. Entrants had to submit papers describing an advertising campaign and how it was evaluated. 130 papers were submitted. The best were given awards and commendations. Thirty-six of these have been published in hardback by Holt, Rinehart and Winston under the titles *Advertising Works* (1981) and *Advertising Works 2* (1983). The twenty case histories here have been chosen from these thirty-six. More details of the scheme, and general comments on campaign evaluation, may be found in these volumes as well as sixteen more case histories.

The source used has some advantages and some disadvantages for students.

The main claim for the case histories is that they are real. The products and services are those you can go out and see for yourself. They give us the opportunity to be a fly on the wall in the decision-taking which actually went on in real life. We see the actual problems faced in making marketing decisions, and in creating and judging advertising.

Because of the prestige attached to winning an Advertising Effectiveness Award, and because the value of the prizes was significant, the scheme attracted a large number of papers of high quality and unusual frankness. The papers were written to convince a panel of professional judges who were intolerant of loose thinking or overclaiming. This collection is in fact unique and the Institute is proud to have made it available.

Incidentally, the papers give a good impression of the variety of advertising. Half the examples here are launches of new products; half are about the maintenance or relaunch of existing products. The selection was made to demonstrate the range of tasks advertising can tackle as well as of evaluation techniques.

So we see fast-moving packaged goods like a margarine, a shampoo, a beer. There are services like an estate agency and a holiday company. The advertisers range from major international companies to small businesses, from profit-seeking entrepreneurs to public service.

The disadvantages are three.

First, these are all success stories, intended to show advertising as a sales-effective, and often profitable, part of the marketing mix. The student should not be led to think that every campaign is effective and worthwhile. There are no examples of failure, though it is as important to diagnose and to learn from disaster as it is from success.

Second, the competition emphasized the evaluation of advertising in the field and in all cases the results of the campaigns were carefully measured. While essential to show what happened, this does exaggerate the part evaluation normally plays. It is not always as prominent as it is here.

Nor were the papers written as case studies. They were not structured to test the student's ability to analyse, diagnose, propose action or argue an alternative approach. They do not explicitly teach general rules (if there are any!). The principles involved have to be deduced by the reader. However, the questions asked below in the 'Guide to Using the Cases' are intended to correct this. Conscientiously used, the examples give many opportunities to practise the skills of marketing and advertising, as well as to absorb what practitioners do.

MANAGING ADVERTISING

The papers cover the whole process of advertising. The same words may not always be used, or the same structure, but the steps are essentially as follows.

Business background

The manufacturers review their market and their product (or their planned product) and decide to involve an advertising agency. The business decisions are made: investment in plant, raw material, labour, distribution and so on. The return expected depends on the pricing and promotion decisions and resultant sales.

Marketing objectives

The manufacturers, often with their agency, agree how sales targets are to be met, who they will sell to, why they should expect this share of market, how the brand is to be positioned, packaged and so on.

Advertising objectives

These predict how advertising will inform and influence the target and how it will play its part, among other marketing tools, in helping to meet the marketing objectives. Budget and timing constraints are laid down.

Campaign

The description of the advertising agency's work breaks broadly into creative and media. The first is about the advertisements themselves; the second is about planning and buying for them time on television, radio and cinema, or space in press, posters, direct mail and so on.

The creative work starts with a brief: the idea or message that the advertisements are to carry to meet the advertising objectives. Then creative development research helps to guide the choice between one execution and another, or to improve details in an execution. Finally, the advertising is executed: film or photographs are shot, copy set and so on.

At the same time the medium has been chosen and a media plan drawn up. Negotiations with media owners are completed.

Post-campaign evaluation

After the advertisements have appeared we know exactly what has been spent. We have adequate measures of the amount our targets have been exposed to the advertising.

We also know what the manufacturer sold to wholesalers and retailers. We have reasonable figures from audits and surveys on who bought from the retailers, what they paid, how the product was used and so on.

We usually have similar information on any competitive media activity and consumer sales. We get this from the same industry and syndicated services.

This can help us assess what our advertising achieved – and we can ourselves try to work out if we did so profitably. That is, have we finished the campaign better off than had we not advertised?

In these examples, the campaign was often planned so that evaluation was possible. Deliberate experiments or additional measures – and certainly extra, critical thinking – played an unusually prominent role. The authors have tried their best to explain not only what happened, but how, in their opinion, these results were obtained.

Thus, the intentions in the marketing and advertising objectives are compared with achievements. In the real world, the next series of planning and execution starts on a sounder footing. But we do not follow through as far as this; we see usually only a single cycle.

GUIDE TO USING THE CASES

This section is not intended as a full description of how to use case studies. It gives a few key ideas and some suggestions specific to this collection. Also see, among other guides, Geoff Easton's *Learning from Case Studies* (Prentice Hall, 1982). He points out that 'The central function of the case method is to teach students to solve complex unstructured problems. There is no analytical technique or approach which can solve these kinds of problems. Some can help, but in the case method their use will always be subsidiary to the central purpose of using cases as a learning method.'

His book also suggests that case histories may be either discussed or presented. In discussion the instructor may ask questions about the case and invite comments about specific issues. The whole class takes part in the analysis and comments on the techniques used and decisions made, with more or less direction from the teacher. In the second method a single student or team is asked to work on the case, or the class is split into groups working separately. The comments and answers to questions may be written or talked through. There may be some days allowed to prepare answers or the work may be done under examination conditions.

It is essential, to get the best out of this book, to use it actively. The student should not simply absorb the facts presented (which are in any case unique) or only master the techniques described. It is the attitude of problem-solving, of finding the best way to market and advertise a brand, which is most valuable. As Gordon Wills points out in the notes on the case study method used at the Management Centre from Buckingham, 'The objective in the use of the case study method is to develop the ability to think in a constructive, orderly manner when facing new situations. The appropriate use of theory and the acquisition, through experience, of knowledge and procedural skills are important subsidiary objectives. The heart of the case study method, however, is the use of problems to discover and fix in one's mind productive ways of thinking, ways of feeling and ways of doing.'

Going further, Gordon Wills also points out, 'The basic purpose of case studies is to provide students of management with simulated experience in making decisions. The case study provides a vehicle for identifying problems, analysing them, deriving solutions, and considering the difficulties in implementing these solutions. These last two aspects of the case study method are important. It is easy to devote most of the available time on analysis, leaving very little time for developing solutions, and none at all for considering the problem of implementing the solution. This "disease" has been termed "analysis paralysis". Beware of it. It is also important to practise persuading others that your proposed actions make sense, and to experience being persuaded by others.' Students may play the different roles in the real team that faced the problem. On the manufacturers' side we can think of a marketing director and financial director; at the agency, a planner or researcher, a creative and a media person, coordinated by client service.

The papers printed here are not impartial. They demonstrate current good practice but are of course not above criticism. The case histories are examples of marketing and advertising principles being applied in the real world, with all the uncertainties, pressures and mistakes this implies. The facts are correct, but they have been selected. The cases were written to make a point: that the advertising campaign was a success. Students should approach them sceptically, like a lawyer cross-examining. You are invited to detect errors in judgement, weaknesses in argument and over-optimism in interpretation. Can you see other explanations for sales, and for image and attitude shifts? Usually the cases stand up well to these questions and we are satisfied that a point has been reasonably made, but not necessarily always.

The papers may not be complete, in the sense that the student would like more information to answer the questions below. You will gain most by: (a) answering in terms of your own beliefs, or what you think likely, but make your assumptions clear; (b) describing what you need to know and how you would set about getting it.

Any success story also appears to have a straightforward structure. The steps we have listed above are taken in order and the result looks automatic and guaranteed. In real life there are short cuts, steps backward and disappointments. The teacher may add a note of verisimilitude by suggesting stages at which the findings or decisions were not those described. How would the team find their way back? In this way the complexity of real life, the additional costs and extra time spent, may be introduced.

The cases also describe techniques which may be used in separate exercises set by the instructor, who thus may bring to life methods which might otherwise seem rather abstract or artificial. Remember, however, that you see them here in the way data was actually collected and analysed because someone had a need to know and a duty to summarize the facts.

The individual techniques are pointed out in the questions suggested about each paper. You can write down for yourself what the method was, how the data were collected and analysed and what the conclusions were. You see one application only, but you may ask yourself what other situations could be illuminated by the method, what other findings could have resulted and what other action suggested.

Because the case studies all have the same broad structure, they have similar natural breaks at which students should pause. You can then ask yourself the following obvious questions. In addition, each case has its own particular features and further special questions are suggested later.

Read the general and special questions *before* you read each paper. The breaks where you should stop in your reading are when you should ask yourself the questions set. In this way you can tackle the problems facing the people doing the real job, and then compare your answers with the decisions actually taken. Other questions ask you to set down formally, and to try on your own or on other data, the techniques used.

After the business background and marketing objectives are explained:

1. Say whether the objectives are clear to you.
2. State in your own words the opportunities seen by the company.
3. Describe exactly the product's advantages and how you think consumers perceive them.
4. Say what marketing objectives you would have set.
5. List the changes in consumer behaviour needed to meet the targets.
6. Describe other information you would have liked at this stage.

After the campaign plan has been described:

1. Discuss the advertising budget set.
2. Say what alternative advertising objectives you would have considered.
3. Describe the target chosen and other reasonable targets.
4. Comment on the media choice.
5. Show how creative research might have improved the advertising.
6. Draw up a campaign and research plan in which evaluation might have been improved.
7. Draw up an alternative campaign plan.

After the evaluation:

1. Say whether you consider the conclusions justified.
2. List ways in which a cynic might otherwise explain the results.
3. List ways in which the evaluation method used could have been made more watertight, or could have explained more.
4. List other methods which might have been used to measure and explain the results.
5. Draw up new marketing objectives and campaign plans, with the benefit of hindsight.

It is also useful to go through these examples to draw up for yourself a checklist, set of questions or list of methods in order to:

1. Write marketing and advertising objectives.
2. Brief creative people.
3. Judge creative work.
4. Write a media plan.
5. Draw up an evaluation scheme.
6. List situations where each method of evaluation might be used – and where it cannot.

HOW ADVERTISING HELPED MAKE KRONA BRAND LEADER

1. Discuss the positioning of the brand. What alternatives were there, and what evidence that the positioning was correct?

2. Describe the relative importance of trial and repeat purchase in this case.
3. Has the part played by advertising (rather than product quality or price) been convincingly argued?

NATIONAL SAVINGS BANK INVESTMENT ACCOUNT 'SAVE-BY-POST'

1. Choose three publications from Table 2.2, Figures 2.1 and 2.2, and speculate about the reasons for their position in these lists.
2. Could other media have been used for the Save-by-Post campaign?
3. Argue the case for direct mail marketing of some other product.

ADVERTISING: KEY TO THE SUCCESS OF KELLOGG'S SUPER NOODLES

1. From Figure 3.1 extract approximately the sales and distribution data. Investigate whether they are related. What does this show?
2. Put into words any connection you can see in Figure 3.5 between advertising and sales.
3. Explain 'price elasticity' and 'advertising elasticity'. How may these numbers be used?

WHITEGATES: A REGIONAL SUCCESS STORY

1. For new products and new companies, the effect of advertising is particularly hard to disentangle from other factors. Has the attempt succeeded in this case?
2. Put the case for the use of other media than television in launching Whitegates.
3. Write a more formal plan to evaluate the contribution of advertising in this case. Would the increased complexity be worth while?

THE CASE FOR ALL CLEAR SHAMPOO

1. What exactly has been shown about the effectiveness of different media in this case? How far could this be generalized?
2. Could the effect of pricing and promotions together explain sales share, without an advertising effect?
3. Should Elida Gibbs have spent more on advertising All Clear? If so, why?

HOME PROTECTION: HOW ADVERTISING HELPS FIGHT CRIME

1. Purely in cost-effectiveness, was the campaign worth while?
2. Write an alternative campaign objective and advertising strategy.
3. Do you find the consumer survey or the retail audit the more convincing evidence?

HOW ADVERTISING HAS HELPED IN THE LAUNCH OF BIRDS EYE OVEN CRISPY COD STEAKS

1. Do you find Table 7.1 or Figure 7.2 the clearer demonstration of advertising effects? Why?
2. What is 'substitution', how is it measured, and was it avoided in this case?
3. Write a questionnaire to give results like those in the 'quantified communication check'. What else would you have asked?

THE EFFECT OF TELEVISION ADVERTISING ON THE LAUNCH OF DEEP CLEAN

1. The media plan included national press as well as TV. What was its contribution?
2. Write your own comments on Figures 8.1, 8.2 and 8.3.
3. Write an explanation in your own words of how the data in Figure 8.1 gave Figure 8.5.

THE LAUNCH OF TJAEREBORG REJSER

1. In what other ways is a direct-response product different from a retailed product?
2. Write a different marketing strategy to sell holidays direct.
3. Which do you find the most convincing argument that advertising was worth while?

FINE FARE: THE LAUNCH OF THE BIRCHWOOD SUPERSTORE

1. If pedestrian traffic had been important to the Birchwood superstore, would the media plan have changed?
2. The final tables are given as evidence of advertising effectiveness. Could there be any other explanation?
3. Define a different type of retail outlet. Argue the case for siting it in a chosen location. How would you promote its opening?

THE 'BIG JOHN' CAMPAIGN: ADVERTISING IN THE BEER MARKET

1. List the difficulties in measuring advertising effects in the beer market.
2. Is it critical that this work was carried out in Yorkshire? What differences would you expect to find in other regions?
3. Design a new survey to check the results in Tables 11.3–11.5 and 11.12–11.15.

DETTOL: A CASE HISTORY

1. Before 1978 what factors affected Dettol sales? What creative brief would you have written in 1977?
2. Define and calculate approximately from Figure 12.5 price elasticity. Define and calculate approximately from Figure 12.6 disposable income elasticity. Compare your results with Table 12.7.
3. Why is it necessary to know 'the precise shape of the advertising sales relationship' (in the 'Economic implications section')?

THE QUALCAST CONCORDE

1. In 1981 Qualcast advertising expenditure rose; so did their prices. Was this cause and effect?
2. Design a pre- and post-campaign questionnaire for recent lawnmower buyers to study how advertising might have affected them in 1980 and 1981.
3. Describe another durables market with a visible difference between product types. Write a TV script to demonstrate this difference.

KELLOGG'S RICE KRISPIES: THE EFFECT OF A NEW CREATIVE EXECUTION

1. Was the previous advertising working?
2. Define a 'demand curve' in your own words. What are the implications of (a) the line drawn through the 'After' points in Figure 14.1 and (b) the change between 'Before' and 'After'.
3. Define 'dynamic difference'. Draw a graph like Figure 14.3 for your own data.

THE RENAISSANCE OF MANGER'S SUGAR SOAP

1. What other research might you have done before the campaign?
2. Turn the data graphed in Figure 15.2 into an approximate, suitable table. Which do you find more convincing?
3. After TV advertising in Granada, sales rose in other regions. A reason is put forward for this; suggest others.

THE REPOSITIONING OF LUCOZADE

1. A single new strategy was chosen. Discuss whether two strategies could have been followed simultaneously.
2. A women's press campaign was used as well as TV. How would you have evaluated it?
3. Describe the principles of AMTES in your own words. From your own or made-up data, predict the sales for three periods in one area, knowing sales in another area for these periods, sales in both areas for ten previous periods, and having measures for a causative factor for all thirteen periods for both areas.

THE EFFECT OF ADVERTISING ON SANATOGEN MULTIVITAMINS

1. Given the results of aiming at Objective One, do you think Objective Two required a media change?
2. From Figure 17.1, Table 17.12 and Table 17.13, speculate on the changed pattern of purchase by age.
3. Use Tables 17.5–17.13 to make in your own words a case for advertising effectiveness.

SWAN VESTA MATCHES

1. For your own data, plot a figure like 18.1. What do you conclude?
2. Use Tables 18.1 and 18.2 to comment on the effect of advertising on awareness.
3. Discuss whether area TV weight tests would have helped, given Figure 18.1.

HOW ADVERTISING ON MILK BOTTLES INCREASED CONSUMPTION OF KELLOGG'S CORN FLAKES

1. How could the 'expected' column in Table 19.6 have been calculated?
2. Plan and describe a test for advertising on: supermarket trolleys, taxi-sides, parking meters or delivery vans.
3. Describe how you would use a consumer panel to measure the effect of local newspaper advertising.

DAILY MAIL CLASSIFIED

1. Actual revenue and profit figures are not given. Make your own estimates.
2. Enlarge the media selection section.
3. Advertising to advertisers is not very common. Discuss.

1

How Advertising Helped
Make Krona Brand Leader

INTRODUCTION

This case history analyses the launch of Krona margarine, a new product from Van den Berghs, into the Harlech and Westward TV areas.

The brand was sold in from 9th October 1978 and TV advertising broke on 20th October 1978. The case history covers a period of twelve months from launch in the two test areas.

Krona was launched to exploit the widening gap in price between butter and margarine and to attract butter users who were trading down. The brand succeeded beyond all expectations and by the end of the first year was established as brand leader in the launch areas with a national equivalent turnover of £32m at RSP.

Following this successful test market Krona has been extended to other areas. In all but one of these Krona is now brand leader or Number 2 brand.

Substantial problems existed in promoting Krona but these were wholly overcome by an extremely unusual advertising campaign. Very rapid trial was achieved and consumers identified advertising as their prime motivation. Subsequent research showed that the advertising had become an important element in the continuing satisfaction provided by Krona to its users.

BUSINESS BACKGROUND

The Yellow Fats Market

Krona operates within the Yellow Fats Market, which comprises butter, margarine and low fat spreads.

This is a huge market worth £600m at RSP in 1979, but it is not showing many signs of real growth. Indeed, it has declined by about one per cent since 1975.

Within this total picture there have been major shifts in the consumption of butter and margarine. A number of factors are at work here. After the war and with the ending of rationing, consumers switched back to butter in a big way, a trend which reached its peak in the 1960s (although per capita consumption never reached the prewar level). Since then the picture has gradually been reversed so that, by the end of 1979, butter and margarine shared the market equally. The trend to margarine has continued strongly in 1980.

The reasons for this are partly the major improvements in the quality of margarine, in particular the development of soft margarine in tubs, partly the development of specialist margarines and low fat spreads designed to tap concerns about health and diet but, most of all, changes in relative price.

Movements in relative price are quite clearly the dominant influence on sector shares of the Yellow Fats Market. Since a period of roughly level-pegging in the early 1970s, the rate of increase of butter prices has been significantly ahead of that of margarine. Because butter does not operate in a free market but is subject to import quotas and subsidies the precise movement of prices is difficult to predict, but all forecasts assume that a substantial premium for butter over margarine will remain.

Van den Berghs in the Market

Van den Berghs are the leading manufacturers in the market with a share well in excess of 50 per cent. They have the long established brand leader in Stork and have pioneered most of the major technical developments both in soft margarine – with Blue Band – and in opening up the specialist sectors with Flora and Outline.

With a substantial share of the market already, Van den Berghs see the best prospects for profit growth as being, therefore, the further development of the more profitable premium brands but, more importantly, increasing the size of the total sector by maximizing gains from butter.

Market Opportunity

The motivation and mechanism of the move to margarine from butter can vary. The major reason will inevitably be economy and any brand priced below butter may benefit. But there are other triggers too. The softness and ease of spreading of tub margarines are attractive to housewives who have a lot of spreading to do and in cookery too. In some families the taste of margarine becomes preferred to that of butter. The health and slimming claims of Flora and Outline obviously work on certain minority sections of butter users.

But the inescapable common element of all these examples is the fact that butter users are moving – indeed, until Krona, are forced to move – to very different products, which match neither the physical characteristics, the taste, nor the texture of butter. Now while, as explained above, this may be the precise reason for the move for some consumers, it does leave unsatisfied that large potential group of consumers who find the increasing price of butter a problem but are unwilling to sacrifice what they see as the unique qualities of butter. So as the price gap widened, a major opportunity was seen to exist for a margarine which duplicated the characteristics of butter but at a significantly lower price.

The search for a genuine butter substitute is not new. For many years Stork claimed to be indistinguishable from butter and, while arguably falling short of this in practice, was built to brand leader. More recently, Unigate launched St Ivel Gold: not strictly a margarine but a mixture of butter and vegetable oils offering a close-to-butter taste and texture. But it came in semi-soft form in a tub, did not have a generally acceptable taste and was limited to use as a spread. So there existed both a technical problem in making an acceptable product and a considerable credibility problem in persuading consumers that such a product could exist.

The margarine that raised questions in an Australian parliament.

In Sydney Australia, several years ago, an extraordinary rumour started amongst housewives.

It grew to such proportions that the New South Wales Government became involved. And it all began over something as simple as a margarine.

So successful did this margarine become, that housewives were even buying it by the caseful. People were taking it off lorries when it was delivered at supermarkets, to be certain of buying some.

All this activity led to the Minister of Agriculture being asked questions about the product in parliament.

For the rumour was that it wasn't margarine at all. Its taste was that good.

The counterpart of this Australian Margarine is on sale in Britain.

It's called Krona.

The Background to Krona

A few years ago a Unilever Company in Australia, E.O.I., had a considerable success with a margarine called Fairy. This was a hard block margarine which bore a remarkable likeness to butter. Samples of the product were tested by Van den Berghs in the UK. In a blind product test 40 per cent of the sample thought Fairy was butter, compared with only 7 per cent for Stork. A lengthy development process then ensued to match Fairy using UK production facilities and in due course this was more than achieved. Launch date was then finally determined by a judgement on the optimum price gap between butter and margarine. The brand was launched as Krona margarine in 1978 with TV advertising breaking in October 1978. It was a block margarine in a foil wrapper initially selling at around 20p for $\frac{1}{2}$ lb, compared with the average butter price of 30p.

MARKETING AND ADVERTISING OBJECTIVES

Marketing Objectives

To increase the Company's market share in the premium sector by securing for Krona a share of at least 5 per cent.

Advertising Objectives

To encourage trial of new Krona margarine by establishing that it is the first margarine with a taste and texture indistinguishable from butter.

CREATIVE STRATEGY AND EXECUTION

Prime Target Group

Housewives currently spreading salted butter, who are being forced to trade down because of the increasing price of butter, but who do not wish to sacrifice the taste and texture of butter.

Basic Consumer Benefit

Krona margarine has a taste and texture indistinguishable from butter.

Supporting Evidence

When the counterpart of Krona was on sale in New South Wales, housewives could not believe it was margarine and a rumour that in fact it was New Zealand butter re-wrapped as margarine spread round the State. The result was the brand became brand leader within weeks.

A brief word of explanation is needed both for the strategy and the execution. Any brand with a claim and a position such as Krona faces two substantial problems in putting these across:

(a) The Margarine Regulations, which are Government regulations prohibiting any presentation of a margarine which either implicitly or explicitly compares it to, likens it to, or refers to butter. Thus there is no legal way in which Krona's benefit can be directly expressed to the consumer.
(b) There exists a legacy of distrust of claims of butter parity deriving from Stork. In addition, Stork has pre-empted a number of possible advertising routes to the extent that they are closed to Krona.

Out of a number of possible creative routes identified, a campaign was therefore developed in which a long established and well respected reporter - René Cutforth - talked about the astonishing success of the Fairy brand in Australia: how a rumour spread that it was not margarine at all and how it became an almost overnight brand leader. The counterpart of this Australian product was now on sale in the UK and called Krona margarine. No direct claim was made for Krona itself. The implication was, however, that a similar success might occur in the UK. Three commercials were produced for the launch campaign, each explaining different aspects of the 'Fairy Story'.

The campaign had been pretested in rough video form and qualitative research was also carried out on the finished commercials. This confirmed that the commercials communicated strongly that Krona would be very like butter. Respondents were certainly very willing to try the product although there was a degree of disbelief that the product would live up to its claim and therefore that Krona would be used as a butter substitute for spreading. There was also a strong, positive response to what was seen as the original 'documentary' style of the advertising.

MEDIA STRATEGY AND PLAN

Budget

The national equivalent launch budget was set at £1.5m. This figure was based on an assessment of what the brand could afford in Year 2, assuming targets were met, upweighted by 20 per cent for the launch year. Company experience on necessary weights for launching premium brands was also influential.

Target Group

The target consumers were seen primarily as housewives trading down from butter and secondly as soft margarine spreaders who still preferred the taste of butter. This definition was not of value in media selection. In fact the profile of margarine and butter users closely matches the population as a whole and demographics were expected to be less significant in selecting Krona users than attitude of mind. For the launch period the target group was therefore defined for media purposes as All Housewives.

Area Choice

Westward and Harlech (82 per cent Test Market Area) were selected for the launch of Krona for the following reasons:

1. Approximately 10 per cent of the UK would be covered – a sample judged to be large enough to assist in network forecasting, yet small enough to minimize capital investment.
2. The area was strong for butter and relatively poor for all margarine. If Krona achieved target, then it was likely to be successful elsewhere.
3. The area is strong for sweet cream (salted) as opposed to lactic (unsalted) butter.
4. St Ivel Gold had begun testing in the same region – consumer acceptance of the two new yellow fat concepts (Krona, a butter grade margarine; St Ivel Gold, a butter/margarine spread) could therefore easily be monitored.
5. The area is strong for packet margarine: it therefore provided the best opportunity to assess whether housewives would perceive Krona as a conventional packet margarine or a butter substitute.

Media Group Selection

Television was the most appropriate medium for announcing Krona. Its various advantages, in combination, were judged to outweigh the disadvantages associated with its sole use:

1. It was felt that the recommended creative approach would be less effective in any other medium.
2. High coverage of the broad target audience of all housewives could be attained (90 per cent).
3. Fast coverage could be achieved.
4. Television is intrusive: important when advertising a basic commodity.
5. Other media groups could not supply appropriate regional test market facilities (unsatisfactory coverage and/or high cost).
6. Test market discounts offered by ITV contractors are helpful.
7. Television advertising tends to be seen by the retail trade as a confident sign of marketing intention.
8. The facility to upweight advertising at short notice was a plus point.

The disadvantage associated with television is that of inadequate coverage/frequency against the light- and non-ITV housewife viewing group. Figures suggested that housewives responsible for a sizeable proportion of total butter and margarine consumption would receive a disproportionately low measure of advertising weight.

The problem was noted, but the recommendation for the solus use of television remained for the launch year. Additional media in the test area would have to be funded from the (National Equivalent) budget, and this would have meant a disproportionate reduction in weight for the preferred medium. It was proposed that a secondary medium, press, would be employed once relatively low weight ITV continuation bursts were bought in Year 2.

Rate of Strike

The theoretical budget would buy approximately 2400 TVR (45 seconds) during the launch year. High and rapid awareness of the new product amongst housewives was considered to be vital to the success of the brand.

It was therefore proposed that the ratings be deployed in short bursts rather than spread over a longer period at a much reduced rate of strike. The launch burst target was set at 1000 H/W TVRs over four weeks to minimize the coverage problems associated with light- and non-ITV viewers and achieve adequate exposure of the three launch commercials.

CAMPAIGN EVALUATION

Brand Performance

DELIVERIES

Despite two major interruptions, Krona deliveries during the first twelve months exceeded expectations and by the end of the period were running at four to five times initial levels.

The pattern was affected by two industrial disputes, the lorry drivers' strike (2nd January to 5th February 1979) and a dispute at Van den Berghs' Bromborough factory. The former sharply reduced deliveries in cycles 1 and 2 1979 while the latter meant that there were no deliveries of Krona (or of other of Van den Berghs' brands) between the beginning of April and the beginning of May 1979.

The resumption of deliveries after the strike was not uniform across all Van den Berghs' brands and Krona received priority. This, to a degree, explains a peak in deliveries in cycles 12 and 13 1979. However, this was not, as might have been expected, a temporary pheno- menon and Krona sales were established at a new high level up to cycle 20.

Overall, the figures show a pipe-line filling phase at the end of 1978, a confused period in the first quarter of 1979, a further pipe-line filling phase in cycle 11 but then evidence of very substantial sales when normal deliveries could be resumed.

DISTRIBUTION

Figures are available only for sterling weighted distribution in the two areas combined, in Multiples and Co-ops only (Table 1.1).

Very strong distribution was thus achieved within two or three months and growth in distribution cannot fully explain the growth in deliveries.

TABLE 1.1:   KRONA STERLING DISTRIBUTION, HARLECH AND WESTWARD

October/November 1978	78%
December 1978/January 1979	95%
February/March	95%
April/May	89%
June/July	95%
August/September	86%
October/November	93%

Stats MR.

CONSUMER SALES/SHARE

Within three TCA periods, Krona had achieved a 10 per cent share, making it Number 2 brand in the market (Table 1.2).

TABLE 1.2:   KRONA VOLUME BRAND SHARE

1978			4 w/e:					1979				
14/10	11/11	9/12	6/1	3/2	3/3	31/3	28/4	26/5	23/6	21/7	18/8	15/9
–	5	10	9	5	8	12	5	3	14	15	18	16

TCA.

This was a time of rapid sampling. Cumulative penetration had reached 24 per cent by November (see below).

There was a temporary set-back as a result of the lorry drivers strike but share recovered strongly by March, only to be hit again by the Van den Berghs strike. As explained earlier, Krona benefited by a shortage of other Van den Berghs brands in June, but, far from falling back when normal supplies were resumed, it actually made large volume gains in subsequent periods. By the end of the first twelve months, Krona was brand leader, with around twice the share of the next brand.

The Consumer

AWARENESS

The first post-check showed that awareness after only five weeks of advertising had already reached a high level and this was then maintained in subsequent months despite the interruptions in supply caused by strikes early in 1979. Considering the very substantial brand shares achieved, the level of spontaneous awareness could seem on the low side. However, viewed in the context of the lowish figures for long established brands such as Stork and Blue Band, Krona's achievement may be judged satisfactory. Certainly prompted awareness was at a very high level for a new brand (Table 1.3).

TABLE 1.3:   KRONA AWARENESS (SPONTANEOUS/PROMPTED)

November	*February*	*July/August*
20/79	22/86	25/80

Quick Read

TRIAL

To be tried by one quarter of all housewives within little more than a month was obviously an exceptional achievement and the brand continued to gain trial in the succeeding months (Table 1.4).

TABLE 1.4:   KRONA TRIAL (% BOUGHT IN LAST SIX MONTHS)

November	*February*	*July/August*
24%	38%	43%

Quick Read.

Obviously, the advertising cannot take sole credit for initial trial. A door-to-door coupon was dropped during October and there were a number of in-store demonstrations. By the end of 1978, distribution in Multiples and Co-ops exceeded 90 per cent sterling. However, there is good evidence that advertising played a major role:

INFLUENCES ON FIRST PURCHASE

The November Quick Read Survey showed:

Coupon received or not

No. of respondents aware of Krona:	248
Yes	47%
No	50%
Don't know, etc.	3%

Whether coupon first encouraged trial

No. of respondents	44
Yes	34%
No	66%
Don't know, etc.	–

Awareness of Krona TV advertising

No. of respondents aware of Krona:	248
Yes	91%
No	7%
Don't know, etc.	2%

A separate survey was carried out at the end of November 1978 among Krona buyers in the two areas:

Source of awareness of Krona

No. ever bought	186
TV advertising	66%
Leaflet/Coupon	13%
Friend told me	13%
In-Store	11%

Seen Krona advertised on TV

No. not mentioning TV above	63
Yes	68%
No	17%
Don't know	14%

Combined with those mentioning TV previously this gives a total of 89 per cent who claimed to have seen Krona advertising on TV, while only a small percentage related their awareness of Krona to the coupon.

Similar information was sought in the March/April Taylor Nelson Survey. This showed that among trialists a majority of both acceptors (59 per cent) and rejectors (63 per cent) gave TV advertising as the main reason for trying Krona in the first place. Obviously, by this time, some while had elapsed since the coupon drop, while there had been a substantial weight of TV advertising, but at the very least it demonstrates the importance advertising was seen to have as a source of information on the brand.

This information should be seen against the context of the general reluctance of consumers to admit advertising as an influence on their behaviour.

REPEAT PURCHASE

The Quick Read Monitors show a steady increase in the numbers of housewives intending to purchase Krona next time (17 per cent of respondents by July/August). By July/August, more than two thirds of buyers had bought more than one pack. Obviously the recruitment rate of new users shows a sharp drop over the period of the surveys, although sampling was still going on. As long after the launch as July/August 1979, over one third of housewives who had ever bought Krona had bought Krona as their last purchase. The November 1978 Krona Buyers' Survey confirmed that, within not much more than a month, 50 to 60 per cent of buyers had bought more than one pack.

The March Taylor Nelson Survey showed that 50 per cent of buyers said that they would definitely buy again and a further 29 per cent would probably buy again. Outright rejection was at a minimal level. Over two thirds of buyers had at that point bought more than one pack.

PRODUCT POSITIONING

The aim of Krona advertising was to present the brand as a high quality spreading margarine, indistinguishable from butter. Was this being borne out in practice in the market-place?

The November 1978 Buyers' Survey indicated that even in the earliest stage of the brand's life, when sampling was at its peak, around half of current Krona buyers felt they had stopped buying other brands or cut down on them. In each case the largest single source of Krona business was butter.

The March 1979 Taylor Nelson Study confirmed this picture, around half acceptors and a quarter of rejectors who had substituted Krona for another product having switched from butter.

Switching from other margarine brands at this point did not show any clear pattern, but certainly there was no demonstrable association of Krona with cheap packet cooking margarine.

HOW THE ADVERTISING WORKS

The brand, then, in its first twelve months in the two areas was clearly highly successful in sales and share terms. A high level of trial had been achieved in a short period and the brand had largely been received by consumers in the way intended. It had lived up to or exceeded expectation for a substantial body of consumers and good levels of repeat purchase were achieved.

Advertising had been identified by consumers as the primary influence on their initial purchase and this is confirmed by the most sensible interpretation of the sales and attitude data discussed.

A fair amount of evidence exists to explain how the Krona launch campaign works.

Sources

We derive our understanding of how the advertising works, as opposed to the influences it has on purchasing behaviour, from several sources:

(a) The various quantitative surveys already quoted.
(b) Qualitative research into the finished commercials prior to transmission and two qualitative studies carried out to assist creative development.

Communication

Our analysis can be divided into two sections: communication and persuasion.

We know from a lot of past research that the concept of a margarine identical to butter (and at a lower price) is highly appealing.

The problem, as we discussed earlier, is to overcome the hurdles provided by restrictive regulation and credibility and communicate the concept effectively and persuasively.

It is clear from the evidence that the communication was understood. In the qualitative studies the main message was seen as:

'It's as good as butter'
'Closer to butter than other margarines'
'Tastes more like butter'
'Alternative to butter'
'Implying it was as good as butter'

The March Taylor Nelson Study showed that over half of acceptors and 42 per cent of rejectors expected either a new brand of butter or something similar.

Persuasion

In terms of persuasion, we have the evidence of image statements from the various Quick Read Studies. These show that:

(a) Despite the legacy of incredibility and the current status of packet margarines, communication *and* persuasion that Krona was a high quality margarine with a butter-like taste was well achieved.
(b) Levels of agreement were high, even in November 1978 *when a substantial majority had only the evidence of the advertising to go on.*

Not surprisingly, acceptance or otherwise of this message became a touchstone of trial of Krona and subsequent repurchase, and in research carried out after the launch there is a substantial division on this issue between acceptors and rejectors.

The advertising had clearly established the pretensions of Krona. It was up to the brand itself to live up to the claims or not.

How was persuasion achieved to the point of trial? The following interpretation is a distillation of the findings of the various qualitative studies mentioned earlier:

STYLE AND TONE

The novel 'documentary' style of the commercials was liked because:

(i) It was different from other, particularly margarine, advertisements.
(ii) The tone was 'telling not selling'. It left the choice to the consumer; it treated her as an adult; it did not talk down to her. The personality of René Cutforth was important here.
(iii) The tone was serious and gave stature to the product.

All combined strongly to enhance credibility.

LOCATION

The Australian context worked in a number of ways:

(i) It was interesting and different.
(ii) It took Krona out of the conventional margarine context.
(iii) It had definite 'dairy' connotations.
(iv) It was related to the UK, though not part of it.
(v) It was a desirable place to be – redolent not so much of affluence, but of a good, healthy, open-air life.

Trial and Repeat Purchase

Finally, the evidence suggested that the campaign was trial *and* repeat purchase orientated. While for some people it clearly on its own could not overcome rooted scepticism about margarine claims, for the majority it provided a strong inducement to try. Once people had tried and accepted the product, the advertising was seen as a confirmation of their experience. They too had made this discovery. They too could not believe it was a margarine. What had happened in Australia was only to be expected. In addition, the intelligent tone of the commercials complimented them as consumers and confirmed the good sense of their choice of Krona. It is quite reasonable on the evidence, then, to claim that the Krona advertising, far from simply conveying a highly desirable message, has by its distinctive character become an essential part of the brand's character and therefore a crucial element in the success of this very major grocery brand.

CONCLUSION

That Krona represented a major marketing success in Harlech and Westward over the period under review is amply demonstrated by the facts. Nor was it a temporary phenomenon. Krona is achieving similar results in other areas as it is extended and has more than maintained its dominance in its original test areas.

We say 'marketing success' deliberately because, as we all know, the successful launch of a new product depends on many related factors. In the case of Krona these were:

1. TIMING

The increasing price premium of butter over margarine provided the opportunity for a brand aimed at people forced to trade down.

2. PRODUCT QUALITY

Krona was the first margarine successfully to simulate butter. It exceeds expectations and arouses almost a religious fervour among converts.

3. NAMING AND PACKAGING

The presentation of the brand communicates the required positioning and reinforces the belief of users that Krona is closer to butter than margarine.

4. PRICING

While Krona is clearly a premium-priced margarine, it is sufficiently cheaper than butter to make the incentive to switch as strong as possible.

5. MARKETING INVESTMENT

Van den Berghs recognized the potential of the brand and were prepared to spend heavily behind it, above and below the line, in its first year. Significantly, the bulk of this money was spent on the consumer in order to encourage the critically important first purchase and not to reduce price at point-of-sale.

6. ADVERTISING

Because of these factors it would be easy to argue that almost any advertising would have worked for Krona. This is not the case, for these reasons:

1. The problem in persuading housewives to accept Krona was formidable. Conventionally, packet margarines were cheap cooking media. Yet here was a premium-priced brand. Previous claims of butter-parity had proved to be excessive. Yet here was a brand ringing the same bell again. Regulations forbade explicit or implicit comparisons with butter, yet here was a brand whose whole raison d'être was that it was indistinguishable from butter.

    Krona achieved not only very rapid and high awareness, which could be put down to the substantial TV expenditure, but rapid trial too.

    While hard evidence of precise cause and effect is unavailable and indeed unattainable to apportion credit between advertising, coupon drop and POS, the view of housewives expressed repeatedly in quantitative and qualitative studies puts advertising as the major influence.

2. Krona's role is to be a cheap substitute for butter. Knowing the strong emotional aura surrounding butter, this role is one which legitimately might be expected to reach the housewife's pocket, but not her heart. In fact there is growing evidence that Krona is on the way to becoming a 'religion' for its users. There is a sense of a 'miracle', that the housewife has made 'a discovery' which she wants to pass on to others.

There is no doubt that the advertising, with its serious and intelligent tone and the story which it tells, is contributing importantly to this.

APPENDIX: DATA USED IN KRONA ADVERTISING EVALUATION

Sales

1. Van den Bergh delivery figures
2. TCA
3. Stats MR Distribution Check: Multiples and Co-ops

Consumer

QUICK READ MONITORS

A series of quantitative studies based on the Quick Reading method developed by Unilever Marketing Division was carried out.

Research was among margarine users (who form around 80 per cent of the population) in Harlech and Westward, quota-ed by age and class.

KRONA BUYERS' SURVEY

187 housewives who had ever bought Krona were interviewed in-home in Harlech (95) and Westward (92). Interviewing was conducted between 27th November and 1st December 1978.

KRONA MARKET MONITOR: HARLECH AND WESTWARD (TAYLOR NELSON & ASSOCIATES) MARCH/ APRIL 1979

Main Objectives:

1. Evaluate Krona's success in terms of awareness and penetration.
2. Investigate Krona's future in terms of likelihood of repurchase or trial (non-users).
3. Evaluate effects of experience on perceived product acceptability and positioning.

Method:

Area: Harlech and Westward TV areas.
Sample: Based on contact interviews with a quota sample of 945 housewives, three subsamples were identified, who were taken through an extended interview:

(a) Respondents who had bought Krona and would definitely or probably buy again in the future (acceptors).
(b) Respondents who had bought Krona but did not know or were unlikely to buy again in the future (rejectors).
(c) Respondents who were aware of Krona and had seen a pack in-store (aware non-buyers).

QUALITATIVE RESEARCH: QUICKSEARCH 1979

30 individual interviews: 15 trialists who either had Krona at home at the time of interview or would have had it if it were available. 15 non-trialists. All aware of Krona advertising with a spread by weight of ITV viewing.

Objectives:

(a) To evaluate response to the launch campaign after four months' exposure.
(b) To elicit response to a possible follow-up campaign.

QUALITATIVE RESEARCH: GREGORY LANGMAID ASSOCIATES (MARCH 1979)

This research consisted of four groups and 16 depth interviews in Swansea and Bristol. All respondents were from the BC1C2 social grades, aged between 20 and 55.

Half were users (bought twice or more) of Krona, half were non-users and non-rejectors of the brand. These latter were women who had heard of Krona but who had not bought or tried it.

Objectives:

(a) To examine attitudes to Krona in the test market area among users and non-users as a background to exploring the acceptability and comprehension of two new Krona commercials in terms of their effects on users and non-users.
(b) To examine the continuity of the new films leading on from the earlier Australian films.
(c) To probe the suitability and effectiveness of René Cutforth as a presenter.

2

National Savings Bank Investment Account 'Save-by-Post'

INTRODUCTION

This paper covers a test operation in direct response advertising, undertaken by Dorland Advertising for the National Savings Bank Investment Account, which was designed to be in keeping with existing thematic advertising for this service and for the Department for National Savings as a whole. The campaign took place at the end of February and of March 1981. For an actual investment in press media of £397 280, a total of £42 000 000 was obtained directly from both new and existing investors by the time of the initial analysis. Over £50 000 000 was ultimately reported.

BACKGROUND

The Department for National Savings is a Government Department responsible for the operation of the National Savings Bank and various other forms of investment.

The origins of this range of securities are in the Post Office Savings Bank established in 1861 to promote thrift among the newly emerging industrial working class. It operated as a readily-available money saving service, developing ultimately into the National Savings Bank which became separate from the Post Office in 1969.

The remainder of the DNS portfolio at the time of this exercise comprised:

1. *National Savings Certificates (19th Issue)*: a guaranteed fixed-interest, lump-sum term investment, with a maximum level of £5000, tax-free and available to everyone.
2. *Index-Linked Certificates (Granny Bonds)*: again a tax-free lump sum term product, with a maximum holding of £3000, but restricted at this time to people over 60 years old.
3. *Save As You Earn*: also index-linked, with a maximum deposit then of £20 per month over a five-year basis (plus a bonus if held for seven years), tax-free and available to everyone of 16 years of age and over.
4. *Premium Bonds*: available to all, yielding a series of weekly and monthly cash prizes selected by Ernie.

Each of these products was targeted at disparate market segments and each is very different in character being designed to meet different needs amongst savers.

The possible switching of funds from savings invested in these products was therefore considered to be unlikely and in the event, this proved to be the case, as far as could be checked. New accounts were expected to come either from new savers or from those who had deposits with competitive savings media.

Returning to the National Savings Bank, there are two services offered to the public; the Ordinary Account, the natural successor to the POSB Account, which offers savings bank facilities at a modest rate of interest, currently 5 per cent, with certain tax advantages; and the Investment Account (Invac) in which a highly competitive rate of interest is offered, fluctuating with market conditions, on deposits from £1 to £200 000.

What began as a service for small savers became increasingly a service for larger investors as the maximum holding rose to £200 000. Recent changes in the direction of Government Policy partly superseded even this later role: the Investment Account (Invac), and certain other National Savings securities, became primary sources for funding the Public Sector Borrowing Requirement.

Thus, in the latter part of 1980:

1. The Investment Account became a potential major source of funds.
2. In November, its interest rate was raised to 15 per cent and maintained at this level to keep it above equivalent rates offered by the main competition, i.e. Banks and Building Societies.
3. In order to fulfil its monetary target and to capitalize on its competitive rate, it received heavier advertising than before, and appeared on television for the first time.

Although this resulted in a considerable increase in inflow of funds, the limits of the system of 'selling' the service were felt to be considerable: Invac service was available only through some 22 000 Crown and Sub-Post Offices. The network was thus extensive, and national, and the offices were open on six days a week, yet the need to be present in person, to queue and to make investments thus publicly was felt to militate against potential users who, for a variety of reasons, could not or would not transact business in this way.

Dorland was asked to examine this proposition considering:

1. Could advertising help to tap this potential source of funds?
2. Would it be cost-effective in terms of attracting larger deposits than the existing average, and creating holdings higher than the existing average balance?
3. Could it do so without increasing the number of handling staff at the operating centre in Glasgow?

The remainder of this paper covers the marketing background, how the agency and client handled the operation, results and analysis, recommendations and further action.

NSB INVAC 1980/1981: OVERALL OBJECTIVES AND STRATEGY

As the test marketing operation for Save-by-Post was but part of the total NSB Invac marketing activity, it is necessary first to examine the overall objectives and strategy.

Marketing Objectives

1. To improve the volume of receipts into Invac.
2. To increase the size of the average holding.

Marketing Strategy

To position Invac as an attractive investment medium for private individuals and certain organizations with up to £200 000 to save, by maintaining a competitive interest rate and an accessible service.

Advertising Objectives

1. To attract new users.
2. To position Invac clearly and competitively within the savings market.
3. To encourage increased holdings among existing users.

Target Market

Consumer: ABC1 savers, 35 years old and over.

Others: Clubs, societies and certain other non-profit making bodies and commercial organizations.

Consumer Benefit

A competitive interest rate with ease of access.

Rationale

1. A higher interest rate than equivalent rates from Banks and Building Societies.
2. Interest is paid gross – useful for non-taxpayers.
3. No penalties need be incurred.

NSB INVAC SAVE-BY-POST

Marketing Objectives

Returning to the Save-by-Post test operation, its specific marketing objectives were:

1. To extend the Invac customer base by making it possible for new users to deal direct with the bank; this new franchise would be among those who could not, or would not, use the Post Office for opening or continuing to use an NSB Investment Account.
2. To achieve this at a level of cost-effectiveness acceptable to the bank and in a manner which could be continued in the future as an integral part of the NSB operation.

Method

PROBLEM EXAMINATION

The current 'distribution' was seen to be a bar to certain potential sales, yet of course it remained essential for all the existing business. Any new selling method should not contradict or downrate it. New physical outlets to tap the market posited by this assumption were not practicable; selling through Banks or franchised shops for example. Direct response advertising was therefore the best candidate method.

DIRECT MARKETING

This offered certain client and customer benefits:

(a) direct access to the customer;
(b) a potential for cost-effectiveness;
(c) ease of monitoring, and thereby the ability to plan for the future;
(d) convenience for the customer;
(e) no intermediary (answering the need for privacy of security).

MEDIA EVALUATION

Direct response advertising offered benefits over other direct methods – no need to build up a mailing list, for example, and also the opportunity to derive additional strength from the existing advertising style. A couponed press advertisement was decided upon rather than television because of the need to explain carefully the details of the investment account, and because of the known ability of press advertising to generate money 'off the page'.

DECISION ON PRESS

Three main criteria were going to be used to analyse the effectiveness of Save-by-Post, namely:

(a) the average amount of money returned per insertion by publication;
(b) the average number of coupons returned per insertion by publication;
(c) the return of money per £ invested (space cost).

Therefore a wide range of national and regional newspapers was used, with the inclusion of the *Radio Times*, for the following reasons:

1. The advertisements had to run within a strict period of time in a changing market, therefore magazines with long copy dates could not be considered.
2. The broad policy of offering a National Savings medium nationally was followed – this also would contribute to the volume of returns in line with the marketing objective.
3. Regional newspapers were used, however, to exploit known areas of strength and to upweight where necessary the coverage afforded by the nationals, as previous experience and the records of the Bank showed potential geographical areas of strength – high earners, retired people and so on.

All of the publications, insertion by insertion (up to five per publication per burst) carried key numbers so that the specific responses could be accurately monitored, and the results used to tailor further activity after the test.

Creative Execution

Although a popular theory exists that good financial products sell themselves without the aid of the normal marketing tools, much care had to be taken with the creative approach. Competition is just as fierce in this market as in any other and, therefore, the effectiveness of good advertising naturally relates and responds to other competitive appeals. As it was known that in this market the reader is bombarded with a variety of competitive claims, often expressed in terms of percentages, it was recognized that simplicity would be of paramount importance to the advertising being developed. Therefore, a decision of fundamental significance was taken by the agency that it was *the new service* and not the percentage return on investment which should be given prominence.

CONSTRUCTION

The advertisement followed the style used for much National Savings activity including the use of a reversed-out headline and a simple type-set format. By adopting this format, it would be possible for the campaign to contribute to the presence of National Savings beyond the immediate results of the coupon response.

The advertisement featured:

— a new name: Save-by-Post;
— a new service: the opportunity to invest by post;
— information: a competitive interest rate, ease of access by Freepost, ease of withdrawal;
— a response device: the coupon.

In addition, it provided information for existing users who could also now save by post, and pointed out that all the existing facilities through post offices remained. The other NSB service, the Ordinary Account, also featured.

The coupon was very carefully designed. The minimum of information was requested, consistent with security and ease of processing, so that it was easy to fill in. The coupons all had to be precisely the same size for handling purposes – they had to comply with existing mechanical handling procedures, and over 20 000 were thus processed – so that each piece of artwork had to be carefully checked.

A copy of one of the advertisements is included on p. 21.

Media Execution

TIMING

February 1981 was chosen as the start month – clear of the Christmas period which was historically an active time even without the heavy advertising activity of 1980 – and it offered a period within which any activity from the campaign could be accommodated at the Bank without imposing a strain on resources.

As interest on the account is credited from the first day of the month *following* deposit, it was necessary for the customers' benefit for the coupons to be displayed, filled in and returned to Glasgow *before* the end of the preceding month. Activity had therefore to be planned near the end of the month with enough time to allow for postage (although in fact deposits received in the first few days of March would not have been disadvantaged).

The first burst took place between 18 and 25 February, with a follow-up between 20 and 27 March. The full media list is shown in Table 2.1.

SPACE SIZE

Full tabloid pages and 38 × 6 columns in broadsheets were used in the first phase:

1.   For impact and dominance.

National Savings Bank
Save-by-Post
A new service for investors from the better value bank

In the past three months over 140,000 people have opened Investment Accounts with the National Savings Bank.

Money earns interest at competitive rates, currently 15%p.a.

Interest is paid gross. And now there's a new easy way to open new accounts and make deposits.

1 New service for savers.

The National Savings Bank is introducing a new Save-by-Post service to make it easier for you to open an account or make deposits.

To open an NSB Investment Account simply fill in the coupon and send with your cheque. Your bank book will be sent to you within a few days.

If you already have an NSB Investment Account, you can now make deposits direct by post. Just send your bank book and remittance to the NSB.

2 Present interest rate 15%p.a.

To earn interest from March 1st, send your remittance to arrive by February 28th. Interest,

at present 15%, accrues from the first of the following month and is credited annually.

Any changes in interest rate are publicised at least one month in advance. Whatever happens to interest rates, the Investment Account rate will remain competitive.

3 Interest paid in full.

Interest is paid gross, which is especially beneficial if you are a non-taxpayer. Interest on every full pound is payable from the first of the month following your deposit, and for every full calendar month it remains invested.

4 Easy to deposit.

You can make deposits direct by Freepost or at post offices. The new maximum holding for an Investment Account is £200,000.

If you use the new Save-by-Post service, don't forget to send your bank book. This will be returned promptly with a pre-paid envelope for your next deposit.

5 Easy to withdraw.

You need give only one month's notice of withdrawal. Forms are available at post offices.

Post Office service.

This new Save-by-Post service is in addition to existing NSB facilities, which continue to be available at post offices.

What to do.

New accounts To open an Investment Account just complete the coupon, cut round the dotted line and send with your cheque (payable to the Director of Savings) to:

Department for National Savings.
(Dept. CDS1B),
National Savings Bank
FREEPOST,
Glasgow G58 2BR

Existing accounts Send deposits with your bank book to the above address. **No coupon or covering letter is required.** Your book will be returned to the address in the book – please make sure it is your current address, and keep a note of your account number.

Fill in for new accounts only.

To: National Savings Bank (Dept. CDS1B), Glasgow G58 2BR
I wish to open an NSB Investment Account.

SURNAME:..MR/MRS/MISS

FORENAMES:
(In full)

DATE OF BIRTH	DATE	MONTH	YEAR

(Essential for children under 7 years)

ADDRESS:
(including postcode)

AMOUNT DEPOSITED	POUNDS	PENCE

I declare that the information given by me on this form is correct.

USUAL SIGNATURE:
(If child under 7, signature of person opening account).
If you hold any other NSB Account(s), please quote account number(s):

NSB Ordinary Account.

For your day-to-day needs, open an NSB Ordinary Account at your post office. Every whole pound in your Ordinary Account earns 5%p.a. and the first £70 of interest is tax-free.

You can now withdraw up to £100 on demand – even on Saturday mornings.

Full details are available at over 20,000 post offices throughout the country.

NSB Ordinary Account deposits should be made at the post office, please note that the new Save-by-Post service is for NSB Investment Accounts only.

TABLE 2.1:   MEDIA SCHEDULE OF CAMPAIGNS

| Publication | Number of insertions | | |
	Campaign 1	Campaign 2	Totals
Daily Express	3	4	7
Daily Mail	4	5	9
Daily Mirror	2	2	4
Daily Telegraph	3	5	8
Financial Times	2	–	2
Guardian	3	–	3
Sun	2	1	3
The Times	3	–	3
Observer	1	1	2
Sunday Express	1	1	2
Sunday People	–	1	1
Sunday Telegraph	–	1	1
Sunday Times	–	1	1
Daily Record	1	2	3
Sunday Mail	–	1	1
Aberdeen Press	2	2	4
Glasgow Herald	2	2	4
The Scotsman	2	2	4
Birmingham Post	2	2	4
Cardiff Western Mail	2	2	4
Liverpool Post	2	2	4
Manchester Evening News	2	2	4
Newcastle Journal	2	2	4
New Standard	1	–	1
Yorkshire Post	2	2	4
Radio Times	–	1	1
Jewish Chronicle	–	1	1
	£182 238	£215 042	£397 280

2.   To complement the existing style of advertising.

3.   To allow room to launch and explain the new service and to give the required amount of 'small print'.

INSERTIONS

Up to five insertions in each publication were used, partly to maximize coverage and awareness within the budget limits and partly to provide data, if required, on the optimum number of insertions needed in subsequent activity.

POSITIONING

The inclusion of the coupons suggested the obvious desirability of right-hand pages. The buying of a high proportion of early right-hand pages was as much a measure of effectiveness as was the securing of discounts against rate card costs: cost-effective buying contributed to one of the principal objectives of the scheme and to the necessary safeguarding of public money.

CONSUMER SERVICE

The overall effectiveness of a direct response campaign depends substantially on the handling of the response. In this case the handling was performed entirely by the client's staff at the National Savings Bank in Glasgow and it had to be done without disrupting existing arrangements.

It was essential to overcome the three negatives which the public was likely to perceive in a governmental operation: inefficiency, slow turn-round, bureaucracy.

Efficiency

It was vital that not one reply was imperfectly dealt with, money lost or wrongly applied. To this end, the best staff were selected and fully briefed and trained, all this consistent with normal day-to-day operations.

Rapid Turn-round

There was a danger, with the expected volume of response, that there could be handling delays. It was decided not to include a 'please allow 28 days for delivery' note, but to set instead an objective that replies would be handled within one day of receipt. This was fulfilled for the vast majority of responses.

Absence of Bureaucracy

The procedure was kept as simple as possible, especially in the vital follow-up phase so that respondents were not subsequently disillusioned. The coupon was kept to essentials, as described. Each respondent received with his bank book a pre-paid addressed envelope for subsequent deposits, for which there was *no paperwork at all* – this is probably unique in the field of investment: the customer simply had to send his remittance and bank book in the envelope supplied. The attraction of this simplicity was reflected in the substantial number of subsequent deposits, £3.25 million of which were coded to press advertisements.

CAMPAIGN RESULTS

The results of the February and March activity were analysed on the basis of data received from the National Savings Bank. Certain confidential cost information has had to be removed. To summarize, some £42 million was brought in by June at a media cost of £397 280 traceable directly to the campaign, three-quarters of it coming from new users; this entirely validated the assumption upon which this test activity was based. All of the new accounts thus opened were specially coded, within the existing rules of the Bank's activities, so that their benefit over time could be monitored. This provided a valuable source of data relevant to the Bank as a whole and to further Save-by-Post activity.

The detailed analysis provided a highly effective appraisal of the strengths of the individual publications chosen.

CAMPAIGN ANALYSIS

A detailed analysis was made of deposits against investment, of coupons per insertion of average deposits per insertion and of volume per insertion (see Table 2.2). These analyses provided a bank of data essential in the consideration of further Save-by-Post activity. In the event, the 'saturation coverage' of February and March was trimmed to a list of six publications in the autumn of that year.

TABLE 2.2:   AVERAGE NUMBER OF COUPONS RETURNED PER INSERTION

Publication	No. of Insertions	Coupons returned		Deposits	
		Average	Total	Average	Total
Sunday Express	2	924	1848	1 562.93	2 888 285
Radio Times	1	717	717	1 268.24	909 325
Sunday Telegraph	1	571	571	2 331.54	1 331 309
Daily Telegraph	8	460	3680	2 023.97	7 448 204
Daily Express	7	446	3125	1 584.97	4 953 026
Daily Mail	9	442	3802	1 263.52	4 803 921
Sun	3	392	1177	664.65	782 291
Daily Mirror	4	371	1485	808.25	1 200 244
Observer	2	279	577	1 400.84	808 287
Sunday People	1	248	248	1 442.36	357 705
Sunday Times	1	203	203	2 769.18	562 143
Guardian	3	195	586	1 179.28	691 054
New Standard	1	177	177	1 312.89	232 381
The Times	3	149	448	1 670.46	748 366
Financial Times	2	67	133	2 478.35	329 620
The Scotsman	4	56	224	1 776.19	397 866
Glasgow Herald	4	55	218	1 457.06	317 638
Yorkshire Post	4	41	162	2 403.94	389 443
Manchester Evening News	4	39	154	1 204.92	185 557
Daily Record	3	37	110	918.15	100 996
Sunday Mail	1	36	36	567.33	20 424
Birmingham Post	4	20	79	1 899.52	150 062
Liverpool Post	4	17	68	1 859.82	126 468
Cardiff Western Mail	4	16	62	2 103.21	130 399
Jewish Chronicle	1	15	15	2 530.20	37 953
Aberdeen Press	4	14	57	1 146.28	65 338
Newcastle Journal	4	13	51	5 185.49*	264 460*

* Includes one deposit for £200 000

Main Features

1. The quality daily and Sunday press had the greatest response in terms of the number of coupons returned, the value of deposits per insertion and the value of deposits per £ invested. (See Figures 2.1 and 2.2.)
2. During both campaigns, certain daily papers have carried two or more insertions in one week, and from the coded responses, it is possible to show that normally the levels of both coupon responses and deposit value fall with each successive insertion. (See Figures 2.3 and 2.4.)
3. A comparison of the two campaigns was made concerning the average number of coupons per insertion and the average value of deposits per insertion. This revealed a marginal decrease for March as opposed to February.

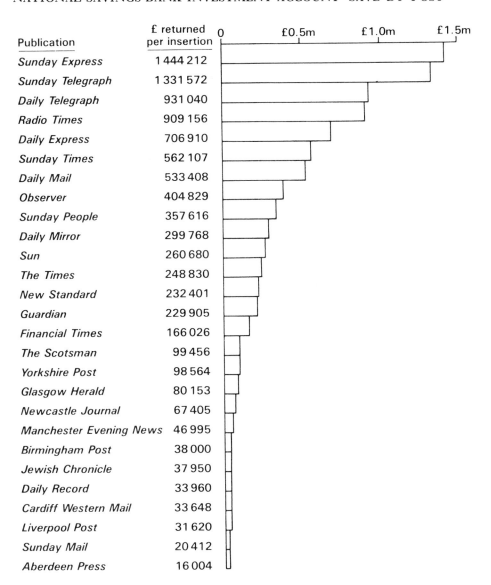

Publication	£ returned per insertion
Sunday Express	1 444 212
Sunday Telegraph	1 331 572
Daily Telegraph	931 040
Radio Times	909 156
Daily Express	706 910
Sunday Times	562 107
Daily Mail	533 408
Observer	404 829
Sunday People	357 616
Daily Mirror	299 768
Sun	260 680
The Times	248 830
New Standard	232 401
Guardian	229 905
Financial Times	166 026
The Scotsman	99 456
Yorkshire Post	98 564
Glasgow Herald	80 153
Newcastle Journal	67 405
Manchester Evening News	46 995
Birmingham Post	38 000
Jewish Chronicle	37 950
Daily Record	33 960
Cardiff Western Mail	33 648
Liverpool Post	31 620
Sunday Mail	20 412
Aberdeen Press	16 004

Figure 2.1　*Average £ return per insertion*

Recommendation

The exercise proved to be a highly important learning operation which allowed the following recommendations to be made to client:

1. Save-by-Post should be repeated at the end of each month.
2. Up-market daily and Sunday newspapers should be used.
3. The number of insertions in daily papers should be limited to two in any one week.
4. Local press should only be considered if it has an up-market readership profile (for example, *The Scotsman*).

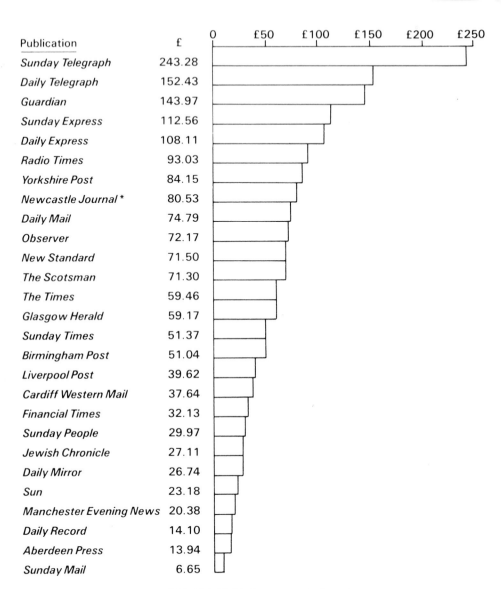

Publication	£
Sunday Telegraph	243.28
Daily Telegraph	152.43
Guardian	143.97
Sunday Express	112.56
Daily Express	108.11
Radio Times	93.03
Yorkshire Post	84.15
Newcastle Journal *	80.53
Daily Mail	74.79
Observer	72.17
New Standard	71.50
The Scotsman	71.30
The Times	59.46
Glasgow Herald	59.17
Sunday Times	51.37
Birmingham Post	51.04
Liverpool Post	39.62
Cardiff Western Mail	37.64
Financial Times	32.13
Sunday People	29.97
Jewish Chronicle	27.11
Daily Mirror	26.74
Sun	23.18
Manchester Evening News	20.38
Daily Record	14.10
Aberdeen Press	13.94
Sunday Mail	6.65

*Includes one deposit for £200 000; if this is removed, the return
per £ invested drops to £19.63 and ranked position drops to
24th.

Figure 2.2   *Amount returned per £ invested*

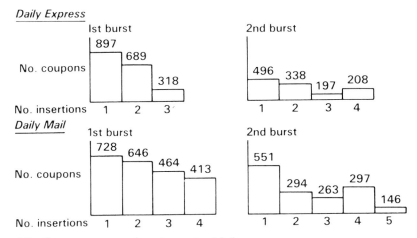

Figure 2.3 *Coupon response per insertion, national daily press*

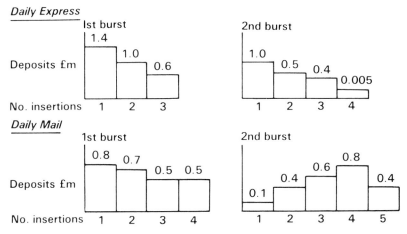

Figure 2.4 *Deposit value per insertion, national daily press*

5. In future campaigns, smaller space sizes should be tested to reduce the investment cost.
6. General interest magazines should be tested to find out whether the success of the *Radio Times* can be repeated.

CONCLUSIONS

1. The two objectives – a new consumer franchise and its cost-effective development – were met.
2. Save-by-Post could become a regular part of the NSB portfolio of investment, without the need for substantial reorganization and at no extra management cost. This test operation was followed up by a further exercise in the autumn of 1981 and again this year.

3. The experience of this test activity allowed for the use in the future of a more limited and even more cost-effective media list of six publications.

4. The results showed the potential attraction of the National Savings Bank Investment Account in surprising ways: amounts up to the £200 000 limit came in; one initial deposit of £5 was succeeded the following month by a subsequent £80 000; and deposits in *cash* arrived, up to £1000, sometimes without even an indication on the coupon of the amount sent in, so that the strict security of the operation's handling was validated.

3
Advertising: Key to the Success of Kellogg's Super Noodles

INTRODUCTION

This case history examines the national launch of Super Noodles, a completely new product from Kellogg. It shows how a modification to the advertising copy, together with sustained advertising expenditure, have taken the brand through the initial launch into a successful brand worth over £5 million at RSP.

The brand was launched nationally on 20 August 1979, with television advertising planned for October. However, the ITV strike meant that posters and black and white press had to be used for the launch and television did not start until January 1980. Since then, however, it can be demonstrated that television advertising has been the key component in its successes.

BUSINESS BACKGROUND

Product Characteristics

Kellogg is the major cereal manufacturer in the UK, with a considerable consumer franchise and reputation. An opportunity existed for Kellogg to harness this consumer reputation outside the cereal business.

The company had available a quick-cooking Japanese noodle product, which was at the time quite unique. Research indicated that the primary appeal of the product, when cooked with added flavouring, was as a main meal accompaniment. Consumers found the product too bland to be consumed on its own as a snack, yet saw it as an acceptable part of a main meal when used as an alternative to potatoes.

Market Opportunity

Having identified the product opportunity, we needed to identify the size of the market-place. We took a market definition of 'starch bulk meal components', which comprised the products shown in Table 3.1.

TABLE 3.1:   STARCH BULK MEAL COMPONENTS

	1977 £m RSP
Fresh potatoes	475
Instant potatoes	19
Packet pasta	13
Canned pasta	33
Packet rice	25
Savoury rice	5
Total	570

Sources: National Food Survey/Mintel

We concluded that if we could successfully position the product as a contender in this category there was a large market opportunity.

The bulk of the market, that is, fresh potatoes, was largely unbranded, yet successful entrants into the category, for example Smash (see Table 3.2), had achieved success despite relatively high price, through consistent and heavy-weight consumer advertising.

TABLE 3.2:   SMASH ADSPEND IN £'000s

1973	1974	1975	1976	1977
561	621	690	898	901

Source: MEAL

For Super Noodles to succeed, the brand had to be clearly positioned with a competitive benefit against an established market category *and* consistently supported with heavy and strongly-branded advertising communicating the desired positioning.

Additionally, the emergence in test market of instant pot noodle products, marketed as snacks, meant that Super Noodles needed to be clearly differentiated from these products, that is, as a main meal accompaniment. In fact, the competitive threat posed by the pot noodle products led to a decision to launch the Kellogg brand nationally, to pre-empt the pot products roll-out.

MARKETING AND ADVERTISING LAUNCH OBJECTIVES

Marketing Objectives

The marketing objectives of Super Noodles were:

— to launch a major new non-cereal Kellogg brand in the UK worth £5 million at RSP within three years;
— to achieve volume sales in first full year of launch of over 9 000 000 packs.

Advertising Objective

The overall advertising objective was to build awareness and trial for the brand, achieving 45 per cent awareness and 9 per cent trial by the end of the first full year of launch.

Creative Strategy

TARGET AUDIENCE

Housewives with children B, C1, C2, particularly instant mashed potato users, who are attitudinally experimental.

CONSUMER PROPOSITION

New Kellogg's Super Noodles are an exciting, easy to prepare alternative to potatoes.

SUPPORT

Noodles with special sachet of seasoning in a range of tasty flavours that cook in just four minutes.

TONE

Introductory, appetizing, modern, fun.

Creative Execution

It was clear from our initial product concept work, that we needed to establish Super Noodles as a highly acceptable alternative to potatoes, in the context of a main meal eating occasion.

We pre-tested animatic material and found that an animated potato extolling the virtues of Super Noodles was a potentially impactful and credible creative vehicle.

It allowed us to make claims for the product without in any way devaluing potatoes, which would have been incredible to consumers.

The finished execution of 'Give potatoes a day off' was further quantitatively tested, and results showed clear communication of the positioning, with good branding.

Budget

In order to help set a budget level for the launch, we used the Leo Burnett Chicago new product model. Based on considerable back data from previous new product launches, this provides forecasts of likely awareness and trial achievements for given levels of television ratings. Given Super Noodles' awareness and trial objectives, a necessary strike rate could be determined from the model. Using the anticipated cost of this amount of air time as a start point, and taking account of the three-year profit target, the budget was set at £1 000 000 for the first year of national launch.

EVERYONE LOVES POTATOES, BUT ONCE IN A WHILE, IT'S NICE TO GIVE THEM A DAY OFF...

AND NOW YOU CAN WITH NEW KELLOGG'S SUPER NOODLES.

THEY SIMMER IN THEIR OWN SPECIAL FLAVOURS.

AND IN ABOUT 4 MINUTES...

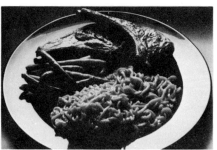

YOU'VE GOT SOMETHING THAT'S GOOD AND FILLING...

AND FULL OF FLAVOUR. CURRY, CHICKEN...

OR BARBECUE FLAVOURS.

NEW KELLOGG'S SUPER NOODLES.
GOOD ENOUGH TO GIVE POTATOES A DAY OFF.

Media Strategy

To make the launch highly visible and to maintain awareness of the product across the first full year of sale, a mixed media schedule was recommended, targeted at housewives with children. Television was recommended as the primary medium to provide rapid build-up of coverage, whilst women's magazines were used at launch to provide additional support, giving the opportunity for couponing and serving suggestions.

The television budget was estimated to deliver 1300 TVRs (30 seconds) during the launch year. Given our desire to build rapid awareness, we aimed to use an opening TV burst of six weeks (of 570 TVRs), in the autumn of 1979, supported by women's and general interest colour magazines. This was to be followed by four bursts of television activity over 1980.

In fact, the brand was launched coincidentally with the start of the ITV strike, and our launch media plans had to be substantially modified over the first three months, with money diverted into black and white press and posters, and only 190 TVRs achieved on television.

LAUNCH CAMPAIGN EVALUATION

Super Noodles' in-market performance was closely evaluated during the first year of launch, using both *consumer studies* and *retail audit data* designed to provide a fast and accurate measure of the brand's standing. On the consumer side, ad hoc dip-stick tracking studies which could be reported quickly were fielded at strategic intervals to monitor awareness, trial and usage. On the retail side, Mars Group Services' continuous grocery audit was chosen to monitor sales and distribution, with data collected on a four-weekly basis and available within a week of measurement. These sales data provided the input for a statistical analysis to determine specifically the effect of advertising on the brand's performance.

The research showed that, after a disappointing start, with the advent of sustained television advertising Super Noodles performed extremely well, achieving pre-set sales and consumer targets. The analysis provided the evidence that advertising was indeed the main reason for the sales gains, and highlighted the fact that the brand was very advertising responsive, albeit in the short term.

Consumer Research

Ad hoc dip-stick tracking studies were conducted by Public Attitude Surveys Ltd amongst nationally representative samples of housewives, in November 1979 and February, May and October 1980, timed to follow successive bursts of advertising.

The results showed that Super Noodles was very slow to respond over the period of initial press and poster advertising in the last quarter of 1979, but that with the start of television advertising in 1980 awareness and trial started to come through, and year-end targets were achieved (Table 3.3).

TABLE 3.3:   SUPER NOODLES AWARENESS AND TRIAL

	Nov. 1979	Feb. 1980	May 1980	Oct. 1980	Year target
Base: All housewives	1872	1292	1014	1063	
Prompted brand awareness	22%	36%	45%	42%	45%
Ever bought	5%	9%	8%	10%	9%

Furthermore, among Super Noodles trialists, an encouraging level of repeat buying was reached during 1980 (Table 3.4.).

TABLE 3.4:   SUPER NOODLES REPEAT PURCHASE

	Nov. 1979	Feb. 1980	May 1980	Oct. 1980
Base: Super Noodles ever bought	98	115	82	111
Bought once only	58%	33%	38%	32%
Bought more than once	42%	67%	62%	68%

Whilst at this stage the effect of advertising per se cannot be isolated, the consumer research did provide some clues as to how it might be working, with sustained television advertising clearly needed to communicate the desired meal accompaniment positioning. By the end of the first year of launch, trialists had understood how the product should be served, as can be seen from their claimed eating habits, but the direct impact of the advertising did appear to be weakening somewhat (Tables 3.5 and 3.6).

TABLE 3.5:   SUPER NOODLES ADVERTISING AWARENESS AND RECALL

	November 1979	February 1980	October 1980
Base: Super Noodles ever bought	98	115	111
Claimed advertising awareness	45%	58%	48%
Of which recall:			
'Give potatoes a rest/use instead of potatoes'	39%	66%	61%

TABLE 3.6:   SUPER NOODLES SERVING PATTERNS

	October 1980
Base: Super Noodles ever bought	111
How Super Noodles served:	
Meal accompaniment	*82%*
Sausages	25%
Chops/steak/mixed grill	17%
Chicken	11%
Beefburgers	8%
Other meat	10%
On their own	*18%*

Mars Retail Audit

Meanwhile, continuous retail audit data were providing further evidence as to Super Noodles performance. Four-weekly sales off-take figures had been showing a poor perform-ance against target in the last quarter of 1979 but the situation improved considerably with the advent of TV support in the new year. (See Figure 3.1.) By inspection, two key factors needed to be taken into account in evaluating Super Noodles' sales – *distribution*, where poor levels would certainly seem to have been hampering initial off-take, and *advertising support*, with each burst associated with an immediate and marked sales gain, which then fell away.

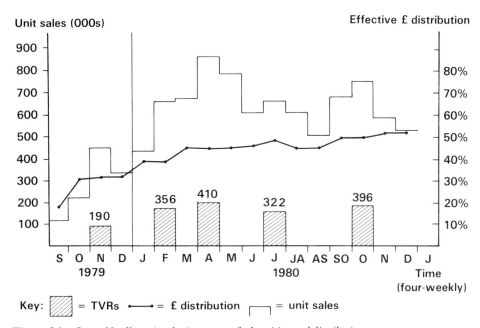

Figure 3.1 *Super Noodles unit sales in context of advertising and distribution*

At this stage, with the data certainly suggesting a link between advertising and sales, a comprehensive statistical analysis was undertaken to provide evidence as to an advertising effect.

Statistical Analysis

INTRODUCTION

In order to provide a more definite assessment of the effect of advertising on Super Noodles' sales an econometric analysis of the data was undertaken. This involves developing a model of the market which sets out to establish the numerical relationship between the brand's sales and a number of variables which could have an effect on those sales, i.e. short-term sales movements are 'explained' as a function of changes in outside factors, in the form of a simple algebraic equation:

$$\text{Brand Sales} = A \times \text{Advertising} + B \times \text{Distribution} + C \times \text{Price} + D$$

The procedure involves computer analysis to find the values of the constants in the equation, to provide the best explanation or fit to actual historical sales data. Judgement and common-sense play a large part in deciding what factors might have an effect on sales, and hence what data to input. The computer analysis then determines whether the factors (singly or in combination) do have an effect, and of what magnitude, with the success of the operation being judged by how good a match the final model equation provides to sales data. In this way the effect of advertising can be isolated from the effect of other factors, and quantified.

The advertising effect itself can be described in terms of four key measures, which together provide an explanation of how advertising is working for the brand in question.

1. The proportion of sales movements 'explained' by advertising and thus its importance in the marketing mix.

2. The 'base' or residual level of sales estimated to exist when advertising support reduces to zero. This tells us about the extent of the longer-term or permanent effects of advertising.

3. The advertising elasticity or short-term responsiveness of the brand, expressed as the increase in sales generated by a given increase in advertising level.

4. The decay rate of the advertising, or how quickly the effect fades away. This is expressed as a 'half-life' or the time taken to reach half the total effect of the advertising.

The econometric analysis provides data on each of these measures, starting with the decay rate. The decay rate is used to notionally spread the advertising over time, to take account of the fact that it has both an immediate effect and also a delayed effect in later time periods. This process of apportionment produces a measure of the effective amount of advertising in any given period (termed 'adstock'), and it is this which has to be used in deducing a direct relationship with sales in the full analysis.

ANALYSIS

For Super Noodles, the model was constructed using four-weekly Mars Audit Data on volume sales (000s units), with an 'explanation' explored on the basis of three variables:

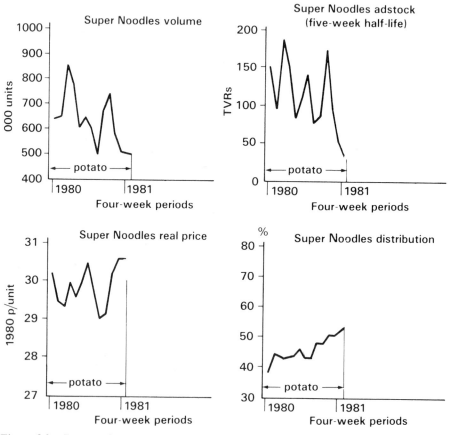

Figure 3.2   *Factors influencing Super Noodles sales*

— advertising (weekly 30-second h/w TVRs converted to four-weekly adstock using an appropriate decay rate)
— distribution (total effective £ weighted)
— price (sales value divided by sales volume for price per unit, deflated by RPI to March 1980 pence)

The time period chosen was one full year from the start of the television advertising with the launch 'Potato' execution (periods 1 to 13 in an analysis spanning February 1980 to January 1981), and Figure 3.2 shows how each of these factors varied over the period.

The first stage of the analysis involved the choice of a decay rate to convert advertising TVRs to adstock, with the model showing how good the data fit was for alternative half-lives by the strength of correlation observed (Table 3.7).

TABLE 3.7:   OPTIMUM DECAY RATE (POTATO)

Decay rate half-life (weeks)	Correlation coefficient (Adstock v. sales volume)
2	0.806
3	0.831
4	0.841
5	0.842
6	0.836
7	0.825
8	0.810
10	0.767

The analysis revealed two key findings for Super Noodles advertising:

— A half-life of five weeks provided the optimum fit, though three to six weeks was an acceptable range
— The correlation here was so strong that adstock or advertising *alone* provided a very good explanation of sales (the coefficient of 0.842 is equivalent to explaining over 70 per cent of the variation in sales).

Having established the parameters of the advertising component, the next stage of the analysis involved a step-wise linear regression, to look at the contribution of other factors as well as advertising in explaining sales. As can be seen below (Table 3.8), price and distribution did not in fact improve the explanation (increase the correlation) substantially.

TABLE 3.8:   STEP-WISE CONTRIBUTION OF FACTORS
IN EXPLAINING SALES (POTATO)

	Multiple correlation coefficient
1. Adstock	0.842
2. Adstock + price	0.897
3. Adstock + price + distribution	0.903

In the first instance, therefore, a model or sales equation was computed from adstock alone, corresponding to the relationship between advertising and sales shown in Figure 6.3.

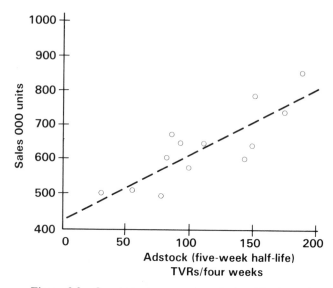

Figure 3.3   *Correlation between sales and advertising (potato)*

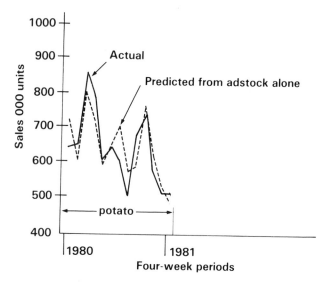

Figure 3.4   *Model predictions v. actual sales (potato)*

KEY FINDINGS

The implications of this analysis in terms of Super Noodles' advertising effectiveness, deduced from the key values identified in the calculations, were as follows.

1. Super Noodles is a very advertising-responsive brand:
    —   Advertising weight alone explained over 70 per cent of the variation in sales;
    —   In any given period, the degree of sales response achieved for increases in adver-

tising was encouragingly high (advertising elasticity = 0.31 compared with a norm of 0.20).

2. The advertising effect has so far appeared to be short term:
   — There was a relatively fast rate of decay of response, such that the effect was half over in five weeks;
   — The base or residual level of sales was not showing signs of increasing over time which would indicate a long-term, more permanent effect.

These findings were validated in the very good fit the model equation achieved in predicting actual sales, as shown in Figure 3.4.

At this stage, therefore, analysis showed that advertising had a key role to play in the launch of Super Noodles, being a major contributor to sales over 1980. There was, however, evidence that it could be made to work even harder for the brand on a longer-term basis, if these sales gains were to be consolidated and built on in 1981, a key requirement for continued success.

MODIFYING THE ADVERTISING AND MARKETING MIX

Whilst the brand had made considerable progress by the end of 1980, it was clearly necessary to continue the momentum into 1981. The research and analysis already conducted to evaluate Super Noodles' performance served to provide guidance as to the brand's current position, and hence how best to exploit its potential further.

In order to build the brand, it was clearly necessary to increase penetration, but over and above that to develop a greater continuity of purchase. The first year's results suggested that Super Noodles was an advertising-led 'impulse' busy, and therefore a key task for the second year would be to make the product part of an established repertoire of main meal accompaniments – a regular rather than intermittent purchase.

Overall, it was apparent that Super Noodles was still in the investment stage, and pressure (from distribution, advertising, point of sale efforts and so on) must be kept up to develop its full potential for longer-term returns. All elements of the marketing mix were re-examined in the light of their contribution to building a sustained presence and interest in the brand, as detailed below.

Product

Super Noodles was launched in three flavours, but it was felt that the introduction of additional varieties could help maintain product interest, thus increasing frequency of purchase and generating incremental volume. In 1981, therefore, three new flavours were introduced, designed to broaden consumer appeal whilst having the additional benefit of strengthening on-shelf presence.

Packaging

With hindsight, it was judged that the initial launch pack did not differentiate individual flavours strongly enough. Given the intention to add flavours to the range to increase frequency of use, it was felt to be essential to increase flavour differentiation.

The packaging was therefore modified for 1982, improving flavour identification, and also strengthening the Super Noodles branding.

The overall effect of the re-packaging was improved modernity, branding and shelf impact. In addition, a new stackable outer was introduced with the new flavours and new packs to increase facings and display opportunities.

Availability

A key requirement for 1981 was to increase distribution to the target level of 65 per cent (£ weighted), concentrating on key multiples as the prime source. With evidence to suggest significant off-take in response to advertising, potential stockists could be convinced as to the value of taking Super Noodles, whilst existing stockists could be encouraged to increase facings and stock-cover to meet demand.

Advertising

CREATIVE

With some evidence to suggest that the impact of launch advertising was diminishing, it was felt that new creative work was required. Further research was therefore conducted to explore the best way of developing the 'Give potatoes a day off' advertising route for the second year in market. At this stage, however, it was found that a strategy setting Super Noodles up as an alternative to potatoes was no longer the best way to go. Whilst necessary at launch to position the product away from pot noodles, now the distinction was clearly drawn, and Super Noodles needed to be established and built up *in its own right* as a different and delicious meal accompaniment, not just in the context of a (potentially infrequent) substitute for potatoes.

The consumer proposition was therefore changed to: 'Super Noodles are a different, delicious tasting, convenient main meal accompaniment,' and a new execution dramatizing the product's appeal and versatility was developed with the broader-based theme of 'Add a new twist to mealtime'.

MEDIA

The experience of 1980 clearly indicated that television advertising had had a major impact on sales, but that further investment was required to maintain momentum and fully develop the brand's potential. Given Super Noodles' responsiveness to adspend, with sales off-take increasing where the brand was stocked during a burst, it was felt that continued advertising support together with a distribution drive should certainly lead to significantly increased volume.

An increased media budget of £1 300 000 was proposed for 1981, giving an estimated total TVR delivery of 1440 (30 seconds). As regards laydown, the 1980 evaluation had shown a relatively fast decay rate for television advertising, which suggested that lengthy gaps between bursts should be minimized. In addition, the key objective of increasing the trial base necessitated a threshold strike rate across the country. The final plan provided for four bursts of 360 TVRs deployed throughout the year, with equal impacts across areas.

Want to add a new twist to mealtimes?

Twist those Super Noodles, Kellogg's . . .
Super . . . Noodles.

Just drop the Noodles in boiling water.

Add the flavour packet, stir and simmer for
four minutes.

Then serve them – with bangers.

Twist those Super Noodles – with burgers.

Kellogg's Super Noodles – with chicken.
Twist those Kellogg's Super Noodles.

Kellogg's Super Noodles add a new twist to
mealtimes.

All the modifications to the marketing mix for Super Noodles, together with the proposed advertising and stocking support, were incorporated into a national plan. With all the evidence to date, it was strongly felt that the changes represented the best way forward for the brand, and that critical time would be lost if regional experimentation were undertaken. Overall, the total new 'package' was designed to generate a significant sales gain in 1981, and an ex-factory sales budget incorporating a 26 per cent increase over 1980 was laid down.

YEAR TWO EVALUATION

Given the ambitious growth strategy planned for Super Noodles in its second year, it was important to continue monitoring the brand closely to evaluate performance in the light of various changes being made to the marketing mix. In particular, of course, guidance was needed as to how the new 'Twist' advertising was working. The methods of evaluation remained essentially the same, with the opportunity being taken to use consumer tracking studies for checking awareness and trial, whilst the ongoing Mars audit data provided basic sales and distribution information as input to a full statistical analysis. In addition, ex-factory sales results provided a useful overview.

The research and analysis showed a continuing successful performance for Super Noodles, with advertising again identified as a major contributor to sales gains. Furthermore, the new 'Twist' copy was shown to be working harder for the brand than the original 'Potato' execution in providing greater *long-term* benefits to Super Noodles.

Ex-factory Sales

On a launch budget index basis, it can be seen (Table 3.9) that ex-factory sales of Super Noodles in year two were significantly higher than those budgeted and achieved in year one. More importantly, shipments were ahead of target for 1981 despite an ambitious growth plan, providing considerable encouragement for the future.

TABLE 3.9:   INDEXED EX-FACTORY SALES

	Budget 1980	Actual 1980	Budget 1981	Actual 1981
Ex-factory unit sales (indexed)	100	102	126	141

Consumer Research

Tracking studies implemented at strategic post advertising points over 1981–2 indicated that awareness and trial were growing steadily over this second year in market (Table 3.10), with the repeat buying rate amongst trialists particularly encouraging (Table 3.11). All this was happening against a backdrop of the new 'Twist' advertising, and suggested that the brand was becoming a more established product in the housewife's buying repertoire.

TABLE 3.10:   SUPER NOODLES AWARENESS AND TRIAL

	Oct. 1980	Mar. 1981	Sept. 1981	June 1982
Base (All housewives)	1063	802	866	794
Prompted brand awareness	42%	45%	49%	63%
Ever bought	10%	12%	14%	16%

TABLE 3.11:   SUPER NOODLES REPEAT PURCHASE

	Oct. 1980	June 1982
Base (Super Noodles ever bought)	111	123
Bought once only	32%	23%
Bought more than once	68%	77%
Buy 2–3 times a month or more often	n/a	36%

Mars Retail Audit

The continuous four-weekly sales data showed clearly that Super Noodles' consumer off-take increased significantly in the second year of launch, with an overall year-on-year gain of 26 per cent over the period of the new television advertising. As in 1980, a pattern of peaks and troughs can be seen which appeared to correspond to the presence or absence of advertising support (Figure 3.5).

The relationship was now a little less clear by inspection alone, however, and the marked improvement in distribution levels (which finally achieved target) needed to be taken into account. Again, this formed the basis for a full statistical analysis to isolate the effect of advertising.

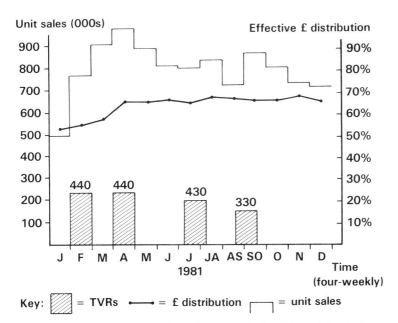

Figure 3.5 *Super Noodles unit sales in the context of advertising and distribution*

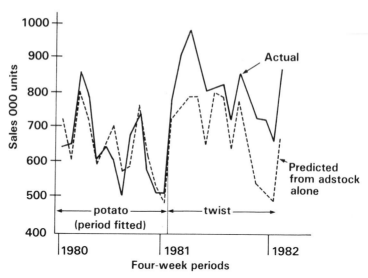

Figure 3.6   *Model predictions (potato) v. actual sales (twist)*

Statistical Analysis

Having already produced an econometric model applicable to 1980 data which provided a very good explanation of Super Noodles sales, the first issue was clearly to explore whether it was still relevant in explaining the sales gains achieved over 1981. Indeed, one of the ways of validating an econometric model is to examine its efficiency in predicting actual sales following the initial period of analysis.

Using the model based on advertising alone, it can be seen that in 1981, with new 'Twist' advertising, sales were significantly higher than would have been expected based on the performance of the original 'Potato' advertising alone, indicating that something different was happening in the market-place from what had gone before (Figure 3.6).

A new analysis was clearly required which would explain what factors were affecting Super Noodles sales in 1981 and to what extent, such that a comparison could be made with 1980. As before, the model was constructed using four-weekly Mars Audit Data on volume sales (actual sales shown above) but this time two analyses were undertaken. One involved the time of the 'Twist' campaign alone, to check differences (periods 14–27 in the analysis, spanning February 1981 to February 1982), whilst the other used *all* the data available (periods 1–27), to provide a full and final explanation. The same three variables were used to try and explain sales, although new levels were operating in each case as indicated below and shown in Figure 3.7.

— Advertising (new 'Twist' commercial and a higher TVR rate).
— Price (lower real prices).
— Distribution (raised to a higher level).

The first stage of the analysis, as before, involved the choice of a suitable decay rate to convert advertising TVRs to adstock. Using the new campaign data (periods 14–27) the fits shown in Table 3.12 were obtained.

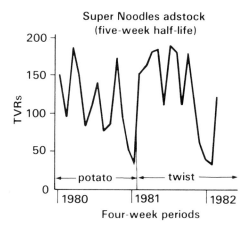

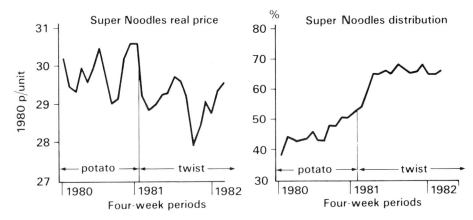

Figure 3.7   *Factors influencing Super Noodles sales*

TABLE 3.12:   OPTIMUM DECAY RATE
(TWIST)

Decay rate half-life (weeks)	Correlation coefficient (Adstock v. sales volume)
2	0.623
3	0.747
4	0.790
5	0.789
6	0.770
7	0.744
8	0.715
10	0.661

It can be seen that either four or five weeks' half-life provided a very good fit or correlation. Since five weeks was chosen before and continued to be adequate, it was used for both sets of periods.

Using this decay rate for both advertising components, the next stage of the analysis (step-wise linear regression) looked at the total contribution of all three factors in explaining sales, this time using the whole of the data for the most reliable determination.

As can be seen in Table 3.13, advertising was again the most important contributor to explaining sales, but now distribution and price were adding significantly, with all three being necessary to provide a good fit (over 80 per cent of sales variation explained).

TABLE 3.13:   STEP-WISE CONTRIBUTION OF
FACTORS IN EXPLAINING SALES
(POTATO + TWIST)

		Multiple correlation coefficient
1.	Adstock	0.719
2.	Adstock + distribution	0.876
3.	Adstock + distribution + price	0.912

Breaking down this full model into its component parts, it was found that the effects of price and distribution were not statistically different across the two periods of the analysis, and that the combined data therefore provided a good estimate to take.

For advertising, a different effect across the two periods was apparent, with year two showing a higher base or residual level of sales (long-term benefit) and a slightly lower advertising elasticity (short-term response). Although not statistically significant, other experience suggested that this was a real difference, with maximum advertising response most likely at the time of a brand's launch, and reducing thereafter. It was therefore decided to take separate estimates for the advertising effect – one for 'Potato' (periods 1–13) and one for 'Twist' (periods 14–27).

Thus, in order to provide a complete picture of the explanation of Super Noodles sales, a final analysis was undertaken using the full two years' data and with the following variables across the two periods:

Advertising: Same decay rate (5 weeks)
               Increase in base
               Different elasticities (0.31 in periods 1–13, 0.20 in periods 14–27)
Price: Same effect/elasticity used (-2.49)
Distribution: Same effect/elasticity used (0.33)

The resulting model equations* provided an excellent explanation of Super Noodles sales, as shown by the fit of predicted to actual sales in Figure 3.8 and confirmed by an overall correlation coefficient of 0.919 (equivalent to explaining 84 per cent of the variation in sales).

---

*Periods 1–13: Sales $= 2079.10 + 1.80$ Adstock $- 61.53$ Price $+ 4.29$ Distribution
 Period 14–27: Sales $= 2157.79 + 1.23$ Adstock $- 61.53$ Price $+ 4.29$ Distribution

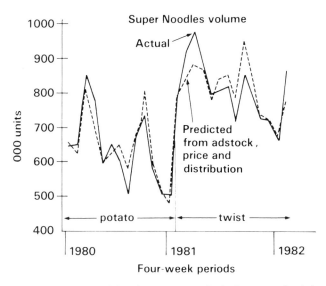

Figure 3.8 *Model predictions v. actual sales (potato and twist)*

KEY FINDINGS

The implications of this analysis in terms of understanding Super Noodles sales and in particular identifying the contribution made by advertising were as follows:

1. *Advertising.* This was the most important factor in generating sales over the first two years of launch, with Super Noodles clearly a very advertising-responsive brand. With the new 'Twist' commercial we made the advertising work harder for the brand by

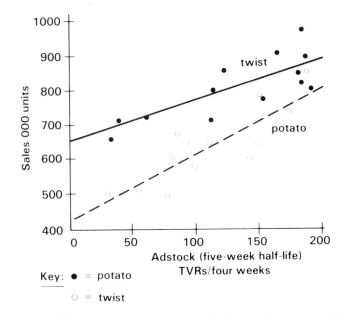

Figure 3.9 *Correlation between sales and advertising (potato v. twist)*

creating a higher base level of sales, indicative of a longer-term or permanent effect, and yet were still obtaining a very satisfactory short-term response with an advertising elasticity of 0.2. This would suggest that Super Noodles was becoming more of an on-going regular purchase than simply an intermittent advertising-led 'impulse' buy. The greater contribution made by the new advertising is indicated above (Figure 3.9), with a permanent base level sales effect equivalent to 224 000 units per four weeks.

2. *Price*. This did not alter much so we cannot be sure of the effect of a large change, but with a high observed price elasticity (-2.5) this meant that Super Noodles could be price sensitive, i.e. a price cut could produce considerable additional volume.

3. *Distribution*. This increased considerably and had a clear but not directly proportional effect.

Overall, therefore, the analysis provided a very believable explanation of Super Noodles' sales over a period of growth and development, and was the means of isolating and quantifying the significant effect of advertising in the marketing mix.

CONCLUSION

The facts presented demonstrate that the launch of Super Noodles nationally has been a major success. Further, the brand has become an established going brand and the volume generated as a result of sustained advertising investment has been profitable.

We have shown the significant role played by advertising in the first year of launch, and of perhaps even more interest, we have shown how modifications to the mix have resulted in an even greater success in year two.

It is significant to note that, unlike many new product launches, media investment was sustained in the year following launch, and that this investment was repaid by a worthwhile volume increase.

The brand achieved its three-year target of £5 million turnover by the end of year two, and established for Kellogg a major introduction outside the cereal market.

4

Whitegates

A Regional Success Story

INTRODUCTION

This paper concerns the launch of not only a new service, but also a new company – a new company in a traditional consumer service sector.

Although to date it can only be presented and titled as 'A Regional Success Story', it is, nevertheless, a case history in which the role of advertising has played a vital, practical and major role. Furthermore, it is the author's contention that, although the level of success which has been achieved is only in a geographically restricted marketing region, this does not in any way diminish the importance of the advertising effectiveness element. The claimed level of success will be demonstrated, as will the part that advertising has played.

Because the submission deals with a 'new service' rather than goods, the measurement criteria cannot be based simply on the 'hard' measurement of sales, but must, of necessity, be based on the equally significant and (in this case) more relevant measurements of behavioural evidence, attitudes and awareness as well as on the sheer growth and success record of the new company. The reason for using these measurement criteria will become obvious in later sections.

The effectiveness of the strategy and campaign involved and the level of marketing achievement can be summarized as follows:

In less than two and a half years, the campaign concerned has successfully launched an entirely new company offering a dramatically different service in a traditionally competitive field of consumer service. It has done so through an aggressive and effective advertising campaign supported by other important elements of the marketing mix to the point where the company concerned can now claim market leadership in the area with a record of growth and expansion far in excess of the most optimistic forecasts.

Whilst it is, overall, a marketing success, the part that advertising has played is recognized as, and agreed to be, enormous. Without the solid foundation stones of truly effective advertising, such a marketing success could not have been built.

BACKGROUND

Provident Financial Group Limited, based in Bradford, is a public company specializing in consumer credit – the largest consumer credit trading organization of its kind. Through a number of subsidiary companies, Provident Personal Credit, Practical Credit Services, etc., the Group provides consumer credit to the weekly paid market and principally serves C2D households. The Group has, for a number of years, been considering areas for diversification and opportunity. The main criteria, in consideration of diversifying markets, were to employ the skills and facilities possessed by the Group. These were identified as in-depth management and marketing skills, finance, and the availability of computer capacity and expertise (the Group has its own massive computer complex designed to service the multiple transactions involved through its various credit trading organizations).

The corporate planning unit within the Group had identified various markets which could make use of these resources and facilities and in 1977 the decision was taken to apply the availability of computer capacity and techniques, linked to management and finance, to enter the field of domestic property estate agency. In-depth research of the domestic estate agency market throughout the United Kingdom and the real estate market in the United States led the company to the conclusion that the concept of using computer time and skills in house marketing presented an opportunity in the United Kingdom.

Consequently, in mid-1977, it was decided to launch, in one region of the country, an entirely new estate agency concept. The new service using the house marketing idea would utilize the computer's capability to match buyers with sellers through a central matching facility. It would also offer a comprehensive computer-backed service featuring fixed fees, a 'no-sale, no-charge' agreement, seven days a week opening, evening opening hours and the production of a computer compiled *Property Weekly* with a highly efficient computer controlled mailing service.

MARKETING AND ADVERTISING OBJECTIVES

The launch of the new service was planned for 1st January 1978 and a decision was taken to promote the completely new house marketing (estate agency) service in the Yorkshire television region.

Desk research showed that Yorkshire represented an area typical of the UK market with profiles of home ownership, households and individuals very much in line with the rest of the country (Tables 4.1, 4.2 and 4.3).

A more precise sample of the United Kingdom could hardly have been obtained. This fact, coupled with the convenience of the area (being the company's home territory, thus

TABLE 4.1:   TYPE OF TENURE

	GB %	Yorkshire %
Owner occupied	52.5	52.8
buying home	31.3	32.8
own outright	21.2	20.0
Rent from Council	35.1	33.8
Other tenure	12.4	13.4
All adults	100.0	100.0

TGI, 1976.

TABLE 4.2:   AGE OF DWELLINGS – DECEMBER 1974

	GB %	Yorkshire %
Pre-1918	33	33
1919–1944	23	23
Post-1944	44	44
Total	100	100

Abstract of Regional Statistics, 1975.

TABLE 4.3:   PROFILES OF HOUSEHOLDS IN YORKSHIRE AND UK

	UK 000s	%	Yorkshire 000s	%	Yorkshire % of UK
All households	19 304	100	2524	100	13.1
Social class:					
AB	2316	12	256	10	11.1
C1	3772	20	442	18	11.7
C2	6690	35	967	38	14.5
DE	6526	34	859	34	13.2

making it more easy to monitor and control), made it the most obvious launch area for the venture.

In light of the competitive nature of the market, coupled with the investment needed, and the uncertainty of the level of success, no detailed expansion plans beyond the Yorkshire television area were set down, although outline proposals were made.

The initial plan was to have two offices operational on 1st January 1978 serving the Leeds and Bradford conurbations and it was at this stage that the Group's agency, Bowden Dyble and Hayes Limited, was brought in to help develop the detailed marketing and advertising plans. The agency's initial brief included the need to develop a title and style for the company: the project at this stage was still being referred to as 'House Marketing Limited'. There was a need to establish a visual styling for the new organization and to prepare detailed advertising proposals covering media strategy, creative treatment, company image, promotional plans, etc.

Part of the marketing brief was to extend the new estate agency service as quickly as possible throughout the Yorkshire region. The precise rate of expansion was to be dependent upon the success of the first branches in operation. In turn, the success of the operation would be dependent upon rapid build-up of consumer awareness, the acceptance of the new company in a competitive and crowded market, establishment of the company's main selling points, and volume throughput of sellers and buyers.

By definition, the estate agency market is a finite one. There is very little, if anything, that marketeers can do to expand it. People's decisions to buy and sell domestic property are influenced by pressures other than marketing and advertising and there could be no expectation of any market growth to satisfy the newly-formulated company.

Consequently, it was recognized that any growth and expansion of the new service would be obtainable only by capturing market share from existing and, in most cases, well established competitors in the market.

The principal marketing and advertising objective, therefore, had to be the forceful and effective projection of the new service in order to ensure that a significant slice of the existing market was captured at the expense of those existing companies.

It was agreed at this early stage that the principal market sector was to be medium-priced property in the domestic market, but, recognizing that the service had an appeal to *all* house buyers and sellers, there was no limit placed on potential users – neither a lower nor a higher value of property was excluded.

The marketing objective in terms of the development of outlets was to move as quickly as possible to the position of having an outlet in each of the main centres of population in the Yorkshire/Humberside region based on the population assessment (centres and hinterland) of the key centres. The location of branches was agreed to be in city or town centre locations on the premise that, if the new service was promoted effectively enough, prospective customers would be willing to visit centrally based units, particularly since these would be open during weekday evenings and at weekends.

The main centres of population throughout the Yorkshire TV region were identified and these became the prime targets for extension of the new services, the principal centres being Sheffield, Leeds, Hull, Bradford, Barnsley and Doncaster.

CAMPAIGN STRATEGIES

Before describing the particular media and creative strategies developed, it is important to understand that the agency and the company had first of all to overcome the basic problem of how to launch two new estate agency offices on 1st January with no properties on the books. By definition, an estate agency cannot be trading, and therefore can hardly advertise the fact that it is trading, without having a product to sell, i.e. without having some properties 'on the books'. This problem was overcome, before the first two offices commenced to trade, by running an incentive offer in the relevant evening newspapers covering the Leeds and Bradford conurbations.

The offer had to be simple, effective and dramatic. A plan was developed to undertake to sell the first 100 houses on the new estate agent's books at an all-in price of £100 – a very aggressive and competitive offer. This offer was featured for a number of weeks prior to the official opening of the branches and the resulting response ensured that, on the due date of 1st January, the new service and the new offices could be advertised because they now had a stock of properties to which they could apply the services they were offering.

The basic media strategy employed following the opening announcement offer (which has since been used in similar form to launch the opening of all other offices) was the extensive use of Yorkshire Television.

This media decision was taken for five main reasons: (1) there was a need to establish the name and the service quickly; (2) there was a need to project the new service as a modern and go-ahead organization; (3) a local rate facility on the Yorkshire Television rate card (whilst only two offices were involved) offered an advantageous rate opportunity; (4) promotion of the name and the service in the areas not yet served by local offices, i.e. the rest of the Yorkshire Television area, represented a 'softening-up' of that wider territory; (5) the use of the medium clearly distinguished the new organization from the traditional local and regional estate agency services.

For only £100, we'll sell your house on TV.

In January, a new kind of estate agent is opening in Bradford.

We're called Whitegates.

And like one or two of the larger estate agents, we'll be publishing a free property weekly carrying details of all our houses.

But what makes us really different is that the Whitegates Weekly will be advertised regularly and frequently on TV, to over 5½ million people.

So if you sell through Whitegates, you can be pretty certain anyone looking for a house in Yorkshire is going to get details of your property.

Of course, we'll also display a photograph and a description of your house in our Property Showrooms.

(We're the only ones in the area to open seven days a week.)

And we'll register all the details of your property on a £1m computer, which accurately and automatically

OPENING HOURS
MONDAY TO FRIDAY
9.00 am to 8.15 pm
SATURDAY
9.00 am to 5.00 pm
SUNDAY
10.30 am to 4.30 pm

matches houses to potential purchasers.

But what's more we offer all these services at extremely competitive fees.

£100, plus 1% of the selling price of your house.

So on a £12,000 house, you'll pay a total of £220.

There are no further costs (except, of course, VAT), no hidden extras whatsoever, and we operate on a strictly no-sale, no-charge basis.

Compare our charges

with those made by other estate agents and we think you'll find there's only one way you can get a better deal if you're selling your house.

And that's by taking advantage of our incredible introductory offer.

We're selling the first 100 houses registered at each office for an all-inclusive fee of only £100. It doesn't matter whether your property is priced at £5,000 or £50,000.

To register your house, 'phone the number below, now.

And from January onwards, we'll be selling it on TV.

*Charges and conditions are based on the understanding that Whitegates are appointed on a 'sole agency' basis.

SELLING PRICE	WHITEGATES ALL-INCLUSIVE FEE
£5,000	£150
£10,000	£200
£15,000	£250
£20,000	£300
£25,000	£350

Whitegates

Tomorrow's kind of estate agent.

BRADFORD (0274) 306611

Whitegates press advertisement.

Stills from Whitegates television advertisement.

It was clear from the outset that the new concept of 'house marketing' required a dramatic and modern creative strategy yet still needed to be presented as relevant to the house buying/selling market.

The first creative problem which had to be overcome was the development of a suitable name and styling. Since time was of the essence, the selection of a name had to be made quickly.

Provident Financial Group Limited has many subsidiary and associated companies and there was obviously going to be some advantage, not least from a timing point of view, if an existing registered name could be adopted. One of the Group's registered but inactive companies was Whitegates Finance Limited, and after deliberation it was agreed that the name 'Whitegates' could be made to work in the 'house marketing' market.

The company was therefore registered and developed as 'Whitegates Estate Agency Ltd and the white gate itself became a clear, simple but memorable logo for use in all advertising and promotional elements. The choice of a 'mon repos' gate was deliberate to enable the mass of the house buying/selling public to identify with it. The name and symbol in close association were used on the fascias of offices, on house specification sheets and on all company stationery. The design itself was naturally taken through to 'For Sale' garden boards, which are essential elements in an estate agent's projection. In order to maintain the developing stance of a very modern, up-to-date company, the traditional garden board, usually made of plywood, hardboard, etc. was rejected and the company, in conjunction with the agency, pioneered the use of a garden board engineered in metal. This development was negotiated through an engineering company specializing in the production of motorway and other road signs. It proved to be a significant development and reflected clearly the forward-looking attitude and style being developed for the new company.

Having resolved the need to find a clear and simple logo in support of the Whitegates name, it became necessary to find a copy statement to be used in association with this logo which would, ideally, encapsulate the basic company philosophy. As a result, the supporting copy statement was developed as 'Tomorrow's kind of estate agent'. This copy claim was again a deliberate attempt to set the new organization apart, in an aggressive and modern way, from the traditional, locally entrenched estate agents. If the marketing and advertising stance was going to be effective then it was felt that a lot of new ground had to be broken in order to establish 'Tomorrow's kind of estate agent'. (By tradition, the field of estate agency is one that attracts little consumer interest and awareness – even the biggest organizations in the market tend to be old-fashioned and appear to have time-worn attitudes towards advertising and promotion. They are incredibly bad at projecting a forward-looking and efficient image.)

Consideration was given to a variety of creative strategies to support the need to project a modern, forward-looking company, and a number of approaches were developed to review stage including the use of various personalities. The idea of using a personality to give credibility and authority to the new service gained ground as the creative work was being developed and a number of candidates were considered.

At this time, when the whole basic creative strategy was being developed, Raymond Baxter had just finished a prolonged period as the presenter of the then highly successful 'Tomorrow's World' programme. The agency decided that he was just the right personality to give aggression, authority, credibility and style to the new company. After detailed negotiations, a series of television commercials was developed using Raymond Baxter (who agreed to undertake the role partly because of the forward-thinking attitude the company represented). Full use was made of Raymond Baxter's presentation style in a dramatic 'limbo' format to add weight to the fact that Whitegates was 'Tomorrow's kind of estate agent'.

The initial series of television advertisements, consisting of two 30-second commercials and four 15-second commercials, all used Raymond Baxter's personality and style to full effect. The 30-second commercials were structured to sell the fullest aspects of the service, one appealing to buyers and one appealing to sellers, with 15-second support commercials being used to accentuate each of the main points in the selling platform, e.g. the efficient computer controlled system, fixed fees, opening hours, the *Property Weekly*, etc. The plan was to use television for an eight-week continuous and heavy burst of activity to establish the Whitegates name and service, making specific reference to the branch offices in both Leeds and Bradford.

As the operation expanded and more branches were opened, so the local Yorkshire TV rate was no longer available to the company. But because of the earlier success and response it was decided to continue to use television at regional rates, supported by a relatively low level of press advertising in selected evening and weekly newspapers. Three follow-up bursts of TV activity took place following the initial eight-week launch campaign: March (four weeks), May/June (nine weeks) and September/October (eight weeks) – all using the same combination of 30-second and 15-second commercials.

MEASURING THE SUCCESS OF THE CAMPAIGN

It will by now be clear that 'hard' measurement criteria such as sales are difficult to apply in this case history. However, the criteria which can be used, and which are most relevant, are the factors of growth and expansion of the new company, measurement of consumer attitudes, awareness and behavioural evidence, and, most significantly, the company's position in the market place (starting from a position of non-existence).

Let's look first at growth and expansion.

Within the first year of trading (1978), Whitegates Estate Agency developed from having just two branches in Leeds and Bradford to having well established and successful offices in eight locations, including the prime centres of Sheffield, Hull and Barnsley.

Eight offices within twelve months – six of which were not even planned at the time the new company was launched in Bradford and Leeds in January 1978.

Because of the level of success and proven reaction to the 1978 television campaign, heavy use of the television medium continued throughout 1979. A new series of television commercials was produced, still featuring Raymond Baxter but now using an even more aggressive and confident style. By this time, more extensive use of local press had also been introduced to support the television activity. Each new branch opening, because of the 'softening' of the ground by the television campaigns, produced an ever-increasing stock of properties, to the extent that, in some cases, the initial stock almost became an embarrassment to the company.

Continued expansion through new branch openings took place in 1979, leading to the position in May 1980 where the company had twenty branches operating. This rapid build-up meant that Whitegates was established in almost all of the major population centres originally identified as the prime targets. Centres not yet represented were largely for reasons of lack of planning permission and/or failure to obtain satisfactory branch locations.

By the end of 1979 (two years after the launch), Whitegates Estate Agency was by far the biggest domestic estate agency in Yorkshire. In market share terms, *the company now (May 1980) holds at least 15 per cent of the total Yorkshire market,* has a stock of properties well in excess of 2000 spanning all types and values of property, and would claim to be the biggest domestic estate agency in the North of England – an incredible performance!

MEASURED BY RESEARCH

The part that effective advertising has had to play in this success story is perhaps best illustrated by an independent image study which was conducted by Scantel Research Limited for Whitegates *only eleven months* after the company commenced to trade.

This research consisted of two stages, using both qualitative and quantitative techniques. The results of the qualitative stage were used as an input into the quantitative stage, and consisted of discussion between Scantel's consultant psychologists, the company's negotiators and an initial number of interviews with respondents known to be selling their homes. The quantitative stage was in two parts, one designed for Whitegates users and one for non-users with interviews carried out in both the Leeds and Bradford areas.

The *unprompted awareness* of Whitegates *was higher than for any competing estate agency* and the *prompted awareness of Whitegates was 100 per cent* – this, in spite of the relatively recent appearance of the company on the market. Almost 85 per cent of Whitegates users mentioned television or press advertisements as their main source of awareness of the company. It must be remembered that many of the company's competitors have been trading in the areas concerned for as many as 50 years and yet *only one* other company achieved an unprompted awareness level comparable to Whitegates.

The following extracts from the Summary, Conclusion and Recommendations of the Research Report are relevant:

(*Scantel Research, Project No. 569, November 1978*)

5.0 SUMMARY AND CONCLUSIONS

'Non-users exhibited *a high level of unprompted awareness of Whitegates* and awareness was *100 per cent under prompted* conditions.

'A significant proportion of non-users claimed that they would have used Whitegates had they known about the company at the time of selecting an agent [the decision having been made to sell, and an estate agent appointed, prior to the Whitegates launch].

'Around 85 per cent of users had come to *know about Whitegates* through either television commercials or press advertisements.

'In contrast, most users of competitors had acquired their knowledge through personal experiences and/or contact.'

6.0 RECOMMENDATIONS

'Television and press campaigns have been extremely powerful in attracting customers to Whitegates. *Indeed on the evidence of this research, the launch campaign has been fundamental to the success of Whitegates, and we have no reason for believing that continued growth could be achieved without heavy and continuous promotional support.*'

The latest research findings re-confirm the part that television advertising has had to play in the Whitegates success. This research, undertaken by the Marketing Division of Provident Financial Group during September 1980, was to examine clients' attitudes immediately after the appointment of Whitegates to handle the sale of their property.

The research was conducted by post among 1000 customers, 42 per cent of whom responded to the survey. The resulting sample (used for analysis) was well stratified in terms of age/social grade of respondents, value of property, and location within Yorkshire.

Within this research questionnaire, clients were asked the source of their knowledge of Whitegates, viz: 'How did you first hear about Whitegates before you approached them?' Provision was made for more than one source to be indicated.

The result of this section of the survey is quoted from the report:

'TV emerges as the most powerful medium of information, being mentioned almost as often as all the other sources combined. TV is weaker in Harrogate and York where viewing is partially split between Yorkshire TV and Tyne Tees TV.

'The three main sources are analysed below:

	Solus mention		Mentioned with other		Total	
	No.	%	No.	%	No.	%
TV	161	38.2	131	31.1	292	69.3
Press	39	9.3	98	23.3	137	32.5
Recommendation	44	10.5	65	15.4	109	25.9

'With nearly 4 out of 10 respondents mentioning TV as the sole source, the strategy of spearheading promotional activity with this medium is confirmed. Detailed analysis of those giving TV a solus mention shows that proportionally rather more under-35s (about 5 per cent) gave this source than the two older age groups. However there was no discernible difference in the levels of TV mention in cases where the respondents were using an estate agent for the first or subsequent times, nor did the value of the property influence the levels.

'Press advertising alone would be unlikely to maintain adequate awareness but has its part to play more probably for the person who is already in a buying or selling situation. It has a rather stronger appeal to the older age groups.'

At a level of 69.4 per cent, TV advertising emerges as the most powerful medium of information – the strongest possible statement of advertising effectiveness!

CONCLUSIONS

Despite involvement in many previous marketing successes over a period of years, the agency has never been associated with an advertising campaign the effectiveness of which can be so clearly demonstrated as has been the case with the launch of Whitegates Estate Agency.

Not only is the company now extremely well established in its territory, having expanded at a rate far in excess of any of the forecasts made, but it has also broken new ground in promoting services which have hitherto not been effectively advertised through the television medium.

Indeed, such is the level of success that Trident Television now consider the Whitegates growth story so highly that they have used it for the promotion of their own television stations, through mailings, press releases and articles.

Of the 22 target centres in the Yorkshire Television region originally planned for the development programme, the company now has representation in almost all of them; and those which are not yet covered are at advanced stages in the future expansion plans.

Whilst the backbone of the advertising effort was effective television, this was supported by many other marketing elements, i.e. press advertising, sales brochures and shop fascias, all clearly showing the creative stance of Whitegates – 'Tomorrow's kind of estate agent'.

We submit that this campaign represents a proven and convincing case for the effectiveness of advertising.

There can be few products or services which have developed to market leadership in an established and highly competitive market in less than two and a half years. Whitegates Estate Agency and ourselves are convinced that this could not have been achieved without the help of the effective advertising campaign and strategy developed for them: a campaign of which our clients and we are justly proud.

5
The Case for All Clear Shampoo

BACKGROUND

Introduction

The anti-dandruff shampoo market is a considerable part of the total shampoo market with the medicated shampoo sector constituting some 35 per cent in 1979 of the total value of the market. It is dominated by Procter and Gamble's Head & Shoulders - brand leader of the entire shampoo markets of both the UK and USA.

In 1978 Elida Gibbs found itself well established in most segments of the shampoo market, but it lacked proper representation in the anti-dandruff shampoo sector.

Market research carried out by Elida had nonetheless revealed a market opportunity not yet exploited by Procter and Gamble. The evidence showed that there was a need for a range of anti-dandruff shampoos for different hair conditions, that is, an anti-dandruff shampoo for greasy hair, one for dry hair, and one for normal hair.

Elida Gibbs developed this range under the brand name All Clear. It was test-marketed for a year in the Southern area. This was successful and Elida Gibbs launched their new anti-dandruff range of shampoos nationally in July 1979.

Marketing and Advertising Objectives

The marketing objective was to gain a significant share of the shampoo market by positioning ourselves in the anti-dandruff segment of the market.

The shampoo market is highly fragmented and very competitive and it was judged that a volume brand share in excess of 5 per cent would be a considerable achievement.

The advertising objectives were:
 (i) to announce All Clear as a new brand in the anti-dandruff shampoo sector;
 (ii) to communicate the unique features of All Clear, namely, that it had a range of three variants, each suitable for a particular hair type: clears dandruff and cares for hair;
 (iii) to position All Clear as a shampoo suitable for men and women.

Description of the Campaign

The launch was scheduled to begin in July 1979 with national TV advertising. Two TV commercials were made, one targeted at the female audience, the other at the male audience. Both commercials lasted 30 seconds.

The ITV strike which occurred a few weeks after the beginning of the launch necessitated a change in the original media plan. The campaign was redirected into press and radio. Only after the strike, in January 1980, did All Clear get the TV support which, it was believed, it needed.

The Period of Time under Consideration

This paper addresses itself to the period of time from the national launch of All Clear in July 1979 to March 1980.

CAMPAIGN EVALUATION

Although the ITV strike coincided with the launch of All Clear, it does enable us to review the effectiveness of the different media employed in the All Clear campaign, and to gauge the importance of television advertising to this brand.

The Methodology of Evaluation

To evaluate the effectiveness of the advertising, it has been necessary to analyse the effect of the individual component parts of the marketing mix and other contiguous factors, for example, competitive advertising activity. This is done below and from it, by a process of elimination, our conclusion is that the TV advertising campaign which started in January 1980 was the single most important influence in the success of the All Clear launch.

The Effect of Pricing

Variations in the sizes of bottles of shampoo make it necessary to convert actual prices to £s per litre of shampoo for comparability between brands. From these figures an index has been constructed to provide a measure of the price advantage which All Clear held over Head & Shoulders during the period under examination. Table 5.1 below shows this index, where 100 would equal price parity with Head & Shoulders, anything less than 100 therefore equalling a price advantage for All Clear.

TABLE 5.1: INDEX OF THE RELATIVE PRICE ADVANTAGE OF ALL CLEAR OVER HEAD & SHOULDERS

| | 1979 | | | | | | 1980 | | |
	July	Aug	Sept	Oct	Nov	Dec	Jan	Feb	Mar
100 = price parity with Head & Shoulders	68	71	72	82	79	82	87	88	90

This index shows that All Clear's price *increased* throughout the period under examination. The price of Head & Shoulders also increased, but at a slower rate than that of All Clear, so that All Clear's price advantage over Head & Shoulders *decreased* during this period.

January and February saw All Clear's price advantage at its then lowest, but Table 5.2 shows that it was these months which saw its brand share at its highest.

The absence of any correlation between price advantage and brand share is clearly demonstrated when volume brand share and the index of relative price advantage (see Table 5.3) are seen together.

m All Clear television advertisement: '**Trouble is, the dandruff keeps coming back.**'

TABLE 5.2:   STERLING BRAND SHARES OF ALL CLEAR AND HEAD & SHOULDERS

| | 1979 | | | | | | 1980 | | |
	July %	*Aug* %	*Sept* %	*Oct* %	*Nov* %	*Dec* %	*Jan* %	*Feb* %	*Mar* %
All Clear	5	7	5	5	6	4	8	8	6
Head & Shoulders	14	13	13	13	13	11	13	16	15

TCPI.

TABLE 5.3:   VOLUME BRAND SHARE AND INDEX OF RELATIVE PRICE ADVANTAGE FOR ALL CLEAR

| | 1979 | | | | | | 1980 | | |
	Jul	*Aug*	*Sept*	*Oct*	*Nov*	*Dec*	*Jan*	*Feb*	*Mar*
% volume brand share (litres)	4	6	4	4	4	3	6	6	4
Index of price advantage	68	71	72	82	79	82	87	88	90

'So it cares for my kind of hair and it really clears my dandruff ...'

The Effect of Consumer Promotions

In measuring the relative pricing of All Clear against Head & Shoulders, price was calculated by dividing volume into a value figure derived from purchases at *actual* prices. By this method all money-off consumer promotions have already been accounted for.

The only consumer promotion which did not involve a 'money-off' offer, a competition, ran in October and November 1979. Its closing date was 31st December 1979. The competition involved a leaflet drop to 10 million households, with cash prizes for the winners.

The objective of this consumer promotion was less to stimulate consumer purchase than

TABLE 5.4:   PERCENTAGE VOLUME BRAND SHARE (LITRES)

	1979 Jul %	Aug %	Sept %	Oct %	Nov %	Dec %	1980 Jan %	Feb %	Mar %
All Clear	4	6	4	4	4	3	6	6	4
Head & Shoulders	9	8	8	8	8	7	8	11	10
Total medicated	26	29	27	28	27	26	29	31	29

l Clear: clears dandruff, cares for hair.'

to increase both consumer and trade awareness of, and interest in, All Clear. The consumer promotion was linked to a trade promotion (see below).

This consumer promotion had little effect on the October–December consumer sales as is shown by volume brand share figures in Table 5.4.

The Effect of Trade Promotions and Distribution

Most of the trade promotional activity, specifically trade discounts, took place very early in the launch programme to obtain shelf-facings and listings with the major Multiples.

The consumer promotion described above was linked to a trade promotion with the aim of increasing awareness and interest in All Clear. The trade promotion, which took the form of a lottery, preceded the consumer promotion and its closing date was 6th November 1979.

TABLE 5.5:   INDEX OF QUARTERLY STERLING DISTRIBUTION FOR ALL CLEAR
IN CHEMISTS AND GROCERS

	July 1979	November 1979	January 1980	March 1980
Grocers	100	130	117	137
Chemists	100	128	134	132

The effect of this promotion would have been reflected in the November and December distribution figures. Table 5.5 shows the quarterly distribution figures for All Clear in chemists and grocers indexed to a base of 100 for July 1979.

As Table 5.5 illustrates, distribution figures did show an increase in November over July 1979, although in grocery outlets distribution started to decline in January. Increasing distribution through to January in the chemists was probably a reflection of their usual increases in stocking at this time to meet the annual increase in consumer purchases of shampoos immediately after Christmas.

Increased distribution in November in both chemists and grocers did not, however, lead to any significant increase in consumer purchase in November and December. Table 5.6 below shows All Clear's performance in absolute volume terms indexed to 100 in July 1979.

TABLE 5.6:   INDEX OF ALL CLEAR'S ABSOLUTE VOLUME PERFORMANCE (LITRES)

| | 1979 | | | | | | 1980 | | |
	Jul	Aug	Sept	Oct	Nov	Dec	Jan	Feb	Mar
	100	128	95	95	97	63	140	115	93

The Product

The product and range remained exactly the same throughout the period under examination. A new 50 ml sized bottle was introduced at the end of February 1980, but distribution was not complete until the end of March. This introduction therefore had no significant influence on performance during the months under consideration.

Competitive Activity

The shampoo market in general is both fragmented (with over 35 advertised brands listed in MEAL over the past two years) and highly competitive with significant levels of advertising expenditure on major brands.

All Clear's media split (based on MEAL figures) for the months under consideration is shown in Table 5.7 below.

So as to assess how much 'interference' there might have been from other shampoo brands advertising at this time, it is useful to look at All Clear's media expenditure in terms of its 'share' of total shampoo advertising expenditure, its 'share of the media voice'. Table 5.8 details All Clear's 'share of voice' and compares it with that achieved by Head & Shoulders.

The 'share of voice' figures show that All Clear achieved its most significant shares of

TABLE 5.7:   MEDIA SPLIT FOR ALL CLEAR (£'000s)

| | 1979 | | | | | | 1980 | | |
	Jul	Aug	Sept	Oct	Nov	Dec	Jan	Feb	Mar
TV	116	29	–	–	–	–	266	59	–
Press	–	–	74	86	72	–	–	3	–
Radio	–	–	–	52	52	–	–	–	–
Total	116	29	74	138	124	–	266	62	–

TABLE 5.8: 'SHARE OF VOICE' FOR ALL CLEAR AND HEAD & SHOULDERS

| | 1979 | | | | | | 1980 | | |
	Jul %	*Aug* %	*Sept* %	*Oct* %	*Nov* %	*Dec* %	*Jan* %	*Feb* %	*Mar* %
All Clear	9	7	33	21	12	–	38	12	–
Head & Shoulders	14	15	–	27	25	44	17	17	22

MEAL.

advertising expenditure in September 1979 and January 1980. The high share in September is largely due to the absence of spending by Head & Shoulders, but this high share did not result in high brand share (see Table 5.2).

The Relationship between Brand Share and Television Advertising

The highest 'share of voice' of advertising expenditure was in fact in January (38 per cent),

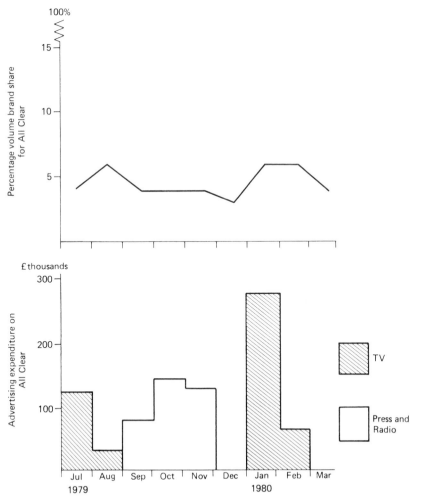

Figure 5.1 *The relationship between volume brand share and advertising expenditure on TV for All Clear.*

the month which did see a dramatic rise in volume share from 3 per cent in December to 6 per cent in January.

It is our contention that brand share doubled in January not only because of the amount of money spent on advertising, but also because the advertising medium had reverted to TV.

Further evidence that television has been the most effective medium for All Clear is that its television spend of £116 000 in late July was reflected in the August volume brand share of 6 per cent. This share dropped immediately to 4 per cent when the ITV strike prevented further advertising on television. All Clear did not regain its 6 per cent volume share until the resumption of commercial television and its advertising in that medium in January 1980.

The clear relationship between All Clear's volume brand share and television advertising is illustrated in Figure 5.1.

THE SIZE OF THE EFFECT

The Effect of Television vs. the Effect of Radio and Press

The £262 000 spent on radio and press advertising in October and November generated £624 000 (according to TCPI) in consumer purchases over the three-month period of October to December.

The £325 000 spent on television advertising in January and February generated £972 000 in consumer purchases in the period January to March.

Thus it may be said that a marginal increase of £63 000 in advertising expenditure (from £262 000 to £325 000) and a change from radio and press to television generated an additional £348 000 (£972 000 − £624 000) in consumer purchases.

Whilst the three months, October to December, in total may be considered 'average' for the year, there is a cyclical annual increase in shampoo sales after Christmas (which between 1979 and 1980 increased by approximately 20 per cent). To take this annual increase into account, 20 per cent is deducted from the January to March figure to give a truer picture of the effectiveness of television advertising.

Thus for a marginal increase of £63 000 and a change to television advertising, a further £278 000 of consumer purchases were generated than would have been had radio and press expenditure continued through to January and February.

To summarize:

	Consumer purchases £	Advertising expenditure £
Jan/Mar 1980	972 000	325 000
Oct/Dec 1979	624 000	262 000
Gross increase	348 000	63 000
Deduct 20% for seasonal increases	70 000	
Net increases	278 000	63 000

The Opportunity Cost of not Advertising at all in January and February

The two months, December and March, in which there was no advertising expenditure are marked in both instances by a fall in value brand share (to 3 per cent in December and 4 per cent in March).

Assuming, then, that a value brand share of 4 per cent represents an achievable brand share without any advertising, the following revenue would have been generated for All Clear in the first three months of 1980:

January	£185 120
February	£172 920
March	£172 240
Total	£530 280

Adding the actual advertising expenditure for January and February to the above, we get a truer picture of Elida Gibbs' potential position without advertising:

Sales	£530 280
Savings on advertising	£325 000
	£855 280

The opportunity cost of not advertising, therefore, is the actual revenue less the potential without advertising:

	£972 000
less	£855 280
	£116 720

Thus the size of the effect of television advertising may be represented by the difference between the actual and potential revenue. Had Elida Gibbs not advertised to the extent they did on television in January and February, they would have lost nearly £117 000 in revenue from consumer purchases (during the first three months of 1980).

6

Home Protection

How advertising helps fight crime

THE ROLE OF ADVERTISING

This study is concerned with an advertising campaign to improve the security of households by encouraging the installation of window locks with the ultimate objective of reducing the number of domestic burglaries.

The following statistics illustrate the scale of domestic burglary.

— Over 340 000 'burglaries in a dwelling' in England and Wales were reported to the police in 1981. This represents about 10 per cent of all indictable crime recorded by the police and is one of the major categories of crime with which they have to deal. It also means that approximately 2 per cent of homes were burgled in 1981.

— The figures almost certainly underestimate the total number of actual and attempted burglaries; the scale of the dark side of crime is unknown but the 1972 and 1979 General Household Surveys suggest that some 30 per cent plus of burglaries are unreported. The British Crime Survey, the data from which are now being analysed, will give a clearer picture.

— The reported value of goods stolen was over £100 million and averaged £440 per burglary in 1980. These figures coincide with payments in 1981 made by members of the British Insurance Association of £106 million and an estimated average claim of £300 to £500. Again these are likely to be underestimates given under-reporting and/or inadequate insurance cover.

— Most burglaries are not solved; in 1981 72 per cent of police-recorded offences were not 'cleared up'.

These bare statistics are enormous in their scale and cost to the community; however they say nothing about the misery that a burglary causes to the victim: the disruption to the physical and emotional security of somebody's home cannot truly be assessed but it is not uncommon for victims to move from their house.

Faced with this enormous problem, it is advisable to consider how advertising can help solve or at least diminish it. The short answer is that it cannot; the causes of crime are inevitably complex (and largely unknown) reflecting a multiplicity of economic, political and moral factors. It is judged unlikely that advertising could directly influence the activities of burglars and thereby bring about a reduction in crime. It does, however, seem more feasible to tackle the problem from the perspective of the potential victim and address the issue of how their actions can reduce the incidence of burglary, or at least the risk of they themselves being burgled. The essential philosophy underlying this approach is that individuals are in a position to protect themselves because improved domestic security reduces the risk of burglary. The obvious qualifications to such an approach are:

(a)   Domestic security is only adequate to the level of skill and determination displayed by the burglar. However, most burglaries are committed by sneak thieves, those who are looking for the more vulnerable and easier 'targets'. Against such attackers, simple precautions are likely to act as an effective deterrent.

(b)   The second qualification to this approach is that one man's security may be another man's downfall. If one dwelling is sufficiently secure to deter a burglar, it does not of course preclude a neighbouring less secure dwelling from being attacked instead.

However, these two qualifications do not invalidate the commonsense hypothesis that a more secure home is less likely to be burgled, and that provided sufficient homes are made secure there is some probability that the incidence of the crime itself may, in the long term, be reduced.

CAMPAIGN OBJECTIVES

There are, of course, a large number of security precautions that a householder should take to minimize the risk of burglary. These range from the simple – ensuring doors and windows are closed and locked when the house is left empty – to the more complex (and possibly expensive) such as installing burglar alarms.

It was decided that window locks should be the principal security measure featured in the advertising campaign, for the following reasons:

(a)   Windows are the most common point of entry for burglars.

(b)   The installation of window locks acts both as a practical deterrent in making forced entry more hazardous, requiring glass to be broken or frames forced; and as a visual deterrent to prevent an attempt being made in the first place.

(c)   Window locks are relatively inexpensive, available through ironmonger and DIY outlets, and can be installed fairly easily by anyone with a minimum proficiency in DIY.

(d)   While the main objective of the advertising was to encourage the installation of window locks, it was hoped that this would not preclude some spin-off effect on other security measures.

Thus the primary and behavioural objective of the advertising campaign was *to encourage householders to install window locks*.

In addition to this primary objective, a secondary campaign objective was to encourage and stimulate the activities of others concerned with advising the public about domestic security. These included:

—   Crime prevention officers within each police force division and the lay crime prevention panels that have been set up by most forces.

—   Lock manufacturers, wholesalers and retailers, persuading them to stock, feature and, ideally, promote window locks.

This supportive objective is analogous with, for example, the way in which an advertising campaign can act as a stimulus to sales force and retailer in the area of packaged goods to increase the distribution or shelf displays of a particular product. In this instance, this objective was to be achieved by press releases prior to the campaign, consultation with the appropriate organizations and trade federations and the provision of promotional material such as window stickers, radio tapes, miniature posters etc. reflecting the overall campaign theme.

In summary, the objectives of the campaign were to encourage householders to install window locks and to act as a focus for the supportive activities of the police and suppliers/retailers of window locks.

CAMPAIGN DETAILS

Target Audience

The target audience for the campaign was defined as *all householders*, for three reasons:

(a)   75 to 85 per cent of houses do not have window locks. (It is important to emphasize that window locks are not the same as 'catches' with which all windows are conventionally fitted.)

(b)   Qualitative evidence suggested that both men and women were likely to be involved in the decision to install and purchase window locks: women, who are more emotionally concerned about burglary, providing an important stimulus to purchase; men, more 'matter of fact' in their comments, being more concerned with the choice and installation of window locks.

(c)   It seemed wrong to exclude in creative or media terms any sub-group given the objective and nature of the campaign offering advice about self-protection.

Advertising Strategy

The underlying principle behind the advertising strategy was to arouse the public's fear of the risk and consequences of burglary, and to demonstrate window locks as an effective deterrent to the burglar. The basic model for this advertising strategy was to highlight and dramatize the problem – burglary – and to offer a solution to that problem – installing window locks.

From initial qualitative research, it was evident that the prospect of burglary was viewed with considerable alarm. In particular, the invasion of the house, the loss of property and the expectation of vandalistic behaviour were all felt to be among the worst aspects of burglary; the experience of burglary was frequently likened, particularly by women, to that of rape.

These understandable anxieties appeared to be a powerful way of dramatizing the prospect of burglary and by doing so to position window locks as a simple and easy solution to the problem. This juxtaposition of the horror of burglary with the simplicity of the solution appeared to be a route to overcome two commonly-expressed attitudes.

1.   Fatalism ('burglary happens to others, it won't happen to me'). If presented in a credible and convincing manner, it was believed that showing the full horror of burglary would break down this barrier.

2. Helplessness ('There's nothing you can do to stop a determined burglar'). The point of the campaign was to say that there *was* something that could be done – the solution was to install window locks.

It was felt that this combination of 'fear arousal' and positive advice would be the foundation of a powerful advertising strategy acting synergetically. Either on its own was likely to be a far weaker proposition: fear arousal alone merely resulting in increasing the public's feelings of helplessness and fatalism; positive advice lacking the necessary impact to make it seem worthwhile.

However, while this primary and emotional strategy appeared to be likely to succeed in encouraging the installation of window locks, it was evident that some more information-based communication was required in order to overcome certain concerns. These included the availability of window locks for different types of window, their cost and ease of installation. While the advertising was expected to tackle these issues, it was felt they were to an extent subsidiary to the primary strategy outlined above: if enough people were sufficiently aroused by the advertising and absorbed the message about window locks, they would tend not to require reassurance on these dimensions. Also it was hoped that the other activity stimulated by the campaign through Crime Prevention Officers, retailers etc. would help in overcoming these concerns.

Figure 6.1 represents the advertising strategy diagrammatically.

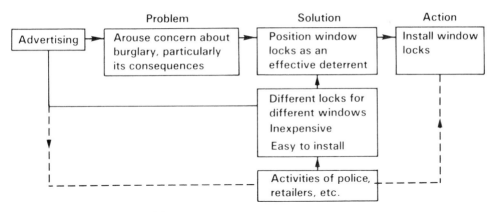

Figure 6.1 *Advertising model*

Creative Executions

From the requirements of the strategy and target audience a mixed media schedule was adopted: television to consolidate high media impact with the necessary dramatic qualities, press to convey more detailed information about window locks, and posters to act as reminder medium.

From the exploratory qualitative research mentioned above a campaign was developed with the common theme: 'A window is always open to a thief. Unless it's locked.' The campaign included:

(a) Two television commercials, one highlighting the physical and emotional consequences of being burgled ('Scars'), the other showing a potential burglar menacingly stalking a house but being thwarted by the presence of window locks ('No windows').

How a thief could get to know you. Intimately.

A window without window locks is an open invitation to a thief.

All too easily he can let himself in and start looking through your personal belongings.

But he can be discouraged by window locks, like those we've illustrated.

Take the simple lock designed for wooden sash windows.

They cost £4 a pair and take only minutes to fit if you do it yourself.

The window security bolt is sold at most D.I.Y. and hardware shops in a choice of colours, so it won't spoil the looks of your window frames.

The push lock is specifically designed for side or top hung casement windows, whether they're aluminium or wood.

And the transom lock is made to protect metal and wooden windows.

If you're not sure which locks would make your windows most secure, ask the Crime Prevention Officer at your local Police Station.

His advice is free and he'll be pleased to help you avoid letting a burglar get to know you.

A window is always open to a thief. Unless it's locked.

(b) Three press executions all of which provided more detail about the costs, availability and ease of installation of window locks.

(c) One poster which appeared on 4- and 16-sheet sites in residential areas.

Media Summary

The campaign ran in the Granada and Yorkshire television regions in two bursts from October to November 1981 and from January to February 1982. In both bursts, television and press were simultaneous to achieve maximum impact and synergy; the posters appeared in February to act in a reminder role and to supplement the somewhat lower strike rate of this second burst.

Total campaign expenditure was £360 000 which equals a national equivalent expenditure of approximately £1 600 000, assuming that national press publications are substituted for the enforced use of local press in the two regions.

CAMPAIGN RESULTS

Methodology

Given the principal objective of increasing the installation of window locks, it was decided that this behavioural measure should be assessed through the establishment of a *retail audit* of hardware/ironmonger/DIY outlets in the advertised areas for the duration of the campaign. In addition a random sample *survey of householders* was carried out to assess behaviour, attitudes and advertising awareness.

The research programme was underpinned by two methodological principles:

(a) Frequent monitoring, to establish the effect of each burst of advertising and thus involving four fieldwork stages, before and after each advertising burst.

(b) Advertising versus control area comparisons to establish that changes in the advertised areas were not due to other unknown factors. The control area chosen was the non-overlap Midlands television region.

The rationale for these two projects was to be able to synthesize hard sales data from the retail audit with any observed changes in the public's behaviour or attitudes. Although the technique of a retail panel is itself not new, it should be noted that it represents a departure for the Central Office of Information and Home Office in their methodology of campaign evaluation. Its use was justified not only because of the tangible advertising objective of increasing the penetration of window locks, but also because it was likely that the campaign effect might be insufficiently large to be shown with any statistical confidence in a household survey.

Purchases of Window Locks

The results of the retail audit (Figure 6.2) were dramatic, with sales of window locks showing, from similar initial levels, a large and statistically significant increase of 128 per cent in the advertised areas compared with the control area.

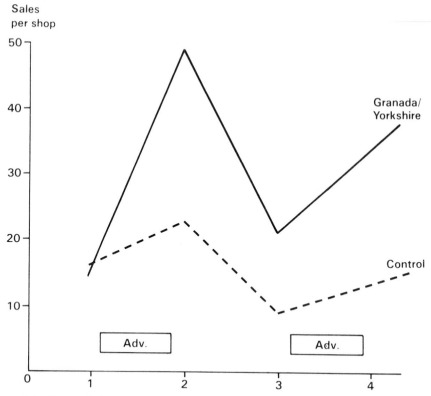

Figure 6.2 *Window lock sales per sample shop*

Commenting on these results we can observe:

(a) A short-term increase of 127 per cent in Granada and Yorkshire at the end of the first burst compared with a small but statistically insignificant increase in the control area.

(b) In both areas a decline of similar proportions (approximately 60 per cent) in period 3, probably explained by the fact that this period covers the two months of November and December. However, sales in Granada and Yorkshire continued above their pre-advertising level (compared with a lower level in the control area) and therefore were maintained at similar levels as Table 6.1 illustrates.

TABLE 6.1:   INDEX OF SALES IN ADVERTISED
AREAS

Period	Control area %	Advertised areas %
Pre-1	100	95
Post-2	100	212
Pre-3	100	227
Post-4	100	252

(c) Increases in both advertised and control areas after this second burst of advertising, with sales in Granada and Yorkshire returning to a level only slightly lower than that following the first burst.

It has been possible to substantiate the evidence of the retail audit through other indirect evidence. In the advertised areas eight out of the 25 sample shops claimed to be out of stock of at least one brand of window lock (compared with four out of 25 in the control area) suggesting that demand exceeded supply. Subsequent telephone interviews with eight major window-lock wholesalers confirmed not only evidence of increased demand but also, in four instances, of supply difficulties with at least one manufacturer.

The demonstration of higher levels of sales of window locks measured during and between bursts of advertising presents a prima facie case for the effectiveness of the campaign. Moreover, other measurable factors do not explain the higher sales levels.

— MEAL records no advertising expenditure by security device manufacturers during the campaign.
— Some Crime Prevention 'fillers' were screened in both advertised and control areas. (Fillers are public service films screened at the discretion of the television contractors.) However, the control area, Midlands, screened more fillers (475 adult TVRs) than either Granada (395 adult TVRs) or Yorkshire (99 adult TVRs) *and* their subject matter will not have featured window locks specifically.
— Reports from Crime Prevention officers on their own activities, media coverage, retailer support etc. have not yet been analysed, so that we are unable to assess the extent and impact of such activity. However, as mentioned earlier, an objective of this campaign was to help to create a momentum that would aid the efforts of those organizations concerned with domestic security and thus such activity may be seen as a direct result of the campaign rather than an independent variable.

In overall terms, then, it would seem that the campaign was the only known variable that could explain the sales increase of 128 per cent.

Intermediate measures

Confidence in the efficacy of the campaign can be further increased by examining intermediary measures and specifically by assessing the advertising model outlined earlier (Figure 6.1). In particular we can examine five elements, drawing on the results of the household survey.

ADVERTISING AWARENESS

There seems no doubt that the campaign was noticed by the public. Spontaneous awareness of advertising in the last three months (Table 6.2) increased significantly from 33 to 78 per cent with a small drop in the period between bursts.

TABLE 6.2: PERCENTAGE CLAIMING TO HAVE SEEN ANY SECURITY/BURGLARY ADVERTISING IN THE LAST 3 MONTHS

Period	Granada / Yorkshire %	Control %
Pre-1	33	39
Post-2	68	48
Pre-3	58	43
Post-4	78	52

Prompted recognition of the campaign (Table 6.3) using photographs of the creative material suggested that 93 per cent recognized some element of the campaign, with television dominating recall.

TABLE 6.3:   PERCENTAGE CLAIMING TO RECOGNIZE

Period	Any %	TV %	Press %	Posters %
Post-2	75	70	32	15
Pre-3	75	64	38	16
Post-4	93	86	53	27

As a digression on monitoring advertising recall, we expect some claimed recognition of advertising which people are unlikely to have seen. For example 50 per cent of householders in the area without advertising claim to have recognized some part of the campaign and 15 or 16 per cent in the advertised areas claim to have seen the poster before it appeared. In this instance, we believe the problem of incorrect recall may have been exacerbated by the theme of anti-burglary advertising which is socially and 'morally' positive and which may have resulted in people wanting to recall a campaign they had not in fact seen.

CONCERN ABOUT BURGLARY

The advertising model discussed earlier indicated the need to heighten personal concern about burglary. However, the household survey suggested that there was very little change over the period (Table 6.4).

TABLE 6.4:   PERCENTAGE AGREEING
WITH 'I AM VERY WORRIED ABOUT BEING
BURGLED'

Period	Advertised areas %	Control %
Pre-1	59	56
Post-2	61	51
Pre-3	55	63
Post-4	60	59

The campaign appears to be exploiting the generally-held perception of the risk of burglary rather than causing more people to believe that they are more likely to be burgled. Obviously, risk assessment is made up of a complex interrelationship of factors (experience, psychology, environment, etc.) and the advertising campaign appears to be *reinforcing existing beliefs* rather than changing them and to be providing a new and positive course of action – namely installing window locks.

WINDOW LOCKS AS AN EFFECTIVE DETERRENT

This conclusion is reinforced by the fact that, over the campaign period, the proportion of the public agreeing with the statement 'Window locks will deter sneak thieves' increased compared with a small decline in the control area (Table 6.5).

TABLE 6.5:   PERCENTAGE AGREEING WITH 'WINDOW
LOCKS WILL DETER SNEAK THIEVES'

Period	Advertised areas %	Control %
Pre-1	58	76
Post-2	67	65
Pre-3	67	70
Post-4	71	68

KNOWLEDGE ABOUT WINDOW LOCKS

The public's knowledge about window locks (availability, cost, ease of installation) did not appear to change; however this disguises the fact that there were a large number of the public claiming to 'not know' and of those giving an opinion, most expressed a positive view.

It is believed that, while this aspect of the advertising strategy warrants further consideration, the prime motivator lies less in educating the public about window locks than in providing a powerful trigger to take action.

WINDOW LOCK INSTALLATION

Finally, the household survey measured both actual and intended installation of window locks. Claimed installation of window locks showed no significant change; however, measuring this behavioural change would have required substantially larger sample sizes than those actually used (200 to 220 per area per check). For this reason, the use of the retail audit was justified as a more cost-effective method of establishing a change in behaviour against the stated advertising objective.

However, Table 6.6 shows increases in the number of people claiming they were 'likely to install window locks in the next 6 months'.

TABLE 6.6:   PERCENTAGE CLAIMING TO BE LIKELY TO
INSTALL WINDOW LOCKS IN THE NEXT 6 MONTHS

Period	Advertised areas %	Control area %
Pre-1	7	12
Post-2	18	13
Pre-3	11	11
Post-4	14	13

It is interesting to observe the similarity of trend in the advertised areas with the audit data: namely a larger initial increase than was shown after the second burst. Although not statistically significant the changes in periods 3 and 4 do, in relation to periods 1 and 2, mirror the findings of the retail audit (Table 6.7).

TABLE 6.7:   PERCENTAGE CHANGE PERIOD ON PERIOD

Period	Sales (audit) %	Intention to install %
Post–2	+217	+157
Pre–3	−57	−38
Post–4	+85	+27

In concluding this section on strategy evaluation the evidence suggests that the advertising 'worked' according to the model discussed earlier.

— The advertising was noticed.
— Window locks were seen as an effective deterrent by an increasing number of people.
— Claimed intention to install did improve, which on the basis of the retail audit, appears to have been translated into action.

However, in one particular area – concern about burglary – the model requires some amendment. Concern among the public about being burgled does not appear to have increased. We would conclude that the advertising has worked by reinforcing existing beliefs and providing a positive focus for action for those who, already somewhat concerned, seek assistance and advice in the protection of their homes.

This hypothesis is supported by Table 6.8 which demonstrates that those who are concerned about burglary show a higher claimed intention to install window locks and that this proportion increases after each burst of advertising.

TABLE 6.8:   PERCENTAGE CLAIMING TO BE LIKELY TO
INSTALL WINDOW LOCKS IN GRANADA AND YORKSHIRE

	Total %	Concerned about burglary %	Not concerned about burglary %
Pre–1	7	9	5
Post–2	18	22	10
Pre–3	11	12	11
Post–4	14	17	10

From Table 15.8, it is possible to estimate how and on whom the advertising worked. If we start with 1000 in the target group, we can say that, before the campaign began, 600 expressed concern about burglary whereas 400 did not. As Table 6.8 shows 9 per cent of the 'concerned' (54) and 5 per cent of the 'unconcerned' (20) claimed they were likely to install window locks.

After the first burst of advertising, there was no change in the number professing concern about burglary but there was an increase in intention to install of 13 per cent among the 'concerned' and 5 per cent among the 'unconcerned'. Among our 1000 target, these translate into an extra 78 and 20 respectively; Figure 6.3 illustrates the advertising model diagrammatically.

Advertising does not seem to have worked by simply moving people through a hierarchy of effect i.e. from unconcern to concern, and from concern to action. Lock sales increased,

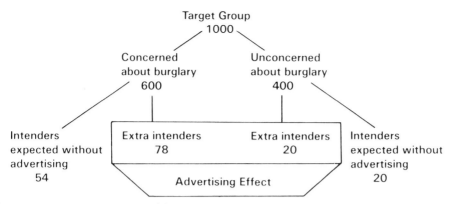

Figure 6.3 *Revised advertising model*

yet the number concerned about burglary did not. Our model suggests that 80 per cent of extra 'intenders' came from those already concerned, and that 20 per cent of 'intenders' came from the 'unconcerned' who did not pass through the intermediary stage of concern about burglary.

ASSESSMENT OF THE CAMPAIGN

Unlike other, commercial case histories, the contribution of advertising cannot be demonstrated by reference to profitability – spending money to make money. Notwithstanding this difficulty, we believe some attempt to justify the expenditure of public funds should be made.

The retail audit suggests that more than twice as many window locks were sold in areas with advertising as would otherwise have been the case. Assuming that retail distribution and consumer purchasing patterns were similar this would imply that for every 100 households who would have bought window locks a further 120 did so as a result of the advertising. On a national basis, tentative estimates suggest that about 130 000 households would have installed window locks in the mid-October to mid-February period and that the campaign would have increased this by about 170 000 households to 300 000.

Furthermore there is some evidence that the campaign would have some additional longer-term effect as window lock sales in the period between bursts remained at a higher level in the areas with advertising than in the control area (see Figure 6.2 and Table 6.1).

It is believed that this level of achievement, when set against the media expenditure, is highly satisfactory. To have more than doubled the numbers of households purchasing window locks is itself a major achievement; if their installation has prevented a burglary from being committed a number of costs have been saved as a result of the campaign: the average property loss of £400, the emotional cost to the family concerned and the police time and resources involved.

Finally, the advertising has been judged to be sufficiently successful to justify a national campaign in 1983.

7

How Advertising has Worked in the Launch of Birds Eye Oven Crispy Cod Steaks

INTRODUCTION

Birds Eye introduced their new Oven Crispy Cod Steaks in Batter into the Midlands in October, 1981. The product is truly a breakthrough in frozen food production. Its unique batter can be cooked in the oven or grilled, giving a perfect crisp golden coating without any of the fuss and bother of frying.

In launching this product, the company were most concerned about the risk of high substitution with their existing Crispy Fish in Batter range - particularly the two cod steaks product, which accounted for over 40 per cent of sales. There was a need for extremely careful product positioning and marketing, in which advertising had the vital role of promoting sales by communicating clearly the unique benefits of the new product, without in any way suggesting that it was a substitute for the existing cod in batter products.

The remarkably high trial of Oven Crispy Cod (60 per cent) and the low level of substitution with existing products resulted in Birds Eye's market share increasing by 9 per cent and the total market growing by 30 per cent. Advertising was shown to generate a significant increase in sales which allowed the advertising investment to be paid for after only 14 weeks.

BACKGROUND

The Development of the Frozen Fish in Batter Market

Fish in batter is traditional British fare with strong emotive associations - everyone has enjoyed 'fish 'n' chips' at some time.

Birds Eye pioneered the frozen fish in batter market in 1967 with its launch of a product range made to a special recipe designed to survive freezing and re-cooking, whilst giving all the taste and crispness expected from the fish shop variety.

Competitive entries from Findus, Ross and others soon followed and the market grew so that today it is a massive 10 000 tonnes, worth over £28 million and accounting for full 8 per cent of all frozen fish products.

By 1980, however, after a decade of steady growth, the market had started to decline. The character of the market had also started to change; with a proliferation of both branded and dealers' own brand products all fighting for share, it was beginning to show the classic commodity trends of price sensitivity and bulk packs.

Birds Eye had suffered quite considerably in face of this competitive pressure and by 1981, their share had fallen from over 60 per cent (in the mid 70s) to 55 per cent. Obviously, the company wanted to redress the balance and as market leader, they also had a responsibility to build and revitalize this profitable but flagging market.

In what is nowadays becoming a classic market scenario of commodity trends and dealers' own brand/retailer pressures, the company realized that a minor product relaunch, perhaps with new packaging or advertising, was not the answer. They believed that one of the main reasons for market decline was the lack of any real investment since the late 60s behind product innovation or development. They recognized the need for a major product breakthrough to restore health and vitality to their brand and to the market.

The Market Opportunity

The new oven cook product which Birds Eye developed, researched extremely well amongst housewives, who were particularly impressed with the quality of the batter when cooked – many regarded it as better than the products they usually bought. This was very important, because a really crisp, light golden batter is known to be the key consumer discriminator between brands in this market. Superior product performance in this respect was likely to be axiomatic to the brand's success.

But was there a real market opportunity for an oven cook product?

Birds Eye had noted with interest the success of the McCains Oven Chips launch. The chip market almost doubled in size with the launch of oven chips and there was only 30 per cent substitution with existing deep fry business. Importantly, in a special study conducted by the company, 63 per cent of chip buyers had tried the new oven chips, 60 per cent of oven chip users were non or infrequent frozen chip buyers and 50 per cent of housewives said they cooked something else in the oven at the same time.

This success tallied with various other trends in food preparation that the company had noted – the trend towards convenience foods with the increasing number of working women and the breakdown of formal meal occasions, the growth of freezer ownership and more particularly, the trend to easier cooking methods – especially a move away from the fuss, bother and unpleasantness of frying. (The company noted that over 50 per cent of people now grill fish fingers and even amongst current Birds Eye crispy fish users, there had been a marked switch in the past two years towards shallow frying instead of the more traditional deep frying.)

Marketing Considerations

So Birds Eye decided to launch the new product in test market, but in doing so, they faced a rather difficult marketing problem.

The company were very concerned about the risk of high substitution with their exisiting fish in batter range – particularly the two cod steaks product, which accounted for over 40 per cent of sales. High substitution would completely negate the value of the product launch. On the other hand, there was an equally real risk that if the company delayed, competitors might launch their own oven cook products which would certainly threaten existing Birds Eye business. On balance, it was agreed to be preferable to have a new Birds Eye product taking sales from the existing 'Crispy' range than to have competitors doing so.

The need for extremely careful product positioning to minimize the risk of substitution was obviously vital.

The Role of Advertising

With this background, the company and Lintas agreed that advertising would play a very important part in the marketing strategy. Aside from its usual role of announcing the new product launch, advertising would have the important task of positioning Oven Crispy Cod very clearly as a new and excellent way of preparing traditional fish in batter, but without in any way suggesting that it was better than and therefore a substitute for existing Bird Eye crispy fish products.

Advertising would also need to provide reassurance of consistent and good product performance in terms of taste and crispness versus the traditional image of fish 'n' chip shop fish, ordinary frozen fish in batter products, and also against other oven cook products of which housewives had experience. This was because product tests had shown that whilst there was very high acceptance of the product once tried, there was quite a high level of scepticism on product performance initially – would it be as good as the traditionally held image of fish in batter and would the all-important batter be really crisp and light? Many people had been disappointed by McCains Oven Chips' performance in terms of crispness and crunchiness – would the Birds Eye oven product suffer similarly?

MARKETING AND ADVERTISING OBJECTIVES

Marketing Objectives: Test Market

To increase total 7-ounce sales of Crispy Cod Steaks (both traditional and oven varieties) by 50 per cent, allowing Oven Crispy 40 per cent substitution with the existing product.

Advertising Objectives: Test Market

To build rapid, high awareness and induce trial of Birds Eye's new Oven Crispy Cod Steaks – a more convenient way of preparing traditional cod in batter.

CREATIVE STRATEGY AND EXECUTION

Prime Target Group

All women, principally B,C1,C2 housewives who either: (a) are current users of fish in batter; or (b) like fish in batter but don't buy currently because of the fuss and bother attached to cooking it; and (c) are probably also purchasers of oven chips, but not necessarily.

Main Consumer Benefit

New Birds Eye Oven Crispy Cod Steaks offer you an easier, better way of cooking fish in batter, with all the taste and crispness you'd expect from deep fried fish.

Based on this strategy, SSC&B: Lintas developed two creative routes which were explored in qualitative research. One route emphasized traditional quality values with added convenience, the other majored on convenience and was more up-beat in mood and tone.

The convenience route was preferred as housewives really appreciated the ease of preparation of the product and wanted this to be communicated clearly. Importantly though, they still wanted reassurance that the finished product would be of good quality and taste just like battered fish fried in the traditional way. The tradition of fish in batter was important to them.

Based on these findings, Lintas developed a 30-second television commercial on the theme that new Birds Eye Oven Crispy Cod is 'thoroughly modern but tastes traditional'. Borrowing interest from the film 'Thoroughly Modern Millie' it featured a 'Millie' type singing her way gleefully through an explanation of the product's benefits to the 'Thoroughly Modern Millie' theme tune.

The television advertising, which featured only the new Oven Crispy product, was supported by tactical press advertising carrying a 10p-off coupon and featuring both the new oven product and the existing Crispy Cod Steaks product. The objective behind this advertisement was to make clear that both products were being actively sold by Birds Eye, that they both delivered the same high quality result and that the only difference was the method of preparation.

MEDIA PLANNING

Area Choice

With 17 per cent of the United Kingdom housewife population, the Midlands was large enough to give reasonable results on which to base test market assessments without too much financial risk. In the case of Oven Crispy it had a number of other advantages:

Media Selection

Television was chosen as the main medium to support the launch. Its advantages in the light of the overall advertising objectives were:

1. In creative terms, it allowed for a clear and succinct expression of the key product benefit whilst adding enormously to the communication of taste reassurance and appetite appeal with the use of movement and colour.
2. High coverage of the target audience which was necessarily broadly defined.
3. Fast coverage could be achieved.
4. Television is intrusive which was important in building high awareness of this unique product breakthrough.
5. There were no other appropriate regional media opportunities.
6. Television is appreciated by both the retail trade and the sales force as a sign that the company is making a serious marketing bid.

Additionally, local daily press was used to give tactical support to both the new product and the existing Crispy Cod Steaks product.

The Media Plan

The television burst broke two weeks after launch and ran for five weeks; 650 housewife TVRs with 87 per cent coverage of the target audience.

The press campaign broke a week after the television and two rounds of insertions were booked on Thursdays or Fridays on consecutive weeks in all the major local daily and evening papers giving 72 per cent coverage of the target audience.

The total national equivalent spend for this campaign was £550 000.

CAMPAIGN EVALUATION

Birds Eye have collected a great deal of data which cover distribution, trial, repeat purchase etc. But for this report we will concentrate only on the data which build a very strong case for the vital role which advertising has played in this launch namely, depot sales and a quantitative communication check.

Ex-depot Sales Results

The success of the test market launch is shown clearly in Figure 7.1. Comparison with the baseline index of 100 which represents the sales level prior to launch, demonstrates that the marketing objective of 50 per cent tonnage increase was not only achieved but in fact doubled. Importantly also, sales targets were exceeded not only on the new Oven Crispy Cod product but also on the existing Crispy Cod product. Furthermore, the very low level of substitution with the existing Crispy Cod product of around 11 per cent was far better than the 40 per cent level expected and allowed for.

The weekly sales index comparison with the rest of the country in Table 7.1 highlights the success of the Oven Crispy Cod test market still further.

BIRDS EYE OVEN CRISPY COD

COD IN BATTER IN THE OVEN YOU POP

... OLD FRYING PAN

BIRDS EYE OVEN CRISPY IS

GOODBYE ....

Singing:
EV'RYTHING TODAY IS
THOROUGHLY MODERN

TRADITIONAL DELICIOUSNESS

Sfx:
Crunch

Singing:
VO DI OH DOH

Sfx:
Drumstick on cymbal

SO HEAR THAT ....

V/O:
NEW BIRDS EYE OVEN CRISPY
COD. IT'S THOROUGHLY
MODERN BUT IT TASTES
TRADITIONAL

I'M CHANGING AND HOW

BIRDS EYE COD HAS
THOROUGHLY MODERN
BATTER NOW

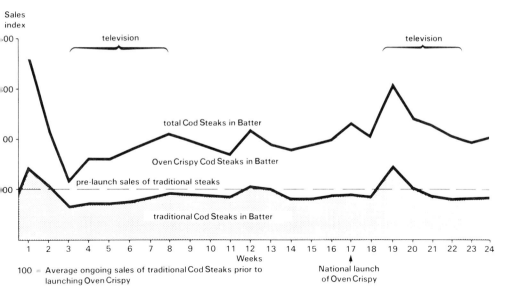

Figure 7.1 *Total Crispy Cod Steaks test market sales response*

TABLE 7.1:   INDEXED COMPARISON OF TOTAL CRISPY COD
STEAKS SALES PERFORMANCE IN TEST MARKET AND REST OF THE
COUNTRY

Week	Total Crispy Cod Steaks (Oven + Original) in test market	Total Crispy Cod Steaks (Original only) in rest of country	Percentage sales achievement in test market v. rest of country*
1	363	159	+128
2	215	142	+51
3	109	90	+21
4	170	95	+79
5	160	98	+63
6	175	99	+77
7	198	102	+94
8	216	112	+93
9	132	87	+52
10	105	55	+91
11	168	102	+65
12	225	113	+99

100 = Average ongoing tonnage level of standard Crispy Cod Steaks prior
        to launch of Oven Crispy
*NB Marketing objective = +50%

However, it is when a closer look is taken and the individual ex-depot sales are examined
that the effectiveness of the advertising is fully demonstrated. Figure 7.2 looks at the ex-
depot sales of Bromsgrove and Peterborough. The figures are for sales of Oven Crispy Cod
only and the data are expressed as a national annual sales projection index.

It should be noted that these sales projections have been calculated to allow for several factors which may differ across the areas. Thus the variations due to population and sales profiles, trade mix, product distribution, trade listings levels, competitive pressures and below the line activity have been compensated for as far as possible in the two areas to allow for direct comparison.

The important difference between the two depots is that 90 per cent of the Bromsgrove area received television during the test market whereas only 15 per cent of the Peterborough area was exposed to advertising.

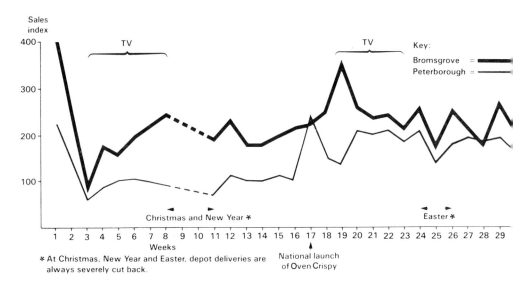

Figure 7.2   *Oven Crispy Cod Steaks Bromsgrove and Peterborough depots sales response*

The difference in national annual projections in the test market period is startling, with Bromsgrove selling on average, approximately double the volume of Peterborough. Having compensated for other variables, the *only* key difference between the two areas that could have affected sales is the level of advertising exposure.

To bring the strength of this hypothesis into sharp focus, the graph continues to plot the sales from both depots after national launch in February 1982, at which time it will be seen that the Peterborough sales level virtually doubled overnight to nearly the same on-going level as that of Bromsgrove. At national launch of course, both depots received full television exposure. (The different sales peaks in weeks 16 to 19 are due to slightly different national launch 'selling-in' times.)

Quantified Communication Check

A communication check was carried out in the heart of the Midlands test market area at the beginning of December, seven weeks after launch and five weeks after advertising broke. Two hundred and five street interviews were conducted with respondents defined very broadly as ITV viewers who bought frozen foods.

FINDINGS

Product awareness. Both spontaneously and when prompted (i.e. by mentioning *Birds Eye* or *battered* fish) Birds Eye Oven Crispy Cod was the most frequently mentioned new frozen fish product:

TABLE 7.2:   PRODUCT AWARENESS

Base	Spontaneous 205	Prompted 205
Recall of Birds Eye Oven Crispy Cod	11%	23%

Source: RBL

Where seen or heard. Television was most frequently mentioned spontaneously as having been the source of information about oven crispy cod:

TABLE 7.3:   WHERE SEEN OR HEARD

Base (All who knew full product name)	47
TV	87%
In shops	21%
Magazine	4%
Newspaper	4%
NB: multiple response	

Source: RBL

Advertising recognition. When shown a still from the commercial, 80 per cent of respondents claimed to have seen it before and 50 per cent of frozen fish buyers correctly identified the commercials being for Oven Crispy Cod or Birds Eye Oven Crispy Cod. These figures compare very favourably with recall of other Birds Eye commercials for such well known products as fish fingers. In particular, the 80 per cent recognition score is a very high figure for a new product.

Perceived advertising message. Respondents were asked directly what the advertisement they recognized had been telling them about the product. 75 per cent of the sample mentioned cooking in the oven or not needing to fry as the main message and only a very few seemed not to know what the commercial had been saying.

Convenience was the attribute most often associated with the product (58 per cent) followed by good quality (48 per cent) with modern (35 per cent) and very appetizing (25 per cent) following.

Reaction to product. Interest in the product was high:

Base (recognizing photo and identifying product)	101
People who would certainly, or might be interested to try	83%
Expecting product to be good, very good or excellent	85%
Expecting product to be at least as good as fried frozen fish in batter	84%

(Source: RBL)

COMMENTS ON FINDINGS

These scores are extremely encouraging. The spontaneous and prompted product awareness scores are considered to be very good given quite a complex name and the fact that these measurements were taken only five weeks after advertising broke.

Although respondents can often be expected to attribute knowledge of a new product to having seen it on television, the fact that the television score is significantly higher than the other scores, does indicate that some respondents do genuinely recall spontaneously hearing about the product on television.

The advertising recognition score is also very good – there is no chance that respondents are confusing it with any other advertising.

The scores on perceived advertising message may have been guesses based on the product name which would have been mentioned by that stage in the interview, but the high level of correct message recall after only a photo prompt and name mention does suggest that advertising is communicating the oven cooking message very clearly. Furthermore, the good scores on attribute associations again suggest that the message of added convenience without loss of quality is well perceived. In short, the advertising is achieving its communication objectives well.

The final set of figures relating to reactions to the product can normally be expected to be reasonably high given general consumer interest in new products and in Birds Eye in particular. However, again the very high levels of interest and product quality expectation do suggest that the advertising has further enhanced consumers' quality perceptions and desire to try the new product.

CONCLUSION

The Market Achievement

In a highly competitive, hitherto declining market, the success of Birds Eye's Oven Crispy Cod in Midlands test market has been remarkable.

The very high trial of 60 per cent and resultant excellent sales of the new product coupled with the very low substitution with the existing crispy cod steaks product, (about 15 per cent) increased Birds Eye's market share by 9 per cent. The total market grew by 30 per cent in volume terms and Birds Eye successfully created a new market segment with their Oven Crispy Cod which alone is projected to be worth £8 million in 1982.

Other Factors Affecting Brand's Performance

The Company and their agency, Lintas are convinced that advertising played a key role in the brand's success. However, there are of course other factors which it can be argued might have affected the launch success and these should be taken into consideration.

First, the product launch was supported by a 7p on-pack offer and 10p-off coupons in press advertising and in-store. These sources of money off may have prompted high sale. However, redemption levels were not significantly high and sales of Oven Crispy Cod have been sustained at the same high level, long after the effect of the money off activity could have been expected to finish.

Neither was price advantage a particular incentive for purchase. The brand was deliberately priced on a par with the existing crispy cod product and at a price premium over the major branded and own-brand competitors.

The success of oven chips launched eighteen months before, had undoubtedly eased the communication job and may have even allowed Oven Crispy Cod to be launched 'on the back of' oven chips. Certainly research showed that people readily accepted the 'oven cook instead of frying' concept. However, research had also shown that there was quite a high level of quality dissatisfaction with oven chips, which could well have had an adverse affect on the Birds Eye product. In the event, the very high scores on perceived product quality indicate that advertising has helped overcome possible negative associations.

Finally, the quality of the product itself is extremely good and must to a certain extent be contributing to the on-going sales success of the brand. However, the proof of a product is only in the eating, and the high trial level of 60 per cent indicates that something more than just good product quality is at work in building such high sales results.

Advertising Pay-back

Even allowing for these other market factors, the company and Lintas remain convinced that the advertising has been a key contributor, if not *the* key contribution towards the brand's success. It is extremely heartening to note that if it is assumed that the difference in average national annual sales projections of the Peterborough and Bromsgrove depots represents the incremental tonnage gained as a result of advertising, then even allowing for up to 20 per cent susbtitution on the existing Crispy Cod Steaks business, the national equivalent advertising investment of £550 000 for the launch burst was paid back in terms of trading direct profit in only 14 weeks from launch.

Further Market Development

Birds Eye Oven Crispy Cod is now fully national and the product has been even more successful than in test market. The market as a whole has shown the same remarkable 30 per cent growth and the company's brand share is very healthy.

The success of Birds Eye's Oven Crispy Cod Steaks has not gone unnoticed by the competition. As expected, both major branded competitors have moved quickly to launch their own oven cook products and own brand market entries may well follow soon.

Having more than proved its worth so far, Birds Eye believe that continued advertising support will be even more important in 1983 - helping to consolidate brand share and highlight the brand's benefits over competition. The need for confidentiality precludes any further detailed discussion of how SSC&B:Lintas and its client intend to learn from the results of the test market and develop the campaign further. However, this very convincing case history has served to endorse fully the company's and Lintas's confidence in the power of advertising and advertising will undoubtedly continue to have a major role in the brand's future development.

8

The Effect of Television Advertising on the Launch of Deep Clean

INTRODUCTION

This paper describes the launch of a new denture cleaning brand, Deep Clean, and the methods used to evaluate the effects of advertising on its initial sales. Generally, it is very difficult to distinguish the influence of advertising from all the other forms of promotional activity that attend the launch of a brand, e.g. money-off coupons, in-store promotional display and the simple fact that the brand is in distribution and therefore available. However, the advertising support for Deep Clean took the form of a national press campaign in newspapers and consumer magazines with an additional substantial weight of television advertising in two areas, Lancashire and Yorkshire. It is the latter feature which is important because it provided the opportunity to isolate the effect of television advertising on sales.

The analysis showed that the additional television activity doubled the brand's market share. This outcome is regarded as a commercial success, since the additional expenditure involved should be repaid within two years.

BACKGROUND TO THE LAUNCH OF DEEP CLEAN

Market Background

In 1978 Steradent (a Reckitt & Colman product) was the brand leader in the large, but declining, specialist denture cleaner market. However, whilst Steradent was the dominant brand, it was also potentially vulnerable, particularly in the grocery trade. There were three or four major manufacturers with both the expertise and resources to challenge Steradent's position in the UK. Efferdent, for example, launched by Warner Lambert in 1970, achieved a 17 per cent brand share during its first year. It was against this background that Reckitt & Colman began to examine ways of securing the specialist denture cleaning market in the UK.

Steradent is an alkaline cleaner which, if used regularly, removes film and plaque from dentures and prevents the build-up of stain carrying deposits on dentures. However, because Steradent is formulated principally to be effective against plaque and film, its efficacy in removing calculus (commonly known as tartar) is limited.

Deep Clean was developed to overcome this problem. An acid denture cleaner in tablet form, it was the first of its kind in the world.

Positioning

The obvious positioning for Deep Clean was as a superior denture cleaner dealing with a particular problem suffered by a segment of the denture wearing population. However, some interesting results emerged from a product placement test carried out in November 1978. Before trial, respondents were shown the pack with a simple product concept statement. Although speed of cleaning was only mentioned in the body copy, this was picked out as the major advantage rather than its superior cleaning effectiveness. This was a truly revealing commentary on the denture cleaning market. Steradent was seen as an overnight steeper taking a long time to work, and being without one's dentures for any long period of time is disliked by many denture wearers. Thus, a quick steeper, which was also effective, was seen by them as a major breakthrough.

The importance of speed as an incentive to trial was confirmed by advertising concept research carried out in April 1979. This showed Deep Clean to be viewed as a modern, fast acting and more effective denture cleaner than Steradent.

Media Strategy

It was decided that, for the launch of Deep Clean, national press advertising would be used, for the following reasons:

(a) The target audience for a specialist denture cleaner is old, defined loosely as all adults 35+, but more precisely four in five are over 45 and two in five are over 65.
(b) Despite the fact that older people tend to watch more television than younger age groups, experience across a wide range of products demonstrates a consistently lower level of advertising recall by older age groups. We would hypothesize that part of the reason for this may be due to the very rapid nature of TV communication. With press, on the other hand, once interested, a denture wearer could take things at his/her own pace.

It was felt, however, that a combination of both press and television advertising could provide a powerful impetus to the product's sales, especially amongst denture wearers under 50 years old, and thus the decision was taken to advertise on television in two regions, Yorkshire and Lancashire. Yorkshire was chosen as a test area on the basis of its average characteristics in terms of denture-wearing population and usership of specialist denture cleaners. A higher level of television advertising support was employed in Lancashire, to counter the test market launch of 'Extradent', a new product from a competitive manufacturer.

Creative Execution

Advertising concept research was conducted in April 1979. On the basis of the findings, a launch press advertisement was developed which emphasized speed and featured a fizzing tablet which communicated speed, activity and freshness. The visual mnemonic was in-

'Clean as a Whistle'

SUNG There's a great denture cleaner that in ten minutes flat

Can get your dentures so fresh and so clean

As clean as a (*whistle*)

in ten minutes they'll be

As clean as a (*whistle*) You'll see!

MVO With Deep Clean stains and bacterial plaque disappear to leave your dentures fresh and clean in just ten minutes

SUNG Oh as clean as a (*whistle*) you'll see what we mean

with super fresh Deep Clean

MVO Deep Clean from Steradent ... For dentures as clean as a (*big whistle effect*)

Stills from Deep Clean television advertisement.

New Steradent Deep Clean. The denture cleaner that only takes 10 minutes!

Try the 10 minute test

Pop your denture into a glass of warm water. Add one Deep Clean tablet. The low pH formula immediately releases the active cleaning ingredients in a fresh effervescent solution which breaks up and dissolves away tartar deposits and stains.

10 minutes later rinse and look–your denture will definitely look cleaner. Really stubborn stains and heavy tartar deposits may need two or three treatments–but you will achieve a really clean denture in a very short time.

Finally try the tongue test (run your tongue over the denture). It doesn't just <u>look</u> much cleaner–it feels it too!

Deep Clean

Your denture has never been so clean–so fast!

cluded in the final TV execution which itself was based on a successful advertising concept, 'clean as a whistle'. It was felt that this would work better in a moving medium than it could in a static medium.

EVALUATION

Analysis of Sales Data

Deep Clean was launched in July 1979 and its sales performance, measured by Nielsen bi-monthly audits, is recorded in Figure 8.1. The graph shows the brand's share of all denture cleaner sales, together with the timing of the press and television advertising. There is clear evidence that, from the beginning of the television advertising, sales in both Lancashire and Yorkshire have increased at a far greater rate than in the rest of the country.

Whilst this is certainly a prima facie case for the effectiveness of television advertising, it is possible that other marketing factors were responsible for the improved sales in these areas. However, there is no evidence that this was the case. The average selling prices of Deep Clean and its competitors have not varied regionally; with the exception of Lancashire, which saw the introduction of Extradent, competitive activity and promotion has been uniform across the country; and consumer promotions for Deep Clean in the form of press coupons appeared nationally.

Another important factor is the availability of the brand, and Figure 8.2 records the growth of sterling-weighted shop distribution. This shows that levels of distribution were initially much the same in all areas, but latterly distribution in the televised areas, Lancashire and Yorkshire, exceeded that in the other areas by some ten points. This improvement could of course be the result of the television activity encouraging retailers to stock the brand. But even if this is not the case, the differences in distribution could not by themselves account for all of the sales improvement in Lancashire and Yorkshire. This is demonstrated in Figure 8.3 which plots the 'rate of sale' (i.e. market share per point of sterling shop distribution) achieved in each period.

Again, in comparison with the other areas, the rate of sale in Lancashire and Yorkshire improved dramatically from the commencement of the television advertising. By January/February the rate of sale in Lancashire was double that of the other areas and in Yorkshire it was fifty per cent higher.

Cumulative Advertising Effects

Both the brand share and rate of sales results show that the brand's performance in Lancashire and Yorkshire was similar up until the January/February audit, at which point sales in Yorkshire fell back whilst sales in Lancashire continued to improve. This disparity can be explained by an examination of the achieved television rating in each area. In the latter months the weight of advertising in Yorkshire was substantially lower than that achieved in Lancashire. By the end of February the cumulative ratings in Yorkshire were 58 per cent of those in Lancashire (Yorkshire 803 TVR, Lancashire 1373 TVR).

To talk in terms of accumulated ratings since launch supposes that the advertising, once seen, is never forgotten. This is obviously fallacious since the effects of an advertising exposure are bound to diminish over time. This concept can be expressed by calculating the

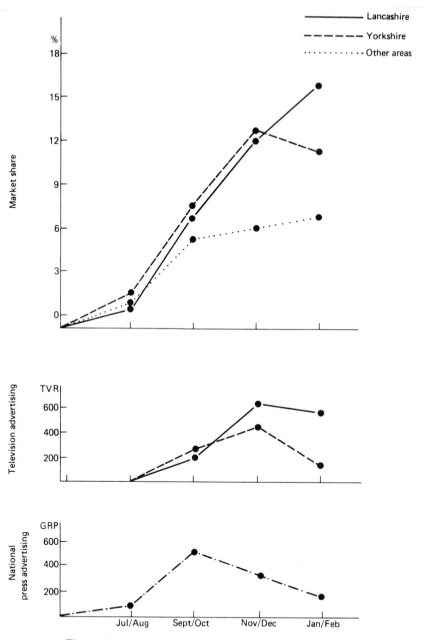

Figure 8.1   Market share and advertising support of Deep Clean.

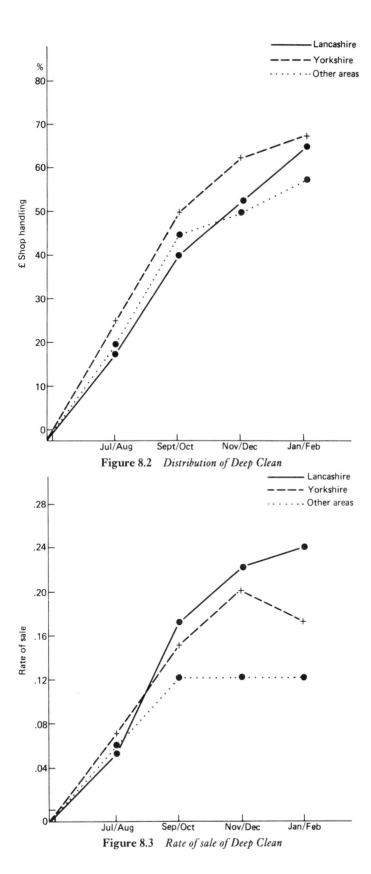

Figure 8.2 *Distribution of Deep Clean*

Figure 8.3 *Rate of sale of Deep Clean*

net accumulated weight of advertising, which is the sum of current advertising plus advertising seen in the past, the latter being discounted by an amount depending on the interval since it was first seen. Specifically, the calculation has the form:

Net accumulated advertising weight
$$= A_0 + \delta A_1 + \delta^2 A_2 + \ldots\ldots\ldots\ldots\ldots$$

where A_0 = Current advertising
$A_1\ldots\ldots A_i$ = Advertising i periods ago
δ = the proportion of the advertising effect carried over to the next period.

The above concept was employed to model the incremental sales achieved by television advertising. A variety of values for the advertising decay rate were tried, the most satisfactory result being obtained by assuming the advertising effects decay at a rate of about 30 per cent per period. This is demonstrated in Figure 8.4, which shows how much of the actual sales variation is explained by alternative assumptions for the decay rate.

Figure 8.5 shows the incremental sales achieved in Lancashire and Yorkshire plotted against the net accumulated weight of advertising, expressed as effective TV ratings per

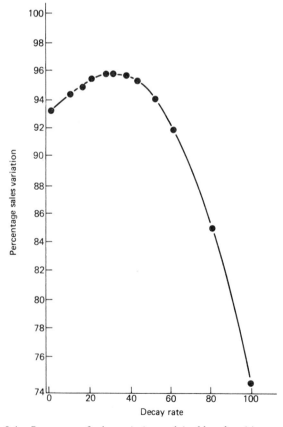

Figure 8.4 *Percentage of sales variation explained by advertising at various decay rates*

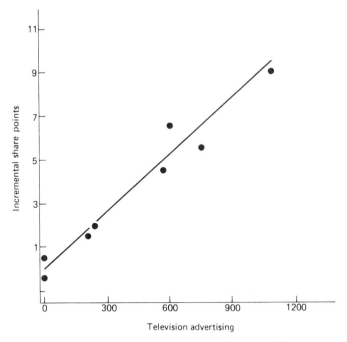

Figure 8.5   *Correlation between incremental sales and TV advertising*

period. Whilst the estimate of the advertising decay rate is based on only a limited number of data points, the hypothesis that the growth of sales during the launch period is dependent on the net accumulated weight of advertising does explain the difference in the brand's performance in the two areas.

Consumer Research

Further evidence for the effect of television advertising is available from an independent national survey of denture wearers carried out in March 1980, shortly after the end of the television campaign. The results are summarized in Table 8.1.

Both the awareness and brand last purchased scores in Lancashire and Yorkshire are roughly double the figures achieved in the rest of the country and this is consistent with the differences in market share shown by the Nielsen data.

TABLE 8.1:   CONSUMER RESEARCH ON DEEP CLEAN, MARCH 1980

	Yorks/Lancs Base = 140	Rest of country Base = 337
Spontaneous brand awareness	8.5%	3.5%
Total brand awareness	31.0%	15.4%
% of people whose last purchase was Deep Clean	6.5%	3.0%

The differences in the awareness scores are statistically significant at the 95 per cent confidence level.

THE PROFITABILITY OF TELEVISION ADVERTISING

The sales attributable to television advertising can be calculated from the differences between the market share achieved in Lancashire and Yorkshire and the rest of the country. To date, the gross profit from these additional sales amounts to 26 per cent of the cost of the television advertising. However, this calculation understates the benefit from advertising for two reasons. Firstly, the residual effects of the advertising which has already appeared will induce further trial purchases, and, secondly, a proportion of those consumers who have already been motivated to make their first purchase will go on to become regular users of the brand. Thus the full benefits of the television advertising will be calculable only when the final levels of trial and repurchase are established. However, if the sales generated by TV advertising were to continue at their current level, then the cost of advertising would be repaid within a year.

Arguably such an assessment is optimistic, but evidence from the consumer survey carried out in March 1980 showed that, even nine months after the launch, a high proportion (58 per cent) of people buying Deep Clean were buying it for the first time, and that the average repurchase rate amongst those who were not first time buyers was 60 per cent. These figures would suggest that sales should continue at least half their current level, which would imply a pay-back period of under two years. Compared with the typical experience of new product launches, this is a highly satisfactory result and demonstrates the effectiveness of the advertising campaign.

9
The Launch of Tjaereborg Rejser

BACKGROUND

Tjaereborg Rejser were founded in 1950 by a Danish pastor! They are now the third largest package holiday tour operator in Europe.

Their growth is based on the simple proposition of selling high quality holidays at prices significantly below other tour operators. The cost saving is achieved primarily by selling direct to the consumer, saving ten to fifteen per cent in travel agent's commission.

The UK was a logical place for Tjaereborg to launch as it is the largest source of package holiday takers in Europe, and a market in which direct sell was embryonic. BMP were appointed in June 1977, and the company officially opened for business on 1st January 1978.

THE BRITISH HOLIDAY MARKET

The package holiday market is a volatile and highly fragmented one. 1972 and 1973 were peak years for the industry with over four and a half million holidays sold each year, but economic recession, the loss of confidence in tour operators following the collapse of Courtline, and the hot summers of 1974 and 1976 had led to a gradual decline in the market.

There were already over a hundred tour operators fighting for a share of this shrinking market, from the giant mainstream companies like Thompsons and Cosmos, to the small specialist outfits like Kuoni and Inghams.

In their first season Tjaereborg aimed to sell 25 000 holidays to consumers in the South East. In 1977 there were 1.3 million package holiday takers from this part of the country, so Tjaereborg were targeting for a modest 2 per cent share. However, as their programme concentrated on popular destinations such as Spain and Majorca, a sector in which there was severe overcapacity and fierce competition, it was evident that without their strong proposition they would have been foolish to enter the market at all.

THE ROLE OF ADVERTISING

Figures 9.1 and 9.2 illustrate the differences in method of operation between a conventional tour operator and a direct-sell tour operator.

Conventional tour operators use travel agents to distribute their brochures, and rely on

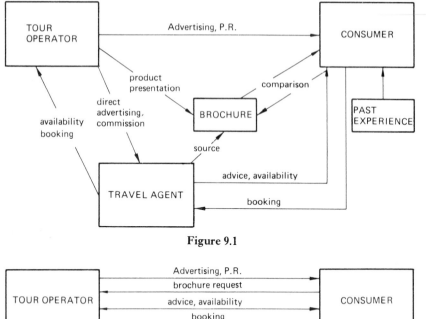

Figure 9.1

Figure 9.2

them to recommend their holidays to consumers when asked for advice. Travel agents also take bookings and collect money for conventional tour operators. The role of advertising is simply to persuade the consumer to consider that operator when choosing a holiday. It is not necessary for the advertising to inform consumers how to go about booking their holiday.

To purchase a holiday from a direct-sell tour operator, the consumer must contact the tour operator to get a brochure, and again to ask for advice or information, and again to make the booking. This is obviously more complex than dropping in on a local travel agent. The advertising thus has the dual role of creating demand and also telling the consumer how to satisfy that demand.

Figure 9.3 illustrates the important stages in the direct-sell booking claim and the role of advertising in each stage.

(i) The advertising must motivate consumers to request a brochure and inform them how to do so.

(ii) The consumer will compare the brochure with competitors' brochures, so it must be consistent with the advertising claims.

(iii) Holidays are a very expensive purchase and consumers are very suspicious of tour operators following the collapse of several notable tour operators in the mid-seventies. At the stage when consumers are actually committing themselves, the advertising has

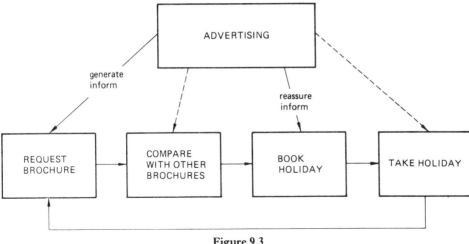

Figure 9.3

a vital role in providing reassurance about the experience and reliability of this new company.

This 'schema' provides the structure for the evaluation of the Tjaereborg launch advertising.

ADVERTISING DEVELOPMENT

Qualitative research was carried out to discover the important factors in planning and booking a holiday and consumers' reactions to the Tjaereborg proposition.

Respondents varied markedly in the thoroughness and degree of premeditation involved in planning and booking their holiday. However, it was evident that, having decided where to go and the standard of facilities required, price was the key factor in deciding which tour operator to travel with.

Not surprisingly, therefore, low price was the primary attraction of the Tjaereborg proposition. Pretesting of the initial executions, however, showed that low price alone tended to imply poor quality, a reaction heightened by the general distrust of tour operators. The best way of reassuring consumers about the quality of the holiday was by a factual explanation of how the low price is achieved. In other words, to say that by cutting out the travel agent, and thus his commission, it was possible to offer holidays of comparable quality to other tour operators, but at prices at least ten per cent cheaper.

No demographic groups stood out as particularly likely to book a Tjaereborg holiday. Inexperienced holiday takers were loath to pioneer an unknown company with a novel booking method, and thus it seemed that the discriminators of potential Tjaereborg bookers would be attitudinal rather than demographic. The target market was therefore defined as all package holiday takers, a group which is biased towards ABC1s and 16 to 44 year olds.

A mixed media schedule was used. Television was included for impact and because of the prestige attached to advertisers in that medium. The primary role of press was brochure generation, and publications with a good history of direct response were chosen for the schedule. In addition the press advertisements provided increased coverage of the primary target group, more information about Tjaereborg and a detailed explanation of the booking method. The total media budget was £83 000. The television advertising was on London and Southern during January 1978; the press insertions carried on until the end of February.

EVALUATING THE ADVERTISING

As mentioned above, the section on advertising evaluation will follow the structure outlined in Figure 9.3.

Generating Brochure Requests

AWARENESS OF TJAEREBORG

A necessary precursor to entering the booking chain is to be aware of its existence. Table 9.1 shows the results of a post-advertising awareness check of 1100 adults.

TABLE 9.1:   POST-ADVERTISING AWARENESS OF TJAEREBORG

	Expenditure[3] (£)	Share of voice[4] %	Prompted awareness %
Tjaereborg (1978)	115 200	8.1	32[1]
Vingressor (1979)	196 600	8.3	17[2]

[1] Respondents intending to holiday in 1978.
[2] Respondents who have taken a foreign holiday in the last five years.
[3] MEAL.
[4] Share of 'foreign tours and holidays'.

By March 1978 32 per cent of the holiday-taking public in the South East were aware of Tjaereborg. In the same survey Thomsons, Cosmos and Cooks achieved scores of ninety plus, which is to be expected given their brand share and length of time in the market. A better comparison is with the prompted awareness achieved by Vingressor, a Swedish direct-sell company, after their UK launch in 1979.

A post-awareness check carried out in March 1979 showed that Vingressor had only 17 per cent prompted awareness, slightly over half that of Tjaereborg, despite a similar share of voice (MEAL has been used for expenditure and share of voice because of the importance of press in both launches; Tjaereborg's press/TV expenditure was split 50:50, Vingressor's 57:43) and, allowing for inflation, a 40 per cent increase in media spend.

Vingressor had the disadvantage of being second into the market. Tjaereborg's novelty, not to say notoriety, within the travel trade meant that they received considerable coverage in industry publications, consumer press and holiday programmes. This would undoubtedly have boosted awareness of Tjaereborg considerably, but, as Table 9.2 shows, advertising was still the primary awareness generator for Tjaereborg.

The post-advertising awareness check also showed that awareness of Tjaereborg was higher amongst the main target group, and moreover that ABC1s were much more likely than C2DEs to have heard of Tjaereborg first through a press advertisement, one of the intentions of the mixed media schedule.

TABLE 9.2:   HOW WAS TJAEREBORG FIRST
HEARD OF? BASE: ALL AWARE OF TJAEREBORG

TV advertisement	66%
Press advertisement	11%
TV programme	10%
Newspaper article	3%
Friends/relatives	4%
On the radio	3%
Others	8%

Fieldwork International Awareness check, March
1978.

BROCHURE GENERATION

Table 9.3 shows the number of brochure requests generated by each medium.

Television is apparently more efficient than the press at generating brochure requests. This is undoubtedly exaggerated as the Ansaphone number was printed on the press advertisements and thus some Ansaphone responses would actually have been generated by the press.

TABLE 9.3:   BROCHURE REQUESTS BY MEDIA, JANUARY/FEBRUARY 1978

Media	Expenditure (£) (actual)	Number of responses	Cost per response (pence)
London	31 637	57 053	55
Southern	10 154	9 898	103
Total TV (Ansaphone)	41 791	66 651	62
Press (coupon)	41 177	57 290	72
Total	82 968	124 241	67

More surprising is the difference in efficiency between London and Southern, with Southern roughly twice as expensive per brochure generated as London. The reasons for this are not fully understood. Although London received 70 more adult TVRs than Southern (398 against 328), the cost per thousand was identical. A partial explanation is probably that the incidence of package holiday taking is 50 per cent higher amongst Londoners than Southerners (BNTS).

There are no directly comparable response data available on either press or TV as there were no comparable advertisers. However, Thames TV have provided anonymous data about their five most successful holiday advertisers to give a yardstick against which to measure Tjaereborg's success. Table 9.4 compares these responses with the weight of the exposure of the five heaviest advertisers (there were only six major advertisers on Thames in 1978 excluding Tjaereborg). While Tjaereborg account for 8 per cent of these advertisers' total adult TVRs, they account for 48 per cent of their total brochure requests. On average the other advertisers generated 13 brochure requests per TVR; the Tjaereborg advertisement generated 143 requests per TVR.

It has been emphasized that these comparisons are quite crude because a mainstream holiday advertiser does not *need* to generate direct brochure requests through its advertising. However, when consumers do ring up to request a brochure they are told that they

TABLE 9.4:   WEIGHT OF EXPOSURE AND NUMBER OF BROCHURE REQUESTS OF FIVE ANONYMOUS
HOLIDAY ADVERTISERS, LONDON, JANUARY/FEBRUARY 1978

	Weight of exposure (adult TVRs)	Number of brochure requests
A	1 610	20 765
B	1 093	17 974
C	949	11 534
D	617	8 928
E	494	2 273
Tjaereborg	398	57 053

Note: Except in the case of Tjaereborg, the numbers in the two columns are not necessarily related to their opposite numbers.

are allowed to ask for up to six brochures. It is significant that, when in a position to obtain a brochure by simply uttering a name, rather than walking down to a travel agent, 70 per cent of consumers who rang up for a Tjaereborg brochure asked *only* for that brochure. That this is the case, when choice is so facile, is an interesting demonstration of the power of Tjaereborg's commercial, and of Tjaereborg's proposition.

Low price was identified as the key element in the advertising strategy, and in fact a postal survey of 1000 brochure requestors, 416 of whom replied (Table 9.5), showed that low price was the most memorable communication of the commercial and the key reason for requesting a brochure.

TABLE 9.5:   POSTAL SURVEY OF 1000 BROCHURE REQUESTORS

	State anything you can remember about the advertisements you saw for Tjaereborg (%)	
	TV	Press
Lower price/cheaper than other companies	45	32
Book direct/no travel agent's fee	37	26
Phone number	10	7
Just the name	2	10

	State the main reason you sent off for a Tjaereborg brochure (%)
Inexpensive/cheaper holidays/lower prices	39
Wanted to compare prices/services	23
No travel agents/direct selling	13
Wanted to see what holidays were offered	10

Fieldwork International 1978 Postal Survey.

Brochure Comparisons

The brochure is a very important, in some ways the most important, part of the overall communication from Tjaereborg to the consumer. Obviously the advertising can have no direct effect on consumers when they are comparing the brochures of different companies. However, the brochure must be consistent, in image and tone of voice, with the advertising.

To cut the cost of your holiday, cut out the travel agent.

Would you like to save 10% on the cost of your holiday?

Like £35 on a fortnight's holiday for two in Majorca?

Or £60 on a holiday in Greece?

These are the sort of savings you can make by cutting out the travel agent and booking your holiday direct with Tjaereborg.

Tjaereborg are one of Europe's biggest holiday companies, and starting this summer, they'll be taking British holidaymakers to Europe's most popular resorts.

Although Tjaereborg save you money, you won't have to give up any quality.

In fact, Tjaereborg share many of their hotels with companies that charge considerably more for the same holiday.

And all Tjaereborg's prices are guaranteed, there are no hidden charges, and there won't be any surcharges.

If you'd like to save money on your holiday, all you have to do is pick one from the Tjaereborg brochure, and book it direct, either by phoning or calling in at the Tjaereborg office.

To get your free Tjaereborg brochure, send off the coupon or phone 01-493 7232.

To cut out the travel agent, cut out the coupon.

NAME_____

(BLOCK CAPITALS)

ADDRESS_____

◆ TJAEREBORG

7–8 Conduit Street, London, W.1.

Tjaereborg press advertisement.

To ensure that this was the case the brochure was researched at the same time as the advertising; consequently it has some unusual features. The shape is landscape rather than portrait, which helps emphasize the uniqueness of Tjaereborg. The copy about hotels and resorts points out problems and faults as well as advantages, thus making Tjaereborg stand out as particularly trustworthy and honest. Finally the prices are clearly marked and 'no surcharges' is guaranteed, thus reinforcing the price claims made in the advertising.

The returns from the postal survey showed that in fact 90 per cent of brochure requestors thought that the Tjaereborg brochure was as good as or better than its competitors.

Conversion to Bookers

The final stage in the booking chain is for the consumer to ring up Tjaereborg and actually book the holiday. As the consumer is at this point committing himself to large sums of money he/she must be fairly sure that Tjaereborg are reliable and trustworthy. If in fact the advertising is effective in reassuring consumers it should be possible to demonstrate that brochure requestors exposed to the advertising are more likely to convert to bookers than requestors not exposed to it.

There were a significant number of brochure requests from outside mainstream TV-advertised areas, due in part to those press insertions which were national or semi-national, but otherwise due, presumably, to national PR exposure.

Table 9.6 shows the conversion to booking ratio in TV-advertised and non-TV-advertised areas. The ratio of brochure requestors to bookers was ten to one in the former and

TABLE 9.6:   CONVERSION OF BROCHURE REQUESTORS TO BOOKERS

	Number of brochure requests	Number of bookers[1]	Conversion ratio
Main advertised areas (London and South East)	94 012	9 573	9.8:1
Rest of England	27 319	1 202	22.7:1
Other areas (Scotland, Wales and overseas)	1 026	225	4.6:1
Total non-advertised areas	28 345	1 427	19.9:1

[1] 2.6 holidays per booker
2 to 3 per cent of data lost due to misaddressing.

twenty to one in the latter. Thus consumers with Tjaereborg brochures exposed to a reasonably heavy weight of advertising were apparently twice as likely to book a holiday with Tjaereborg than those who had not.

However, there is another possible explanation for these findings. In 1978 all Tjaereborg holidays departed from Gatwick airport. By and large the advertised areas are nearer to Gatwick than the non-advertised areas. In other words it could be that the product was inhibiting brochure requestors from outside the TV-advertised areas from booking, rather than the advertising encouraging bookings within the advertised areas.

To control out the product variable, the conversion ratios in six counties which are roughly equidistant from Gatwick and which all have London between them and Gatwick have been compared. Of the six counties – which are Hertfordshire, Essex, Buckinghamshire, Berkshire, Oxfordshire and Bedfordshire – two, namely Oxfordshire and Bedfordshire, fall substantially outside the London and Southern ITV areas.

As Table 9.7 shows, the conversion ratios in the advertised areas is 13 to one, whereas in the non-advertised areas it is 22 to one. This is substantial evidence that the advertising is having an influence on the final stage of the booking claim.

TABLE 9.7:   CONVERSION OF BROCHURE REQUESTORS TO BOOKERS BY COUNTY

County	Number of brochure requests	Number of bookers	Conversion ratio
Hertfordshire	7 695	574	13.4:1
Essex	18 212	1 265	14.4:1
Buckinghamshire	2 180	206	10.6:1
Berkshire	2 822	328	8.6:1
Total advertised	30 910	2 373	13.0:1
Oxfordshire	2 052	69	29.7:1
Bedfordshire	1 796	106	16.9:1
Total non-advertised	3 848	175	22.0:1

WAS THE ADVERTISING EFFECTIVE?

In answer to this question, so far this chapter has looked at the mechanism of the advertising and evaluated it against such criteria as are available and seem sensible.

One fact not yet mentioned is that, although Tjaereborg targeted to sell 25 000 holidays, they actually sold 29 000, thus going 16 per cent over budget. It could be argued that this is, per se, a demonstration of advertising effectiveness. However, it also could be argued that the direct-sell operation, and the advertising which is so integral to it, was not the most cost-effective way of marketing Tjaereborg's holidays, and that a conventional operation could have been equally successful and more cost-effective.

Direct Sell

Table 14.8 lists all the marketing costs which Tjaereborg had during their first season in the UK. Apart from the cost of advertising (media and production) most of the costs relate to the printing and distribution of brochures.

The net sales value (NSV) of the 29 000 holidays which Tjaereborg sold in 1978 was £3 500 000. At £251 000 the advertising and distribution costs were 7.2 per cent of NSV.

TABLE 9.8:   DIRECT SELL COSTS (£)

Advertising	83 000
Production	68 000
200 000 brochures	57 000
Postage and packaging	32 000
Handling house	4 000
Ansaphone costs	7 000
Total	251 000

BMP Estimates.

Conventional

Table 9.9 estimates the costs of marketing these same 29 000 holidays using the conventional brochures distribution mechanism through travel agents.

No advertising other than trade press is costed in, although it could be argued that a moderate amount of advertising would be advisable. However, as Tjaereborg's holidays would be such good value for money they could probably rely on consumers finding them

TABLE 9.9:   CONVENTIONAL COSTS (£)

Advertising	5 000 (trade press)
Production	2 000 (trade press)
300 000 brochures	78 000
Sales force (8)	35 000
Launch	10 000
Travel agents' com.	350 000
Total	480 000

BMP Estimates.

out for themselves and hope that travel agents would reassure consumers about their quality. A vigorous trade press campaign and a prestigious trade launch would be necessary!

There are approximately 1700 travel agents in the South East; however it would not be necessary to service them all, probably the 500 largest would suffice. A well known tour operator employs a sales force of eight and prints 300 000 brochures to cover just such a number of travel agents and the costs for Tjaereborg are based on this.

The largest new cost would be travel agents' commission, which would represent at least ten per cent of the net sales value of the holidays. The total cost of this option is therefore £480 000, which is 13.7 per cent of NSV.

The conventional operation is almost twice as expensive as selling direct, which means that Tjaereborg would have had to sell a considerably higher volume of holidays through travel agents than the 29 000 they sold direct to the consumer to make as much money.

Tjaereborg could pass on the cost of the travel agent to the consumer as do all other tour operators. It appears that if they sold 29 000 holidays this way, they would make more money as there would be no expensive media costs to bear. However, this line of reasoning is invalid as to raise the price of Tjaereborg's holidays would destroy their proposition. To sell their holidays in this situation Tjaereborg would have to segment the market on a different basis than price. For example, they could offer unusual destinations or specialize in certain destinations, though given the mainstream nature of their programme this is not really feasible. Alternatively they could build a proposition around high quality; however, for a new company this in itself would require substantial advertising support, which would be competing head on with the big tour operators without the benefits of their long established and reliable brand names.

As discussed in the introduction it is apparent that if Tjaereborg had not had a distinctive proposition, i.e. low price, they would have been foolhardy to enter the UK holiday market at all. Now it has been demonstrated that direct sell, and the advertising which is such a vital ingredient in direct sell, was by far the most cost-effective way for Tjaereborg to sell their holidays.

SUMMARY OF THE ARGUMENT

Tjaereborg had a requirement to sell 25 000 holidays; they had a mainstream programme of resorts but a distinctive proposition, namely, lower prices achieved by their means of operation – selling direct to the consumer.

Price was the key element in the advertisements which were developed for Tjaereborg. The television commercial used the distinctive 'How much?' device, while the press concentrated on giving consumers information about the quality of the holidays and the size and experience of the company.

There are three stages in the holiday booking chain: (i) brochure requesting, (ii) brochure comparison, (iii) booking the holiday. It has been argued that advertising has a major influence on (i) and (iii).

The scale of the number of requests generated by the television advertising has been demonstrated by comparison with other holiday advertisers; it was, simply, unprecedented. Moreover the percentage of solus requests has been used as evidence of the degree of interest aroused by the advertising.

The importance of the advertising in reassuring consumers that Tjaereborg are a trust-worthy company at the stage at which they are booking a holiday has been demonstrated by comparing the conversion ratios of advertised and non-advertised counties which are equidistant from Gatwick.

Finally, the cost-effectiveness of the advertising has been demonstrated by contrasting the costs and profits of the direct-sell method with the conventional operating system. It is clear that Tjaereborg would have had to sell a considerably higher volume of holidays to achieve the same return if the latter system had been used. In fact, as it was, they sold 16 per cent more holidays than they had originally budgeted to do.

DISCUSSION AND CONCLUSIONS

This case history is direct response because advertising is the means of the advertiser carrying out his business as well as the tool used for creating demand for his products. It differs from most direct-response advertisers in that with Tjaereborg a brand is being created.

The launch of Tjaereborg was the launch of a new sector of the travel industry, and it is important to establish Tjaereborg as number one in that category. The benefit of this is that with repeat bookings and increased personal recommendation from satisfied customers the need for advertising decreases over the years, making the whole operation even more profitable. This contrasts with the lot of the conventional tour operators, where the travel agents' commission is omnipresent.

When seeking to demonstrate the effectiveness of Tjaereborg's advertising it could be argued that the advertising should have generated even more brochure requests or achieved an even lower conversion ratio. However, given the finite number of holidays to sell, and even here Tjaereborg over-achieved, this argument is impossible to validate.

The difficulties of demonstrating anything at all in the real world are immense. Without areas controlled for such variables as PR, distance from Gatwick, media weight, propensity to take package holidays and so on, it is difficult to take these factors into account and impossible validly to assign causes to effects. However, the criteria of the business man are not the same as those of the empirical scientist. The fact that Tjaereborg were successful, and continue to be so, despite the opposition of the travel industry and their dire predictions of doom for Tjaereborg, setting up in such difficult times, is perhaps the best demonstration of advertising effectiveness which could be offered.

10

Fine Fare

The launch of the Birchwood superstore

INTRODUCTION

This is the story of the successful launch of the new Fine Fare superstore at Birchwood outside Warrington in November 1980, and demonstrates the major role that advertising played in contributing to that success.

Warrington was already well supplied with at least three other competitive superstores so novelty alone would be insufficient to attract enough shoppers to the store. An analysis of previous superstore openings suggested that size itself was rarely the key to success, and Birchwood would have to be considerably better than previous Fine Fare launches if it was to achieve its turnover targets.

This report analyses the role and impact of the advertising campaign which accompanied the launch of the store. It seeks to demonstrate that the advertising played a critical role in that it was the key to generating awareness of the store and its location, interest in and reasons for trial well above the levels which would have been predicted from earlier launches. This latter was particularly important because of the comparatively inconvenient situation of the Birchwood site. Research data are used to support the argument for the advertising effect and its contribution to the sales levels achieved.

Although the argument is a simple one it demonstrates dramatically how advertising works in concert with the other elements of the marketing mix.

BUSINESS BACKGROUND

Fine Fare opened its first superstore in 1972 in Scotland and had launched twenty-two stores prior to Birchwood.

Superstores are normally defined as stores with over 25 000 square feet of selling space; there are approximately 300 in the United Kingdom. It is not a discrete description in that consumers have no fixed criteria on what differentiates a superstore from a supermarket.

Any new store has to compete primarily for existing business, whilst it seeks to create incremental business in the operational catchment of its store. Thus, the pulling power of a store is a measure of the business it brings in from areas currently controlled by other stores.

Every catchment is unique and each presents its own marketing opportunities and problems. Perceptions of grocery store brands are very often catchment-specific and are derived from experience of the local product. If a multiple is represented by an ageing, earlier generation supermarket, it is no comfort to shoppers to know that elsewhere sparkling new stores exist under that brand name.

That stores have brand values which are their own and not related to most of the goods they sell is an important factor in this argument. Own labels have grown enormously and not simply because they may be cheaper than the previous brands; in many stores they carry the quality credentials of the store name.

Shoppers do differentiate between stores along the same basic dimensions as any other branded goods, i.e. price/values/quality and personality. The latter is less likely to be consistent on any national base because of the variability of the offer (store size, age, etc.).

LAUNCHING A NEW SUPERSTORE

Although every catchment area is unique its structure and profile dominate strategic planning. The primary considerations are:

(a) Population: density, composition and proximity to the store (and to competition).
(b) Competition: where can we expect to draw our business from and how strong are the established businesses?
(c) Communication: what media are available at the local level and what coverage can we get?

The actual site of the store is important, both relative to the population centres and to competitive stores.

Virtually every retailer depends on meeting the consumer trinity of location, price and range/offer. Whilst this is well tried and well tested it demands that any new store has to produce evidence of superiority in these dimensions in order to compete effectively.

Trial is therefore the effective and real-life consumption measure. Unless you are able to generate high initial trial you risk a low loyalty rating and further marketing effort and expenditure to continually attract new custom and retrial.

THE BIRCHWOOD SUPERSTORE: THE MARKETING CONTEXT

Factual

Location, as previously stated, is of primary importance for any aspect of retailing. Whilst it is strategically well placed at the junction of two motorways, the M6 and the M62, Birchwood has special logistical problems, particularly when compared with previous store openings. The site was both isolated and unfamiliar to the population and was not easy to get to unless you already knew the way.

Its success depended to an unprecedented degree on achieving a very high percentage of car-borne shoppers due to the almost non-existence of local pedestrian traffic.

Superstores were not new and besides having two in the immediate area there were others in the peripheral catchment area. These were all well-established stores which were already offering all the generic advantages associated with large stores.

The price benefits which are an important part of the superstore armoury would be contested by a number of Kwik Save discount stores in the catchment.

The marketing plan for Birchwood acknowledged that to achieve targets we would need to draw substantial numbers of people from outside the immediate trading area up to the twenty-minute travelling time limit.

Attitudes/Predisposition

In order to evaluate how consumers perceived both the current shopping environment and the potential for new development, qualitative research was undertaken. The main findings were as follows.

PRE-LAUNCH RESEARCH (JUNE 1980)

Qualitative research showed that there was no positive predisposition to Fine Fare, primarily because their previous experience of any Fine Fare was limited to a very small older store. Thus the population had to be given strong reasons to travel to the store.

When asked to describe what attracted them to their current store, points in order of importance were:

— low prices
— not too far away
— range
— everything under one roof

The Birchwood centre proved to be an unknown quantity where nobody knew the exact nature of the development and many had not even heard of it. Nobody had any idea what, if any, shops would be opening there.

An earlier piece of research by the Development Corporation (February 1980) had shown:

1. *Reasons for using out-of-town shopping centre*

Cheaper prices	45%
Wide variety of shops	26%
Everything under one roof	17%
Easy to get to	9%

2. *Knowledge of centre*

Nothing	71%
Shopping complex	6%
Near Warrington	4%
New housing complex	3%
Only heard of area	16%

The primary objective was to achieve both the week one sales target and an ongoing sales level commensurate with Fine Fare profit requirements.

Data from previous launches and operating superstores enabled Fine Fare to predict both the catchment potential and share of trade for their new store. Share of trade is calculated by estimating the total food spend for a given population and using share levels refined from previous store data. Whilst the exact data are not necessary to argue the case, it is important to recognize that there was an existing and proven method of forecasting performance.

After the initial calculations for Birchwood had been completed, it became obvious that in order to meet targets it would need to operate at a different level from previous stores. This was summed up in the client brief by:

'We are faced with generating turnover, catchment share and outside draw on a scale which has rarely (if ever) been achieved in the past.'

Thus the task dictated that the advertising campaign had to generate trial rates at an exceptional level, which in turn would result in a regular customer base.

The Role of Advertising

1. To create virtually universal awareness of the store opening in the catchment area determined by the marketing plan.
2. To communicate the unique features and benefits of the store in order to position it as the best store in the vicinity, engendering curiosity and a desire to see the store.
3. This should encourage trial at a level which would both fulfil the initial turnover objectives and deliver sufficient customers for conversion to regular users at the budgeted target.

The great difference between a launch of a new FMCG product and a superstore is in providing journey motivation. Whilst many products are discovered on a shelf during a shopping trip we had to persuade people to:

(a) abandon confirmed shopping habits and familiar journeys;
(b) travel a new way to an untried store in an area they didn't know;
(c) use some means of transport (rail, bus, car) because there was no opportunity to get large-scale pedestrian traffic.

In order to achieve these objectives, one had to place a proposition in front of shoppers that was strong enough to motivate a trial shopping trip. To create interest or curiosity which was product-derived was the target of the creative strategy. Thus we would build a positive predisposition to the unique store benefits which were confirmed by the product experience.

ADVERTISING STRATEGY

The product had key elements which were both superior to existing stores and important to the consumer. The summation of the strategy is the creative work plan which is an agency control designed to select only the critical information in strategy selection.

Key Fact

The new Fine Fare Hypermarket surpassed all other stores in the area in the combination of low prices, wide range (food and non-food), and facilities it offered the shopper.

You can't miss the best shopping around.

The Hypermarket is beautiful as well as big. It's probably no exaggeration that a visit there will be the nicest shopping trip you've ever made.

The store itself is extremely spacious, well laid out and clearly signposted. And the interior decor is a positive work of art.

There are plenty of well-trained, friendly staff. No fewer than 35 checkout points, including express and disabled people's tills.

Easy payment facilities, including cheque cashing. Ziggy's restaurant, serving refreshments and full meals all day. And opening hours from 9am to 8pm every day from Monday to Saturday, for your convenience. There's even a Customer Service Desk to deal with any questions, suggestions or (heaven forbid!) complaints.

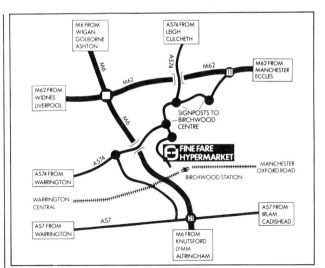

You can't miss your way by train.

The Hypermarket is also very convenient if you're coming by public transport.

Special shoppers' rail fares (a mere 44p off-peak return from Warrington Central, for example) will take you to Birchwood station on the Manchester-Oxford Road – Warrington Central line, which is only 100 yards from our doors.

You can't miss your way by car.

You've probably already noticed us without actually realising it. The Hypermarket is that vast green building by the M6, just south of the M62 intersection. It's a speedy journey in any direction, either along the A574 or off the M62 at Junction 11.

And once you arrive, you'll find a vast car park with ample space for 1500 cars. Each area clearly numbered and with a 'woodland' symbol to make it easy for you to remember.

That's not all. Right next to the car park you'll find very cheap petrol at the Fine Fare filling station.

You can't miss your way by bus.

We're looking after bus travellers too, with 6 free bus services running between the Birchwood Centre and (1) Orford, (2) Westy, (3) Cinnamon Brow, (4) Penketh and Great Sankey, (5) Walton and Stockton Heath and (6) Lymm. There's also the normal service along the A574. Which adds up to what we've been striving for. And you've been waiting for. The cheapest, choicest, most convenient shopping yet.

⊕ FINE FARE HYPERMARKET BIRCHWOOD
It's just too big to miss.

Consumer Problem

All shoppers in the area were (presumably) more or less satisfied with where they shopped, whether it was the local Co-op or one of the supermarkets/stores in the area.

Advertising Objective

To persuade shoppers in the catchment area that the Fine Fare Hypermarket was sufficiently different or superior to where they currently shopped to justify at least a trial visit.

Creative Strategy

Prospect definition:

1. All housewives using Warrington supermarkets.
2. All housewives travelling to shop at superstores in the area.

Principal competition:

1. Warrington supermarkets – smaller, expensive and less appeal visually.
2. Superstores (Asda and Tesco), which are price competitive, but less attractive.

Consumer Benefit

'You'll get more of what you want from the Fine Fare Hypermarket than from any other store you've ever experienced.'

The support for this strategy was the store benefits and the unique proposition offered by Fine Fare.

A core price strategy was already in existence which was delivered as the 'Fine Fare Guarantee'. This promised that week in week out, Fine Fare delivered the cheapest weekly shop and any customer who found this to be false could claim a refund.

The unique 'interiors' are exclusive to Fine Fare and create an ambience which improves the shopping experience.

All the DIY product was contained in a special store within a store called Fix'n'Fit which was heavily service-orientated.

Certain aspects of the Fine Fare offer were original and innovatory, for example, Yellow Packs (generic) and an extensive non-food department.

The totality of the offer was the consumer proposition which had to form the basis for the creative strategy.

MEDIA SELECTION

A multi-media campaign was selected to ensure that the advertising achieved both maximum visibility and media creativity. Television was the primary medium and was selected for its ability to deliver large audiences quickly, whilst generating a high level of awareness and excitement. To build further frequency of communication into the television campaign, radio was chosen, using the two local stations, Piccadilly and City. The creative flexibility of the medium was exploited by tailoring individual executions to key areas of catchment.

Newspaper activity was also planned, using the high penetration local and regional news-papers, to ensure that the wide range of benefits of the store was fully communicated.

MEDIA PLANNING

In order to exploit the strengths of the various media each had a carefully defined role. Television would be used both to create tension and anticipation by using a 'teaser' campaign and to build rapid awareness. Because the ambience of the store was an important part of the offer it was critical to use a medium which could convey the size, the breadth of offer and the unique in-store décor.

Press advertising was used to spell out both the breadth and detail of the offer. Pricing, which is so important, had to be communicated in line listings which can only be handled efficiently by the press.

Besides its customary role of acting as a reminder, radio was used for the first time in a very tactical role. Individual scripts were prepared which addressed themselves to discrete groups of housewives in small areas around the centre but within travelling distance. We addressed them by name 'calling all St. Helens' housewives', and gave them detailed instructions on how to get to the store.

CREATIVE EXECUTION

Every execution, whether television, press or radio, was designed to meet the launch objectives. The message was required to create a reservoir of anticipation and desire to visit the store which would burst on to Birchwood on launch day. The totality of the offer and thus the 'experience' had to be communicated, not simply individual elements of the offer in a competitive framework.

The theme was 'it's too big to miss' which used the store structure as a visual device and detailed all the exciting elements of the offer which was designed to create both interest and enthusiasm.

The television execution used a well-known presenter who developed the store opening from pre-launch. It was designed to communicate the most important retail event that had ever happened in this area. There was an absence of ballyhoo and the script was careful to avoid any 'hype' which might discredit the store's image. One of the store's real strengths was the internal space characterized by its wide aisles and dramatic décor; only after the initial awareness had been built was the full store shown in order to leave the impact to immediate pre-launch.

Press coverage was organized around the local group of Warrington papers and the schedule was carefully matched both to population and expected and desired propensity to travel to the store. The inclusion of a colour supplement meant that we could do some justice to the décor and range benefits of the store.

THE LAUNCH

The store was opened to the public on 11 November 1980. On the opening day 12 000 people visited the store and by the end of the first week's trading this had grown to 76 000.

Turnover during both the launch and subsequent weeks was in excess of targets, and the strength of the product created a conversion to regular use which built a successful business base.

Thus the evidence for trial and traffic size is not contestable – they came! The question is why, and from what source did they get their information?

Because the new store was the largest yet launched there may have been a correlation between size of store and share of business. Thus one could then hypothesize that size alone could be a determinant of success. An analysis of earlier launches showed that no such relationship existed.

POST-LAUNCH EVALUATION

We have two major pieces of quantified research that were carried out after the store had been open for one month.

The first was conducted over a week, in the store itself. Over 500 shoppers were interviewed. Primarily this project was designed to get an accurate profile of shoppers both in demographic and geographic terms. This work showed that 80 per cent of shoppers had come by car and 40 per cent had previously mainly used another superstore.

The other piece of research consisted of a sample of 400 housewives interviewed in their homes in the immediate and extended catchment area. This survey gave both the attitudes and shopping behaviour of the total sample, but additionally the data allowed us to compare attitudes of trialists and non-trialists.

Analysis

TABLE 10.1:   SPONTANEOUS AWARENESS
OF LARGE SUPERMARKETS AND
HYPERMARKETS

	All %	Near %
Birchwood	56	67
Tesco–Irlam	36	26
Any Kwik–Save	37	28
Any Co-op	36	34

Source: Home Interviews

From Table 10.1 it may be seen that within one month the store was top of mind for over half the catchment population. When looking at the immediate catchment, for Birchwood this increased to 67 per cent. Yet the Tesco store was the same size and had been operating for five years.

Advertising recall (Table 10.2) was very high and especially so in the extended areas of the catchment where it was important to gain ground as one of the original objectives. Thus even if seeing the advertising had been an exclusive pre-condition to trial we would have made target.

TABLE 10.2:   HAVE SEEN ADVERTISING FOR
ANY STORES MENTIONED

	All %	Near %	Further %
Birchwood	82	79	85
Tesco–Irlam	30	30	31
Any Kwik–Save	30	28	31
Any Co–op	29	28	30

Source: Home Interviews

TABLE 10.3:   EVER VISITED BIRCHWOOD

	All %	Near %	Further %
Birchwood	50	61	41
Tesco–Irlam	59	62	57
Any Kwik–Save	68	64	71
Any Co–op	83	86	80

Source: Home Interviews

Table 10.3 confirms that not only had half the sample already tried Birchwood but these trial rates were comparable with well-established competitive stores. Of our immediate catchment we had already matched the prime competitive superstore and were on par with a multi-brand operator. These figures suggest that the initial rate of trial so far achieved was in excess of any previous store launch in Warrington.

When asked whether they intended to use the store in the future, 60 per cent answered 'yes'.

TABLE 10.4:   WHERE ADVERTISING SEEN/HEARD

	All %	Near %	Further %
Television	81	81	81
Warrington Guardian series	68	66	69
Radio	5	4	6
Newspaper supplement	2	1	4

Source: Home Interviews

In that the media had different roles it was essential that both the primary ones were intrusive. The figures in Table 10.4 indicate that this particular objective had been achieved.

If we now look at those who came, we can evaluate how and why they decided the trip was worth it (Table 10.5).

For those who visited the store, advertising was by far the single most important source of information. Because of location constraints, all press work had carried a detailed map of how to get to the store from any part of the catchment area.

TABLE 10.5:   HOW FIRST FOUND
OUT THAT THE STORE WAS HERE

	%
Saw or heard advertising	59
Saw building	20
Heard from friends	12
Read article in paper	7

Source: Store Interviews
NB The ad/editorial supplement
was the main 'article in paper'.

TABLE 10.6:   MAIN REASON
FOR FIRST VISIT

	%
Curiosity/to see inside	64
Check/compare prices	7
Close/convenient	7
For a change	3
Like Fine Fare	1

Source: Store Interviews

Perhaps the information in Table 10.6 is the nucleus of the case study. Why were people curious? What had prompted them to want to see inside? As such a high proportion found out about the store from advertising which was specifically designed to create interest or curiosity then the role of advertising was a key one.

Measuring the 'Trial' Propensity

Perhaps the most conclusive evidence about the effectiveness of advertising on changing behaviour is obtained by comparing trialists against non-trialists using advertising awareness as a discriminator.

We have as our base data the results obtained from our two surveys:

1.   All shoppers in catchment area (interviewed at home), 82 per cent ad. awareness, 50 per cent trial.
2.   All Birchwood customers (interviewed in store), 95 per cent ad. awareness, 100 per cent trial.

Using these base data we can compare the levels of trial among shoppers in the catchment area according to whether they were aware or unaware of the advertising.

Figures for all shoppers in the catchment area may thus be broken down as follows.

Base: All shoppers in catchment area.

	All shoppers %	All aware %
Aware and visited	48	59
Aware and not visited	34	41
Total aware	82	100

	All shoppers	All unaware
Unaware and visited	2	11
Unaware and not visited	16	89
Total unaware	18	100

Therefore, when we compare the aware of advertising group with the unaware group, we find that the former were over five times more likely to have visited the store (i.e. 59 v. 11).

CONCLUSION

Whether in absolute terms or when compared with previous launches, the Birchwood launch was a resounding success. The evidence supports the hypothesis that the advertising created high levels of curiosity which in turn generated the targeted trial rates.

11

The 'Big John' Campaign

Advertising in the beer market

INTRODUCTION

This paper attempts to show how the 'Big John' advertising campaign boosted John Smith's Bitter's brand share amongst Yorkshire beers and helped to increase sales at a time of market decline.

It is notoriously difficult to isolate the effect of advertising on beer sales, owing to the complexity of the business and the sheer size of the brands involved, which together mitigate against radical, and therefore easily measurable, changes. The attempt is nonetheless well worth making. As the £6 billion beer market has fallen into decline under the effects of the recession, the fight for brand share has intensified and the brewers have increased their advertising expenditure. In 1981 they spent well over £40 million on television alone, of which more than £12 million went to promote bitters such as John Smith's, an increase over 1980 of some 60 per cent. While this expenditure does not appear to expand the market, it is clearly believed to influence drinkers' brand choice; to determine whether it can do so is the aim of this paper.

With John Smith's Bitter we were fortunate. The number of variables was fewer than usual. Courage and John Smith's have good data from a wide variety of sources over several years, so we were able to measure sales (and consumer response) before the advertising and after, and in the advertised area against non-advertised areas. Thus we were able to estimate the incremental sales stimulated by advertising.

The study is chiefly concerned with brand sales through John Smith's 'tied' public houses. This is for three reasons: retail (pub) sales account for the bulk of brand volume at a secure margin; the brand's problems were most evident in this sector; and better data are available to us for the tied trade than for the 'free' (club) trade.

This analysis is interesting because it represents a first step towards a more thorough understanding of what advertising can do for pub sales in general. We have gained a clearer idea of how advertising can be used and evaluated, and hope we show that, although there are several ways for a brewer to stimulate sales, in this case advertising was the most efficient in that it produced extra sales more cheaply than the alternatives. This experience and the evaluative techniques used will be useful, we believe, in planning future marketing investment.

BACKGROUND

The Brewery

John Smith's Brewery was founded in 1758 and taken over by Courage in 1970. It still produces all its own beers at Tadcaster, Yorkshire. John Smith's 1500 pubs are widespread across the North of England, and account for 15 per cent of all pubs in the heartland of Yorkshire. Tied houses account for some 60 per cent of total sales; the remainder goes through the free trade (mainly clubs). These proportions are roughly in line with those of other major brewers.

The Brand

John Smith's Bitter accounts for about half of the Company's total sales and is sold in every John Smith's pub. It is a well-established Yorkshire beer, whose formulation was last altered in the mid-1970s. It is a medium-strength, session bitter with an original gravity of 1036°. Ales of this type are known as 'Bitter Is' in brewery definitions; they are stronger and more expensive than 'Bitter IIs' or 'Milds', weaker and cheaper than 'Premiums', and constitute the single largest sector in the whole beer market.

The Market

The Bitter I market in the North East was worth some £350 million in 1980 (at retail prices). Bitter Is account for almost half of all draught beers in Yorkshire, though nationally the proportion is nearer one-quarter.

Yorkshire consumers are thus committed bitter drinkers, averaging over 13 pints of bitter a week, and tend to judge brewers by their Bitter Is rather than by their strongest beer or the standard of their pubs. Pub traffic is materially affected by the status of the brewer's Bitter I. The sector therefore is of primary importance.

The Competition

John Smith's chief rivals among the major brewers, who account for some 80 per cent of the Yorkshire market, comprise: Tetley (Allied), with 14 per cent of Yorkshire pubs and a massive free trade presence; Stones (Bass), 16 per cent; Whitbread, 11 per cent; and Webster (Grand Metropolitan), 7 per cent. Competition is fierce: draught bitters accounted for some 30 per cent of all Yorkshire TV beer advertising, against some 20 per cent in England and Wales (1981).

THE PROBLEM

John Smith's Bitter's volume sales started to fall in 1979, even though the Bitter I market was static.

The decline was due to lost pub sales. Sales in the so-called free trade (the largely finance-dependent clubs) continued to grow, reflecting distribution increases (Table 11.1).

TABLE 11.1:   JOHN SMITH'S BITTER TRADE PERFORMANCE, 1976–1980 (1976 = 100)

| John Smith's volume share of: | 12 months to December | | | 6 months to June |
	1977	1978	1979	1980
Pubs	100.7	100.7	95.4	95.4
Free trade	99.5	107.4	113.8	127.4

Source: BMS (see Appendix)
Base: major brewers, north east.

The pub share decline in 1979 represented a loss of 5.7 million pints (worth some £1.9 million at 1979 retail prices). But there is a multiplier effect: bitter drinkers (accompanied by friends) also spend money on fruit machines, bar food and games, so that non-beer sales account for some 30 per cent of pub turnover. Thus the total revenue loss caused by a mainstream bitter's decline is hard to estimate, but may be double the value of its own lost sales.

The BMS 'North East' region includes Yorkshire and Tyne-Tees. Company sales figures, collected on a regional basis from 1979, show that the 1980 sales decline was in Yorkshire. Non-Yorkshire sales were growing, reflecting pub acquisitions (Table 11.2).

TABLE 11.2:   JOHN SMITH'S BITTER VOLUME SALES (PUBS) BY REGION, 1979–1980

12 months to October 1979 (fiscal year)	Percentage change 1980 v. 1979
Yorkshire (75%)	−4
Non-Yorkshire (25%)	+7

Source: Courage (see Appendix)

Several explanations for the sales decline were examined and rejected:

1. *Product*. No change.
2. *Price*. In line with competition (cf. Wyman-Harris LTM; see Appendix).
3. *Pub standards*. No evidence of deterioration. No change in rate of investment in estate. No unusual staff or recruitment problems.
4. *Distribution*. No loss in the universe of tied pubs.
5. *Industrial relations*. No problems of production or availability.
6. *Share of mix*. No product in the portfolio promoted at the expense of John Smith's Bitter.

The fount design was slightly modified in the late 1970s, but this was not thought to be a significant factor.

We turned to consumer research to understand what appeared to be a consumer problem with the brand.

UNDERSTANDING THE CONSUMER PROBLEM

We conducted ten group discussions in June 1980 when reappointed to the brand. The sample comprised regular drinkers of both John Smith's and competitive bitters, in five Yorkshire towns covering strong and weak John Smith's trading areas.

Findings were consistent across locations. Essentially, John Smith's Bitter lacked character. Although acceptable to most drinkers, it did not arouse enthusiasm among its users. It was known to be local and long-established (both positive attributes), but so were its competitors. It was regarded merely as 'one of' Yorkshire's bitters, while Tetley's was the paradigm, especially among young drinkers, who saw John Smith's as an 'old boy's drink'. Younger drinkers in particular spoke highly of handpumped Tetley's (the consumer symbol for cask-conditioned, traditional 'real ale'). We deal with this important point in more detail later.

Survey data corroborated these findings (Table 11.3). The measures reflected but exaggerated the sales loss among drinkers in general, and young drinkers in particular.

TABLE 11.3: CLAIMED 'MOST OFTEN' DRUNK BRAND OF BITTER
(‡) = 18–24-year-olds

	1974	1978	1980
Base: total sample	449	314	264
		Percentage of total sample	
John Smith's	10 (13)	9 (10)	6 (5)
Tetley	19 (19)	27 (34)	29 (32)
Trophy	–	9 (9)	11 (9)
Stones	–	9 (6)	112 (14)

Source: Marplan, Yorks (see Appendix)
Base: All male bitter drinkers weekly or more often

The 'most often' drinkers appeared to decline much more than sales. This, we believe, is because the 'most often' claim measures both behaviour and consumer preference – a greater propensity to think of the brand as 'my brand' when asked a market research question like this. Thus the loss of 'most often' drinkers reflected the loss of commitment to the brand among its users, evident in the group discussions.

We seemed to have a particular problem with young drinkers in Yorkshire (see Table 11.4).

TABLE 11.4:   18–24-YEAR-OLDS AS PROPORTION OF 'MOST
OFTEN' PLUS 'REGULAR' DRINKERS

	Yorkshire		Non-Yorkshire*
	1978	1980	1980
	%	%	%
John Smith's	21	14	22
Tetley	16	23	22

Source: Marplan
* Non-Yorks. = North West/Lancs plus Tyne-Tees.

Image measures also showed a decline, especially among young drinkers; Tetley, however, improved among this group on overall imagery (Table 11.5). The scales in this table have been selected as the most descriptive of drinkers' attitudes to bitter brands on product and user imagery.

TABLE 11.5:   MEAN SCORES ON THREE ATTITUDE SCALES

Base: heard of brands		1976 (223/221)	1978 (179/119)	1979 (157/115)
'Good value for a bitter'				
John Smith's	All	3.43	3.49	3.23
	18–24	3.51	3.72	3.22
Tetley	18–24	3.65	3.99	3.93
'Lots of flavour'				
John Smith's	All	3.48	3.54	3.37
	18–24	3.49	3.48	3.23
Tetley	18–24	3.67	3.90	4.11
'For knowledgeable drinkers'				
John Smith's	All	3.26	3.52	3.34
	18–24	3.24	3.37	3.16
Tetley	18–24	3.28	3.89	4.21

Source: Marplan, Yorks.
Scale: +5 to +1.

The importance of the younger drinkers is threefold. They tend to consume more bitter than older people; they go to more pubs and are more willing to try different drinks; and they represent the market's future and will retain, in later years, the tastes they now develop.

Reasons for Loss of Young Drinkers

There seemed to be two factors affecting the decline in young drinkers. First, there was a change in the market. This period saw the northern revival of handpumped, cask-conditioned 'real ales' from major brewers, of whom Tetley's were in the forefront. Handpumped Bitter Is showed significant share growth: +3 per cent year on year (Table 11.6).

TABLE 11.6:   HANDPUMPED BITTER I'S SHARE OF TOTAL PUB SALES IN THE NORTH OF ENGLAND

	1979				1980	
Quarter	1	2	3	4	1	2
Percentage share	n/a	8.1	10.9	11.5	11.9	11.1

Sources: LTM (Wyman-Harris)

The demand for handpumped ales is most prevalent among young drinkers. The effect of young drinkers on pub beer sales is shown in Table 11.7.

TABLE 11.7:   EFFECT OF UNDER-25s ON HANDPUMPED BITTER'S SHARE OF PUB SALES

	Proportion of Under-25s in Bar		
	Under 10%	11–20%	21–40%
Handpumped bitter's percentage share of all sales (excluding lager)	12.9	14.6	20.6

Source: LTM (Wyman-Harris)

But John Smith's Bitter was not available in handpumped form; John Smith's brewery only produces 'bright' (keg) beers, so the brand could not profit from the new trend amongst young drinkers.

The second factor was a decline in John Smith's Bitter share of advertising voice (see Table 11.8). Moreover its advertisements had stressed the brand's 'Yorkshire heritage' during the 1970s, and similar claims had been adopted by other bitters, so that confusion existed in consumer recall of particular brands' campaigns. Too many competitors had jumped on the same bandwagon.

TABLE 11.8: JOHN SMITH'S BITTER SHARE OF DRAUGHT BITTER ADVERTISING ON YORKSHIRE TV

	1977	1978	1979	1980
Share of Yorkshire's major brands	34	27	22	15
Share of all brewers' brands	26	18	19	12

Source: MEAL (Media Expenditure Analysis Limited)

In conclusion, we believed that sales were down because the brand had declined in appeal, particularly to young drinkers, who had lost interest. It lacked handpumps, and the advertising had failed to offer something new in the face of heavy competition from similar bitter campaigns and more exciting lager commercials.

THE CASE FOR ADVERTISING

The marketing objective was to increase volume sales. Various options were assessed.

Installing cask-conditioned capacity at the brewery and handpump facilities in the pubs was not judged to be financially justifiable. Substantial increases in the rate of investment in the Yorkshire estate (or increasing the size of the estate) were not affordable within budget plans. However, advertising offered a cost-effective way of restoring share, by revitalizing the brand in the eyes of consumers.

The 18–24s appeared to be the most volatile group in terms of brand imagery and choice, and produced the greatest volume return for a given proportional change. If brand advertising could regain the loyalty of only a small proportion of these drinkers, share would be regained, and with that would follow benefits for total pub revenue.

It is worth stating here the rationale for putting media support behind a brand rather than outlets. Direct pub advertising is impractical, because of the infinite variations within the estate: all pubs are different, in size, location, style or 'atmosphere'; that is their charm. Virtually the only elements common to all the pubs are the John Smith's name and the beer on sale. By advertising the mainstream bitter, we could support the brewer whose name endorsed it, as well as his biggest single product, and could promote its sales in both pubs and clubs.

THE ADVERTISING

The Task

The task was to create a more relevant brand image for John Smith's Bitter (without any changes to the product or its presentation at point of sale), which would give the brand greater appeal in the face of increasingly aggressive competition.

Objectives

PRIMARY

The main objective was to restore the commitment of John Smith's Bitter drinkers to the brand, thus increasing their frequency of purchase.

SECONDARY

The secondary objective was to attract lapsed drinkers, both those who had switched to other pubs and those who had adopted other brands in the free trade.

The Role of Advertising

These objectives were realistic because of the significance of brand imagery in brand choice, particularly among younger drinkers. Beer drinking is essentially social and group pressures can be strong. The public selection of a brand of beer reflects the buyer's self-image in the same way as choice of cigarettes, clothes or car. Buyers want to feel that they are making a sensible, defensible choice that reflects well upon them as knowledgeable beer drinkers. This can override actual taste preference; the brewery adage that 'people drink with their eyes' has been repeatedly confirmed by blind and branded product tests, where the brand-names can reverse the preferences expressed 'blind'.

The under-30s tend not to be beer experts: they are too young. Their drinking is more influenced by what is popular and fashionable among their peer group. With them, the problem was to find a brand personality for John Smith's Bitter which could match the appeal of handpumped rivals, be talked about in the pubs, and revive their confidence in the brand.

TARGET MARKET

The primary target market was defined as young bitter drinkers (18-30, C1C2D). They were the most frequent buyers, the future market, the least enthusiastic about John Smith's Bitter and the most interested by advertising.

The proviso was attached that the advertising should not alienate the brand's older drinkers.

THE BRIEF

Alternate strategies to achieve the advertising objectives were investigated in group discussions, in the form of concept boards. Consumer reactions forced us to acknowledge that no single, strong, product-based platform existed. As a mainstream brand in the biggest sector of the beer market, John Smith's Bitter had, to some extent, to be all things to all men; its advertising had to express the essential qualities of a major Yorkshire bitter, and attach them unmistakably to John Smith's.

John Smith's Bitter
'The Forester'

(To the tune of 'Big John')

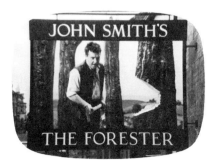

I wish I could get down from chopping these trees, 'cause a John Smith's pub is below my knees.

Now forestry is a worthy career, but stuck up on this sign I miss the big bitter beer that's Big John.

(Chorus) Big John, Big John, Great Big John.

Now don't get me wrong 'cause this job is OK . . . I like trees a lot if they fall the right way.

There's advantages too with Big John Smith's beer – 'cause of the simple fact they've got branches everywhere.

(Chorus) Big John, Big John, Big John (fades)

John Smith's Bitter
'The Cricketer'

(To the tune of 'Big John')

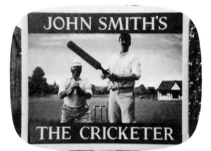

I've had a long innings on this John Smith's sign. In fact I've been here since 1909.

And I wish that bowler there could knock off these bails, 'cause I reckon I deserve a pint of Big John Smith's Ale; that's Big John.

(Chorus) Big John, Big John, Great Big John.

Now that brings my score to 5 million and two. My faithful old bat is nearly worn through.

Hmmm ... must be woodworm, well who'd have thought that!

Now for the big bitter taste of John Smith's. Howzat!

(Chorus) Big John, Big John (fades)

The execution, therefore, needed to be masculine, sociable, working-class and pub-based; drinkers in the commercials must really want the beer and be seen to enjoy it.

The tone should be assertive and the style contemporary, so that it could rival lager advertising in its appeal to young drinkers.

The communication, most importantly, should be that while John Smith's remained proud of its Yorkshire heritage, it was nonetheless as successful, popular and right today as it had ever been. Drinkers of the brand, we wanted consumers to believe, were not the 'old boys' of current criticism, but admirable drinking men who knew their beer.

THE CAMPAIGN

The creative solution was the 'Big John' idea. This stemmed from the fact that drinkers often ask for 'a pint of John's' at the bar.

The advertising aimed to create the impression of John Smith's Bitter as a 'big' pint – popular, widespread, drunk by everyone. 'Big' also implied a flavourful and strong pint.

The ingenuity of the campaign came from the blend of brand and drinker: 'Big John' was also a character, a real drinking man.

Classic values were expressed through the pubs and their signs, the traditional occupations of the characters, and the role of the beer as reward and refreshment after labour. 'Yorkshireness' was not overt – a reversal of earlier campaigns and a distinction from most competitors.

The modern elements of the 'Big Bad John' music, humour and special effects, gave the idea its freshness and strong branding.

Key frames from the two draught commercials are on pp. 18-19, the music track was faithful to the original Country and Western song, well-known by drinkers when tested.

MEDIA

Choice

Television was chosen as the sole medium. This was not only for reasons of cost-efficiency (although heavy drinkers do tend to be heavy ITV watchers too), but because of the nature of the advertising task. First, in a market dominated by brands spending heavily on television, John Smith's Bitter needed to establish a major advertising presence. Second, the chosen strategy involved a change to the brand's perceived character, which only television was felt able to achieve quickly.

Buying

Four bursts ran in Yorkshire. Timing was related to market seasonality and to cost-efficient time periods. Weight was determined by the media budget available (£250 000) and deemed sufficient at over 1500 men TVRs during 1981. Granada received one burst in November/December. Advertising for canned John Smith's was on air with the draught commercials.

Weight

With the launch of the new campaign, John Smith's Bitter's weight and share of advertising expenditure in Yorkshire rose substantially, returning to historic levels (see Table 11.9).

TABLE 11.9   JOHN SMITH'S BITTER SHARE OF DRAUGHT BITTER ADVERTISING SPENT ON
YORKSHIRE TV

	1977 %	1978 %	1979 %	1980 %	1981 %
Share of Yorkshire's major bitters	34	27	22	15	34
Share of all brewers' bitters	26	18	19	12	26

Source: MEAL

RESPONSE TO THE ADVERTISING

Three stages of qualitative research were carried out by BMP (see Appendix) to confirm the relevance and appeal of the strategy, and to develop the executions.

Post-campaign qualitative research revealed that the desired communications were being achieved (as they were during the pre-testing). The following verbatim quotations from the group discussions illustrate the consumer response to 'Big John'.

The beer:
   'It's a big pint, it's good value with a good taste.' (Leeds 18–30)
   'It goes down big and it sells a lot.' (Doncaster 25–40)
   'It says the beer's strong, a man's drink.' (York 18–24)

The drinker:
   'It's drunk by big and manly chaps.' (Leeds 30–45)
   'It's a masculine ad, all macho.' (York 25–40)
   'They're aimed at a big lad who's been knocking down a tree and wants to get down to tap room.' (Leeds 18–30)

The brewer:
   'It shows that John Smith's are still in business, still as good as ever was, as traditional as ever was.' (Leeds 30–45)
   'It's big John Smith.' (Leeds 18–30)
Source: BMP Qualitative

The post-campaign research also indicated positive improvements in the brand's status. A year before, John Smith's was simply overlooked, and placed among the crowd of lesser brands, behind Tetley's. But now its drinkers displayed considerable enthusiasm for the brand, and even most Tetley drinkers acknowledged it as an acceptable choice. Nor was it seen particularly as an 'old boy's drink' – it was for everyone, young and old.

This is not to say that among all drinkers the brand matched Tetley's, but our drinkers now felt justified in stating their preference. It had risen above the competitive brands into clear second place and the renewed commitment of its buyers (our target) had reduced Tetley's predominance.

The 'Big John' campaign seemed to have affected this attitudinal shift more than any other factor. Drinkers vastly enjoyed the advertising and saw the advertiser (John Smith's) in a new light:

   'They're new and something different, not run of the mill adverts like the others.' (Leeds 18–30)
   'The Woodman one was brilliant. They're trendy and they're always bringing them up to date.' (York 18–24)
Source: BMP Qualitative

THE EFFECTS OF ADVERTISING: SALES

The campaign appeared to work in terms of increased sales, and also the intermediate measures we would expect.

The brand's volume sales in its Yorkshire pubs rose in 1981 by 4.8 per cent, even though the Bitter I market there declined by 7.7 per cent. Market share thus increased to its highest ever level, increasing from 97.2 in 1980 to 105.5 in 1981 (1976 = 100).

Year on year, the share improvement continued throughout 1981, although the greatest growth was seen in the first quarter, when the heaviest advertising took place (Table 11.10).

TABLE 11.10:   JOHN SMITH'S BITTER TRADE PERFORMANCE IN 1981 (1980 = 100)

| | 1981 | | | |
	1st quarter	2nd quarter	3rd quarter	4th quarter
John Smith's volume share of pubs	116	106	105	108

Source: BMS
Base: major brewers, north east.

The difference between the 1979 and the 1981 shares represented additional sales of 10.3 million pints, worth some £5.1 million at 1981 retail prices.

The additional effect of the campaign on free trade sales is hard to measure as distribution increased, but the brand's share rose from 100 in 1980, to 114 in 1981.

Comparing sales in the advertised area with those in John Smith's other trading regions, the turn-around in Yorkshire looked all the more remarkable, as sales-growth slowed elsewhere (Table 11.11).

TABLE 11.11:   JOHN SMITH'S BITTER VOLUME SALES (PUBS)
BY REGION, 1980–1981

| 12 months to October 1980 (fiscal year) | % Change year-on-year | |
	1980	1981
Yorkshire (75%)	−4	+5
Non-Yorkshire (25%)	+7	+3

Source: Courage

We examined other possible explanations for the rise in sales:

1. Distribution. Static in Yorkshire; volume improvements were attributable to increased consumer offtake.
2. Pub standards. Investment in the estate and improvements in licensee selection continued, and both are probably more significant than advertising in the long term. But Yorkshire pubs did not receive proportionately more attention than non-Yorkshire ones.
3. Price. In line with competition.

THE EFFECTS OF ADVERTISING: CONSUMER BEHAVIOUR

Consumer research helped us identify a causal link between the advertising and increased sales (see Table 11.12).

TABLE 11.12:   CLAIMED 'MOST OFTEN' DRUNK BRAND OF BITTER () =
18–24s

	Yorkshire		Non-Yorkshire	
	1980	1982	1980	1982
Base: total sample	264	412	540	797
		Percentage of total sample		
John Smith's	6 (5)	19 (19)	3 (3)	4 (3)
Tetley	29 (32)	30 (32)	11 (12)	13 (8)
Trophy	11 (9)	9 (10)	5 (6)	4 (4)
Stones	12 (14)	10 (11)	4 (3)	7 (6)

Source: Marplan
Non-Yorks. = North West/Lancs plus Tyne-Tees.

As with the decline, the rise in claimed 'most often' brand share reflects the Yorkshire sales increase but exaggerates it, suggesting an increase in preference as well as actual consumption. This is also implied by the increase in the proportion of 'most often' drinkers among those who had ever tried John Smith's Bitter (see Table 11.13).

TABLE 11.13:   'MOST OFTEN' DRINKERS as
PROPORTION OF 'EVER TRIED' 1980–1982

	1980 %	1982 %
John Smith's – Yorkshire	13	36
– Non-Yorkshire	10	9
Tetley	47	47
Trophy	21	22
Stones	21	21

Source: Marplan
Base: ever tried brand

Such a large increase may seem incredible, but our confidence that the measures reflect a real change in our drinkers' loyalty to John Smith's was confirmed by the stability of the non-Yorkshire John Smith's and the competitive brand figures.

In claimed behaviour, it seemed that the advertising had more effect on the younger drinker. The proportion of loyal drinkers who were aged 18–24 came back into line with other brands (see Table 11.14).

TABLE 11.14:   18–24s AS PROPORTION OF
'MOST OFTEN' PLUS 'REGULAR' DRINKERS

	1980 %	1982 %
John Smith's – Yorkshire	14	21
– Non-Yorkshire	22	20
Tetley	23	23
Trophy	23	23
Stones	24	21

Source: Marplan

Attitudes to John Smith's

These also showed improvement within the advertised Yorkshire area and, while young drinkers still lagged behind their elders, it appeared that the movements were encouraging (Table 11.15).

TABLE 11.15:   MEAN SCORES ON THREE ATTITUDE SCALES

	Yorkshire		North West/Lancs	
	1980	1982	1980	1982
'Good value for a bitter'				
John Smith's All	3.23	3.60	3.34	3.13
18–24	3.22	3.56		
'Lots of flavour'				
John Smith's All	3.37	3.66	3.39	3.35
18–24	3.23	3.41		
'For knowledgeable drinkers'				
John Smith's All	3.34	3.50	3.45	3.24
18–24	3.16	3.34		

Source: Marplan
Scale: +5 to +1

It is interesting that, despite our success with our primary target, the younger age group, we in fact achieved a turn-round in loyalty and attitudes among John Smith's Bitter drinkers of all ages in Yorkshire. The advertising seemed to have a broader appeal than we anticipated and older drinkers were perhaps more susceptible to brand imagery than they were prepared to admit.

Thus the consumer measure revealed significant improvements both in claimed drinking of John Smith's Bitter and in attitudes towards the brand, improvements which did not occur in non-advertised areas. Moreover, the loyalty and age profiles of drinkers only improved significantly for John Smith's, while other brands and John Smith's in non-advertised areas remained the same.

So the sales turn-round was accompanied by improvements on the same measures that had first prompted us to identify the brand's problem as essentially one of consumer commitment. This, we felt, indicated that the analysis had been sound and that the advertising had addressed the key area in need of change, namely the brand image.

SUMMARY

In a market where advertising can seldom be confidently shown to have an effect on volume, this campaign seems to have succeeded in restoring sales-growth to John Smith's Bitter cost-efficiently.

Whereas in 1980, drinkers appeared to be losing their confidence in the brand and transferring their loyalty to competitors, sales and their claimed behaviour in 1982 indicated renewed commitment to John Smith's Bitter. This turn-round was reflected in drinkers' improved attitudes to the brand on scales relevant to the advertising content.

These improvements in sales, claimed drinking and brand imagery were largely confined to Yorkshire, the only area to receive substantial media support throughout 1981. Competitive brands did not enjoy similar improvements, and indeed the bitter market as a whole declined in the area, in contrast to John Smith's growth.

Qualitative and quantitative consumer research studies underline the role of advertising in stimulating the brand's success. The absence of any identifiable changes in the marketing mix or retail environment, apart from advertising investment and content, help to confirm this role. A total investment of some £300 000 in television advertising thus contributed to a revenue increase for John Smith's draught bitter of some £5 million in the pub trade alone, whilst free trade growth continued, all in a declining market. The profitability of such a return on investment in the tied trade alone is assured.

We believe that, by rejuvenating the brand's imagery amongst younger bitter drinkers in particular, so that they could confidently claim it as their pint in a sales-environment where social pressures predominate, the 'Big John' campaign played a significant part in this improved performance.

CONCLUSIONS

1. Causal relationships can only be inferred, never demonstrated. But the weight of evidence suggests to us that the Big John advertising caused incremental sales.
2. Other marketing investments could have had the same effect, but we doubt whether they would have been so cost-efficient. Within a year, investment in advertising resulted in revenue over fifteen times greater than the investment.
3. It is impossible to judge whether it was the advertisement's content, or merely the increased weight of advertising, that was mainly responsible. Our judgement is that both worked together. A lower weight would have reduced the brand's consumer presence. Inappropriate content would not have regained the loyalty of drinkers. But we still lack measures relating weight to response. That may be the next subject for research.

APPENDIX: MAJOR DATA SOURCES

Beer Market Survey (BMS)   A census of major brewers' sales. Each brewer contributes his sales figures by trade and beer type confidentially. Thus each can monitor market trends and his own share.

Marplan U & A Survey   A regular consumer study commissioned by Courage, covering drinking behaviour and brand imagery. Structured to represent the universe of men drinking bitter once a week or more often. Regional upweights of specific groups (including the 18–24s).

Wyman-Harris Licensed Trade Monitor (LTM)   Quarterly audit of retail trade sales. Data collected by auditor observation in pubs.
    The Northern sample is over 300 pubs.

Courage Sales   Ex-brewery production.

BMP Qualitative   Source, 40 group discussions in Yorkshire over two years.

12
Dettol

A Case History

INTRODUCTION

In this case history we have set out to demonstrate in two distinct ways that Dettol's advertising works and is effective.

Firstly we show that, by virtue of a change in creative strategy that was implemented at the beginning of 1978, consumer attitudes to Dettol have been modified in the directions intended. The research also shows that the use and purchase of Dettol have increased in this period.

Secondly, an econometric analysis of factors affecting Dettol's sales during the period 1974-78 is used to demonstrate that the sales response to the advertising expenditures put behind Dettol generated profitable increases in sales.

Other factors influencing Dettol's sales are also identified and it is clear that two 'non-marketing' variables - seasonal factors and consumer's purchasing power (disposable income) - have a major effect.

We conclude however that it is the long term effects of Dettol advertising that lead consumers to purchase Dettol when these factors are favourable.

In consequence the dramatic decline in Dettol sales that occurred in 1975-77 was converted into an equally dramatic improvement in 1978 and maintained in 1979 (Table 12.1).

TABLE 12.1:   DETTOL EX-FACTORY SALES INDEX

1973	100
1974	100
1975	85
1976	87
1977	83
1978	100
1979	100

Many brands enjoyed increased sales as a result of rising consumer prosperity in 1978, but not to the extent of these figures, which underline the importance of maintaining a brand franchise by sustained and effective advertising support.

BACKGROUND

Dettol has been marketed in the United Kingdom since 1933.

It is promoted as both an antiseptic and a disinfectant and is used in a wide variety of ways ranging from personal antisepsis of cuts and grazes, through to disinfection of surfaces in the kitchen and bathroom and, in some instances, as a more general disinfectant down lavatory bowls, waste pipes and drains. It is sold in three sizes, 100, 250 and 500 ml.

Dettol is not only a mature brand but an extremely well established one. There is universal awareness of it by housewives; 70 per cent of housewives claim to use it nowadays – a figure which has not changed over the past eight years; and it has virtually 100 per cent distribution in chemists and grocers.

Although there are many alternative antiseptics and disinfectants on the market, including many low priced retailer own brands, there is only one other product that is promoted as a direct alternative to Dettol in its range of uses, Savlon Liquid. For many years Savlon had been available only through chemist shops, but since the beginning of 1979 has been heavily advertised and its distribution widened into grocery outlets also.

Advertising support for Dettol has been provided consistently over the last 20 years and is considered to have been a major factor in the brand's development to the position it now occupies as described above. The case history described in the following pages, however, relates to the period 1974–1979 and describes, in particular, the changes to the advertising campaign that were implemented in 1978.

The 1977 Scenario

Sales of Dettol had reached a peak in 1973–74. However, a combination of factors – rapid inflation and declining consumer purchasing power, reduced advertising investment, some production problems – had led to a sharp decline in sales in 1975, 1976 and 1977 (see Table 12.1).

Additionally, a situation had been developing which was of concern to the future promotion of Dettol. A significant personal use of Dettol was in bathing which involved claims which could not be proved or disproved. Therefore, the ITCA would not permit the claims for this area of usage to be advertised.

So the problem that Reckitt & Colman and the agency faced in 1977 can be concisely expressed as: 'How can we restore sales volumes to the 1973–74 levels when a major usage area of Dettol is no longer open to direct advertising, and inflationary pressures are affecting sales volumes?'

DEVELOPMENT OF THE 1978 STRATEGY

Where is Increased Volume Going to be Obtained?

Research had shown that amongst Dettol users its use as an antiseptic was virtually universal; fewer housewives used it in its disinfectant role. Further research using diary panel techniques showed that there were certain household cleaning functions where Dettol was more widely used than others, e.g. in wiping lavatory seats, cleaning up after pets, but even in these instances Dettol's share of products used was relatively low.

We nevertheless argued that, to increase Dettol volume sales to any marked extent:

(i) We could not expect to obtain additional users – household penetration was extremely high (70 per cent).
(ii) And that increased volume was more likely to occur from the advertising of *disinfectant* uses of the product.

But this conclusion presented its own problems:

(i) The earlier success of Dettol had been built on the personal/antiseptic uses of the product: heavy promotion of disinfectant uses could well destroy the extremely favourable attitudes housewives had with regard to its personal benefits.
(ii) Dettol's price was considered to be a problem in the market place (dictated by the high cost of ingredients). If Dettol is looked upon primarily as a disinfectant then the price differential with its main alternatives become particularly large – in some instances two or three times the price of own label disinfectants.

How Should We Approach the Problem of Price?

An econometric analysis (described in full later) had shown that consumers appeared to be relatively insensitive to changes in Dettol's *price*, but sales were found to be affected by the decline in *disposable income*. This apparent anomaly can be explained by the fact that the housewife's need for Dettol has a lower priority than essential items such as food. In other words, for Dettol to be included in a housewife's grocery purchases, she must have sufficient money left after buying the essential items; and relatively small variations in the price of Dettol do not therefore affect her decision to buy. As a result the decision was taken to allow the price to rise generally in line with inflation and to confine any price cutting to short term, tactical retail promotions.

A New Creative Strategy Based on Disinfectant Usage

In developing a creative strategy for Dettol based on disinfectant usage it was essential to be aware of consumer perceptions of Dettol and to provide advertising consonant with them. Research had shown that advertising centred on the *scientific* basis for Dettol's performance in killing bacteria was ineffective in changing consumer attitudes and behaviour. The high regard which consumers have for Dettol is based on confidence and trust derived from its history, its name, its smell and clouding in water. As one interviewee commented: 'You can't see germs being killed. I have to use Dettol to be sure.'

New advertising for Dettol had to reflect such attitudes.

1978 ADVERTISING

At the beginning of 1978 we introduced new TV and press advertising for Dettol which took account of the thinking outlined in the previous section.

TV: Two TV commercials, entitled 'Beginning' and 'Discovery'. These two commercials addressed themselves to the need for environmental protection in the home

Dettol Protects

Pure, safe Dettol keeps your lavatory a safe place for everyone,
day and night. Trust Dettol to protect your family's health.

in the context of a newborn baby and a toddler, Dettol providing protection and confidence. In parallel a TV commercial for Dettol Cream – an antiseptic cream – was also transmitted, assisting in the reinforcement of Dettol's traditional first aid usage.

Press: Full colour page advertisements were produced in both 1978 and 1979 pinpointing specific disinfectant usage areas for Dettol. The subjects chosen were ones in which Dettol already had relatively high usage, although still low in absolute terms, viz: the lavatory seat, kitchen waste bins, cleaning where pets have been, e.g. the kitchen floor.

Media: In each of 1978 and 1979, TV advertising amounted to approximately 20 weeks at an average of 50 to 60 TVR per week in all ITV regions. The press advertisements appeared in women's weekly and monthly magazines providing 70 per cent cover and 7.0 OTS.

To summarize the advertising changes:

CONTENT

A switch from advertising which had been primarily concerned with the antiseptic uses of Dettol to its environmental/disinfectant role.

WEIGHT

Although the budget was maintained in cash terms in 1978, due to media cost inflation the effective weight of advertising was reduced by about 20 per cent compared to 1977.

RESULTS AND EVALUATION

1. Volume sales of Dettol increased substantially in 1978, and this achievement was maintained in 1979 (see Table 5.1).
2. Consumer research clearly indicates the improvements in consumer attitudes to Dettol that occurred during the period of the 1978–79 advertising campaign as well as changes in consumer usage of Dettol.
3. An econometric analysis of the factors affecting Dettol sales volume conducted over the period 1974–78 shows the profitability of the advertising investment throughout that period and suggests also that the long term investment in advertising is a major factor in determining consumer purchasing of Dettol.

It should be noted that the periods covered by the econometric analysis and the consumer research are not exactly coincident. The reason for this is simply that the two pieces of research were not planned as a co-ordinated programme.

Consumer Research

Two disinfectant and antiseptic usage and attitude studies have been carried out amongst consumers: the first in January 1978, the second in January 1980. These two surveys reflect the extent to which the advertising for Dettol has been successful, both in increasing its usage and changing perceptions of the brand.

The broad objectives of these studies were to monitor trends in the usage and image of disinfectants and antiseptics in terms of the following:

  (i) Brand awareness
 (ii) Brand penetration
(iii) User profiles
 (iv) Usage patterns for the major brands
  (v) The image of the major brands
 (vi) Detailed purchasing habits
(vii) Usage and purchase patterns of antiseptic creams
(viii) Advertising recall

THE RESEARCH METHOD

For each of the studies, 1200 housewives were interviewed at 120 sampling points throughout Great Britain by Public Attitude Surveys Ltd. They were located by means of Random Location Sampling. In each case the sample was restricted to housewives aged 15 to 64.

A non-interlocking, two-way quota was set on working status (working full time/others) and whether they had children.

Weighting factors were applied to ensure that the sample was representative of the population.

THE FINDINGS

In the two year period since the beginning of the new Dettol strategy, research indicates that Dettol has:

  (i) Retained its leading position in terms of the penetration measurements.
 (ii) Achieved increases in terms of the frequency with which it is bought and used.
(iii) Achieved increases in the applications for which it is used, reflecting the success of the advertising strategy of the past two years.
 (iv) Achieved positive shifts in its image as a disinfectant.
  (v) Retained its positive image as an antiseptic.

There has been a substantial and significant increase in the frequency with which Dettol is used (Table 12.2). Just over one quarter (an increase of 7 percentage points) of users now use Dettol every day. 53 per cent of housewives use it on average every two to four days.

There has been a substantial and significant increase, of 10 percentage points, in the number of housewives buying Dettol once a month or more often (Table 12.3). These findings are consistent with the increase in ex-factory dispatches during 1978 and 1979 and the improvement in consumer sales audited by Nielsen, which is described overleaf.

In terms of usage, Table 12.4 shows increases in the areas of Dettol usage which clearly reflect the positive effects of the advertising strategy over the past two years. This table also shows that increased household usage has not resulted in a decline in personal usage – in fact, upward movements have been noted in some areas of personal use.

TABLE 12.2:   THE FREQUENCY OF USING DETTOL

Base: all current users	January 1978 835 %	January 1980 849 %	Change 1980 vs. 1978
Every day	19	26	+7[a]
Every 2–3 days	28	27	−1
Every 4–6 days	12	11	−1
Once a week	19	18	−1
Once every 2–3 weeks	6	6	—
Once a month	7	5	−2
Less often	8	7	−1

[a] Statistically significant at 99.9 per cent confidence level.

TABLE 12.3:   THE FREQUENCY OF BUYING DETTOL

Base: all current users	January 1978 835 %	January 1980 849 %	Change 1980 vs. 1978
Once a month or more often	39	49	+10[a]
Once every 6 weeks	22	18	−4
2–3 times a year	29	26	−3
Once a year	7	5	−2
Less often	3	2	−1

[a] Statistically significant at 99.9 per cent confidence level.

TABLE 12.4:   THE USAGE OCCASIONS FOR DETTOL

Base: all current users	January 1978 835 %	January 1980 849 %	Change 1980 vs. 1978
Selected Household Uses			
Cleaning lavatory seat	51	56	+5[a]
Lavatory bowl	43	46	+3
Bath and handbasin	32	36	+4
Kitchen rubbish bins	29	34	+5[a]
Kitchen sink and waste pipe	28	32	+4
Kitchen floor	23	32	+9[c]
After pets	23	25	+2
Kitchen surfaces	16	23	+7[c]
Outside dustbin	13	14	+1
Selected Personal Uses			
Cuts and grazes	64	71	+7[b]
Bath	55	55	—
Bites and stings	38	45	+7[b]

Statistically significant at:
[a] 95 per cent confidence level.
[b] 99 per cent confidence level.
[c] 99.9 per cent confidence level.

The image questions were structured so that respondents could make a free association with attitude couplets by brand. Thus, the respondents were introduced, by a preamble, to mention whatever brands on the list were appropriate to the Stimulus (attitude couplets). The respondents were free to mention as many or as few brands as they wished. In each study half the sample were given a list of antiseptic brands to associate with the attitude couplets while the other half of the sample were given a list of disinfectant brands.

Table 12.5 shows the number of positive mentions achieved by Dettol over several selected dimensions. Aside from illustrating the positive overall image of Dettol, it also shows upward shifts in perceptions of the brand's image in those areas for which it has been advertised.

Table 12.6 shows the number of positive mentions achieved by Dettol when the product is rated amongst a list of other antiseptics, and illustrates the overall stability of the brand in this area.

TABLE 12.5:   THE IMAGE OF DETTOL AS A DISINFECTANT

Base: all rating the disinfectant products	January 1978 583 %	January 1980 592 %	Change 1980 vs. 1978
A product you can really trust	91	94	+ 3[a]
Particularly effective against infection	90	90	—
Strong enough for my needs	83	82	−1
Goes a long way	73	73	—
Particularly suitable for cleaning the lavatory	52	56	+4
Particularly suitable for sinks and drains	47	50	+3
Particularly suitable for kitchen surfaces	37	41	+4

[a] Statistically significant at 95 per cent confidence level.

TABLE 12.6:   THE IMAGE OF DETTOL AS AN ANTISEPTIC

Base: all respondents rating the antiseptic products	January 1978 614 %	January 1980 602 %	Change 1980 vs. 1978
A product you can really trust	92	92	—
Particularly effective against infection	88	86	−2
Strong enough for my needs	82	82	—
Particularly suitable for adding to bath water	78	77	−1
Goes a long way	66	66	—

Econometric Analysis of the Factors Affecting Dettol Sales

OUTLINE OF METHOD OF ANALYSIS

Common sense dictates that variations in the weight or content of the advertising are not the only factors which will influence a brand's sales. Even with the benefit of a carefully controlled area test specifically designed to measure the effects of advertising, it is usually necessary to check and allow for the influence of other marketing factors which may have caused a differential sales effect between areas. In the case of Dettol, no controlled experiment was carried out and thus the evaluation of the sales effects of Dettol's advertising requires that any other influences on sales are isolated.

In essence, the method involves setting up a simple hypothetical model of the market which describes the likely relationship between the brand's sales and the marketing factors which are believed to influence sales. For example, a very simple model might be of the form:

$$\text{Brand Sales} = K_1. \text{ Advertising} - K_2. \text{ Price} + \text{Constant}.$$

This means that for each unit increase in advertising weight the brand's sales increase by K_1 units; and for each unit price increase sales will decrease by K_2 units. The technique of multilinear regression analysis is then used to find the values of the constants in the model (the K's) which provide the best fit to the historical sales data.

There are, of course, many different formulations of the model which are hypothetically possible, which then raises the question as to which is the right one. To answer this, the chosen model must satisfy three basic criteria:

(i)   The model must agree with common sense. In other words, the variables influencing sales must satisfy our intuitive understanding of the market.
(ii) The model must be capable of accounting for a large proportion of the historic sales variation. Unless this is so, one cannot tell whether the marketing variables in the model really do significantly affect sales.
(iii) The model must be able to predict future sales once the new values of the various marketing variables are known. This last condition is an acid test of whether the model really does explain the behaviour of the market.

The mechanics of the analysis involve the use of real-time computer facilities. With this aid it is possible to evaluate many different models rapidly and at low cost, and thereby find a model which meets the three conditions described above. The following sections describe the evaluation of Dettol's sales performance. Details of the statistical analysis are shown in the appendix at the end of this chapter.

THE CONSTRUCTION OF THE MODEL

Dettol occupies a unique position in that it is used both as a disinfectant and an antiseptic; consequently the definition of its competitors, and hence its market share, is somewhat arbitrary. In the event, we found that the most satisfactory explanation of the brand's sales performance was achieved by modelling Dettol's actual volume sales rather than its share of a defined market.

The model was constructed from Nielsen bimonthly consumer sales audit data covering the period 1974–77, and the 1978 data were then used to test the model's predictive capability. (In the initial stages national data were used, which provided 30 observations, and the analysis was subsequently expanded by including the data for five individual regions, giving a total of 150 observations.)

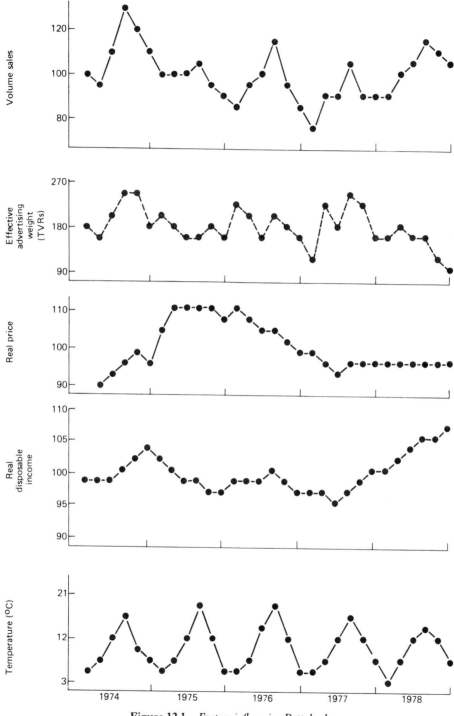

Figure 12.1 *Factors influencing Dettol sales*

Four factors were found to have a statistically significant influence on Dettol sales; they were:

(i) Real personal disposable income.
(ii) Dettol's price (adjusted by the retail price index).
(iii) An underlying seasonal variation (this is common to all disinfectants and antiseptics, sales being higher in the warmer summer months).
(iv) Accumulated advertising weight (described in detail in the next section).

Figure 12.1 shows how each of these factors has varied over time. When combined they account for 90 per cent of all the variations in Dettol's national sales. This is demonstrated in Figure 12.2, which shows the bimonthly sales of Dettol as recorded by Nielsen from 1974 to 1977, together with the fit to these data provided by the model which has the four factors above as its components. In statistical terms the correlation between sales and the component factors is highly satisfactory; the chance that the result is merely a random coincidence is substantially less than one in a thousand.

The significance of the relationship between sales and each individual factor is demonstrated by the cross-plots shown in Figures 12.3 to 12.6. For example, Figure 12.3 shows the correlation between the variation in accumulated advertising weight (expressed as an effective advertising weight in TVRs) and Dettol sales after removing the effect of the other three factors (price, disposable income and seasonal variation).

An important feature of the analysis is the substantial effect that the 'non-marketing' variables have on sales. Together, the underlying seasonal variations and the influence of disposable income account for more than half of the total variation in Dettol's sales. This underlines the need to take account of such effects before examining the influence of factors which are within the control of the advertiser, i.e. price and advertising.

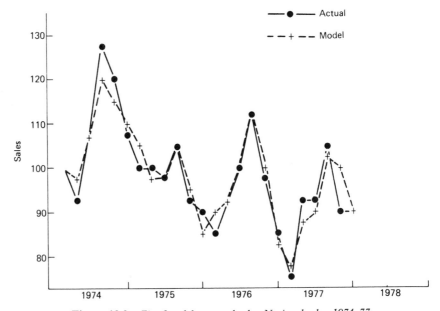

Figure 12.2 *Fit of model to actual sales. National sales, 1974–77*

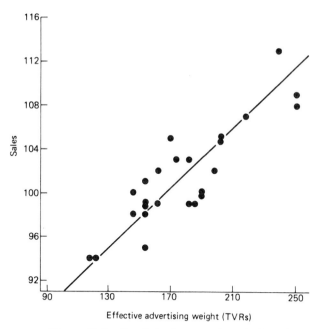

Figure 12.3 *Correlation between sales and advertising*

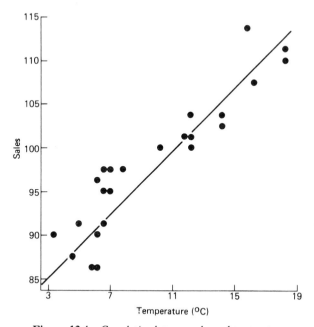

Figure 12.4 *Correlation between sales and temperature*

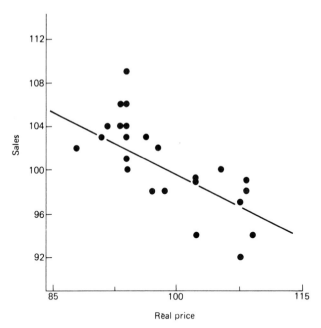

Figure 12.5 *Correlation between sales and price*

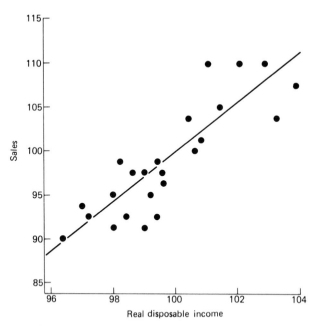

Figure 12.6 *Correlation between sales and disposable income*

The predictive capability of the model was tested by comparing the model's sales forecasts (based on the known values of the four variables during 1978) with the actual sales achieved in that period. This is shown in Figure 12.7. The model estimates closely follow the actual sales achieved, which is a very satisfactory result, particularly in view of the fact that the reversal of the previously declining sales trend has been correctly predicted.

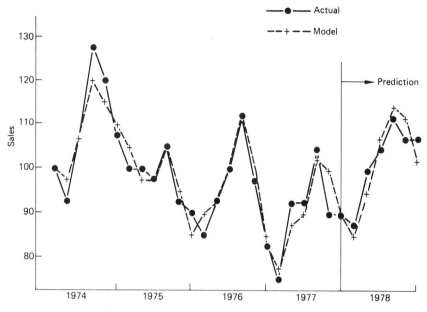

Figure 12.7   *Model predictions vs. actual sales in 1978*

THE EFFECTS OF ADVERTISING

The weight of advertising was expressed in terms of television rating points. Press expenditure, which formed only a small proportion of the total, was included in the television figures assuming it to be equally cost efficient. Using the larger sample of 150 observations available from the regional Nielsen data, it was possible to investigate the duration of the advertising effect, i.e. previous advertising influencing sales in the current period. The analysis (which is described in the appendix) provided strong evidence that the advertising effect decayed over time at a rate of about 10 to 15 per cent per month, i.e. half the full sales effect is achieved within about four months. This is an important result since it means that it is the accumulated weight of advertising which influences sales and not simply the advertising in the current period.

THE ECONOMIC IMPLICATIONS

One of the most important features of this type of statistical analysis is that it is possible to quantify the effects on sales of changing the price and the weight of advertising. Because Nielsen reports at bimonthly intervals, and hence the number of observations is limited, only the average effect over a number of years can be calculated with any degree of reliability.

The results shown in Table 12.7 are presented in the form of elasticities, i.e. the percentage change in sales that results from a 1 per cent change in each of the four variables.

The price and advertising effects are clearly of most interest to the advertiser, since they have a direct bearing on decisions regarding the marketing strategy. The most useful way of interpreting these results is to compare the estimated elasticities with the 'breakeven' values (Table 12.8).

TABLE 12.7:   ELASTICITIES CALCULATED FROM ECONOMETRIC MODEL, 1974–78

	Best estimate	95% confidence range
Advertising elasticity	.19	.11–.26
Price elasticity	−.44	−.64– −.23
Disposable income elasticity	2.26	1.66–2.86
Temperature (pr^0C)	1.85	1.49–2.21

TABLE 12.8:   ESTIMATED ELASTICITIES COMPARED WITH BREAKEVEN VALUES

	Best estimate	Breakeven
Advertising elasticity	.19	0.16
Price elasticity	−0.4	−2.0

For example, the breakeven price elasticity of −2.0 means that a 1 per cent increase in price would generate an increased profit for the brand provided that sales volume did not fall by more than 2 per cent. The estimate of the actual price elasticity is substantially less than this breakeven figure; had price been increased by 1 per cent the best estimate is that sales volume would have declined by 0.44 per cent. Thus, there is strong evidence that the brand has been underpriced.

By contrast, the estimate of Dettol's advertising elasticity, 0.19, is higher than the breakeven figure of 0.16 (this is the percentage increase in sales required to recover the costs of a 1 per cent increase in advertising expenditure).

The implications of this are:

(i) *The advertising expenditure over the period 1974–78 has generated profitable increases in sales for the brand*. Even allowing that a degree of uncertainty is associated with every statistical estimate, there is only a 1 in 5 chance that the advertising was not profitable (i.e. the advertising elasticity was actually less than breakeven).

(ii) Given that our best estimate of the advertising elasticity is correct, the level of expenditure should have been higher to maximize the profit returned. By definition, at the optimum expenditure level the breakeven and actual elasticities will be equal. However, it is not possible to say what the optimum level should have been; to do so requires that the precise shape of the advertising/sales relationship is known.

The consumer research described above showed that the 1978 advertising campaign had generated significant improvements in consumers' attitudes, accompanied by increases in claimed usage. This certainly suggests an increased advertising effectiveness in 1978. Unfortunately, it is not possible to confirm this finding via the econometric analysis, for two reasons:

1. Firstly, as previously stated, there are only a limited number of sales observations for any one year, which means that an estimate of the advertising elasticity based on one year's data will be very unreliable. In fact, a statistically significant result would only have been obtained had the advertising doubled in effectiveness.
2. Secondly, 1978 was a period when consumers' disposable income rose rapidly. In this situation it becomes very difficult to separate the contributions that advertising and disposable income made to the improvement in sales. (A very small change in the weight of importance given to disposable income would allow a substantial improvement in the effectiveness of the 1978 advertising.)

However, the assessment of the average advertising effectiveness over the period 1974–78 almost certainly understates the contribution that advertising made to the substantial improvement in sales during 1978. The rapid increase in consumers' spending power was a necessary precursor, but it is not axiomatic that this increased prosperity should have been directed to purchases of Dettol. Consumers must have a reason for purchasing the brand which involves a belief in its value, and this in large part must depend on the image built up by many years of advertising. Such benefits cannot be readily quantified, but they nevertheless provide additional justification to the value of Dettol's advertising.

CONCLUSION

The change in advertising strategy that occurred in 1978 provided us with the opportunity of demonstrating that Dettol's advertising does influence attitudes and behaviour. There were shifts in consumer usage and attitudes along each of the desired dimensions.

The econometric analysis conducted between 1974 and 1978 has shown that the advertising expenditure on Dettol in this period has been profitable.

Further, in 1978, the combination of past and current advertising allowed Dettol to capitalize on the growth in consumer spending power.

APPENDIX: TECHNICAL APPENDIX TO ECONOMETRIC ANALYSIS

1. *Model Based on National Sales Data*

The results shown below were achieved using stepwise multilinear regression on 24 observations, covering the period 1974–77.
The regression equation is:

Sales Volume = $1.7 \times$ Temperature $+ 2.2 \times$ Disposable Income
$\qquad\qquad + .183 \times$ Accumulated Advertising $- .241 \times$ Real Price
$\qquad\qquad - 131$

With the exception of temperature (which is expressed in degrees centigrade) all other variables were computed as indices about their mean values and hence the coefficients represent the elasticities for each variable.
The key statistics for the regression equation are as follows:

$R^2 = .909$ This shows that 91 per cent of the variation in sales volume has been explained and thus it is unlikely that another factor of major importance has been ignored.

F ratio $= 35.85$ This means that the chance of such an explanation being due to random chance is less than one in a thousand.

Standard error as % of mean volume $= 4.13$
This is a measure of the likely forecasting error.

Durbin-Watson statistic on residuals $= 1.8$
It is important that the error term (residual variation) is randomly distributed. If this is not the case, then the variables are not independent of each other, and errors in estimation are likely. There is no evidence here of colinearity (a value of 2.0 is ideal, with 1.5 to 2.5 being acceptable limits).

The table below shows key statistics for each of the variables in the regression equation.

	Mean[a]	95% Confidence limits upper	lower	T statistic[b]	Partial F[c]
Temperature	1.7	2.15	1.24	7.89	62.2
Disposable income	2.2	1.11	4.25	4.25	18.1
Advertising	0.18	0.07	3.47	3.47	12.1
Real price	-0.24	-0.52	-1.82	-1.82	3.3

[a] The mean is the most likely estimate of the coefficient for each variable, and the 95 per cent confidence limits indicate that there is a 5 per cent chance of the coefficients lying outside the range shown.
[b] The T statistic is a measure of the extent to which the coefficient is significantly different from zero (i.e. the variable has no effect on the regression equation). A value greater than 2.0 is significant at the 95 per cent confidence level.
[c] This is a test of whether the variable in question explains a significant amount of the sales variation. A value of 4.0 would be significant at the 95 per cent confidence level.

2. Model Based on Regional Data

The regional model was based on 150 observations using Nielsen data from the five largest areas (London, Midlands, Lancashire, Yorkshire, Wales and West). Each variable was expressed as its index about the regional mean.

The existence of long-term advertising effects was established by first testing for an immediate advertising effect and then by introducing lagged advertising variables, examining whether the fit of the model (R^2) improved significantly (an R^2 lower than that for the national model is to be expected, since the regional Nielsen shop sample is smaller). With only immediate advertising considered, the R^2 was .50 and the F ratio for immediate advertising 19.1; by including advertising variables successively lagged up to six periods ago, the R^2 improved to .58.

A plot of the lagged advertising coefficients is shown in Figure 5.8. Compared with the coefficient for immediate advertising, those for the lagged variables diminish the longer the lag. The rate of advertising decay implied by this is of the order of 25 per cent per bimonthly period.

This information was used to construct a transformed advertising variable, representing the accumulated advertising effect, assuming a decay rate of 25 per cent per bimonth, viz:

$$\text{Accumulated Advertising Weight} = a_0 + .75a_1 + (.75)^2 a_2 + \ldots\ldots$$
$$\text{where } a_0 = \text{current advertising}$$
$$\text{where } a_i = \text{advertising lagged by i periods}$$

Using this variable the R^2 achieved was .65, with the F ratio for advertising increasing to 57.5.
The full results were as follows:

Sales Volume $= 1.85 \times$ Temperature $+ 2.26 \times$ Disposable Income
$\quad\quad\quad\quad + .188 \times$ Accumulated Advertising $- .44 \times$ Real Price
$\quad\quad\quad$ $R^2 = .653$ $\quad\quad$ F Ratio $= 44.7$
Standard error as $\%$ of mean volume $= 8.3$
Durbin-Watson statistic on residuals $= 2.1$

	95% Confidence limits		T	Partial
	upper	lower	statistic	F
Temperature	2.21	1.49	10.04	100.82
Disposable income	2.86	1.66	7.4	54.9
Advertising	0.264	0.111	4.86	23.6
Real price	-0.23	-0.64	-4.15	17.25

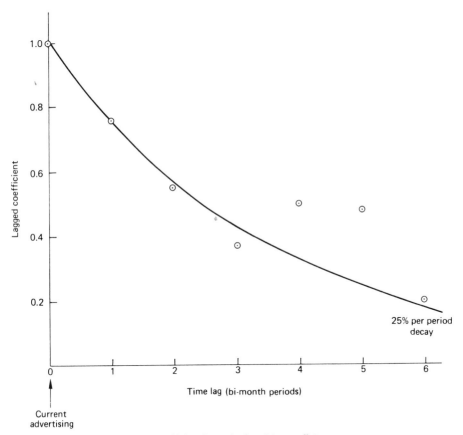

Figure 12.8 *Lagged advertising coefficients*

13

The Qualcast Concorde

INTRODUCTION

Birmid Qualcast have traditionally dominated the UK lawnmower market with their cylinder machines.

For many years technology changed little, allowing Qualcast to refine their production skills as well as the quality of their mowers, becoming a very efficient cylinder mower producer.

But the development of the hover rotary mower was to become a major marketing innovation. In the mid-sixties Flymo, with fifteen years of patent protection ahead of them, introduced their revolutionary rotary grass cutting hover mower.

The first of these machines were expensive, petrol powered and an unlikely threat to the market or Qualcast whose main interest and strength was in the light mains electric machine market. This was the segment that Qualcast had effectively pioneered and which they dominated with their small electric cylinder mower, the Qualcast Concorde.

However, in the mid-1970s Flymo successfully launched into the light mains electric sector with an electric powered hover at a competitive price supported with very effective advertising.

By 1979 Qualcast were beginning to feel the cumulative effect of:

— the rapid growth of the 'more modern' rotary/hover mowers (a 61 per cent increase in five years)
— two summers of drought (in 1976 and 1977) serving to depress the overall lawnmower market
— lack of real product development since the launch of the innovative Concorde in 1972
— lack of investment in advertising

resulting in

— a tired 'yesteryear' image among both the trade and consumers (especially young new entrants to the market).

THE QUALCAST POSITION IN 1979

As can be seen in Table 13.1 Qualcast, although in line with the total market, had suffered a 12 per cent volume decline in 1979 compared with 1978.

TABLE 13.1: QUALCAST CONSUMER SALES –
VOLUME

	1978 '000 Units	1979 '000 Units
Total Qualcast	606	532
Index	100	88
Share of total market	44%	44%

On first sight Qualcast's position did not appear to be any worse than the competition. Surely nothing to get unduly worried about?

However, Table 13.2 clearly demonstrates the critically important dynamic within the market.

TABLE 13.2: CONSUMER SALES – VOLUME

	1978 '000 Units	1979 '000 Units
Total lawnmower market	1386	1216
index	100	88
Total light mains electric	919	886
index	100	96
—Hover & wheeled rotary	526	595
index	100	113
—Cylinder	393	291
index	100	74
Concorde (all cylinder)	270	235
index	100	87

The biggest market sector, 'light mains electric', comprising small electric powered cylinder, rotary and hover mowers, suffered only a 4 per cent decline; it was the cheaper hand mowers and the bigger more expensive machines which were mainly responsible for the 12 per cent decline in total market volume.

The gradual decline of the hand mower market, which Qualcast also dominated (87 per cent share in 1979), was not a problem for Qualcast if people traded up to an electric version of the traditional cylinder mower, i.e. Concorde.

The plain truth was, however, that increasingly more people were trading up instead to the new 'more modern' hover machines.

In 1979 the electric rotary/hover market had grown by 13 per cent whilst the electric *cylinder* market had declined disastrously by 26 per cent. Although Concorde's sales position did not seem unduly pessimistic, this was solely because of Concorde's *share* growth (from 69 per cent to 80 per cent) within the declining 'light mains electric' cylinder sector (Table 13.3). A worrying situation, although some consolation was gleaned from Concorde's resilience within its sector.

The task was clearly spelt out for Qualcast – if Concorde was really to build sales volume it had to reverse the decline in the electric cylinder mower market; it could not achieve the necessary volume simply by continuing to increase brand share alone.

The encouragement to embark upon such a marketing strategy was to come from

TABLE 13.3   CONCORDE SHARE OF THE
LIGHT MAINS ELECTRIC CYLINDER MARKET

1978	1979
%	%
69	80

consumer research – a quantified test where people were given the opportunity to try out Concorde. Based on initial preference, two out of three voted in favour of a hover mower pre-trial (Table 13.4). Post-trial, *half* of these had converted to Concorde. What this meant to Qualcast was that the growth of the hover was reflecting a change in consumer *attitudes and imagery* rather than any fundamental dissatisfaction with Concorder or cylinder technology – in fact quite the opposite: a high level of satisfaction was recorded.

TABLE 13.4:   CONSUMER PREFERENCE BEFORE
AND AFTER CONCORDE TRIAL

	Before Trial %	After Trial %
Concorde E30	38	60
Flymo DLE	47	23
Don't know	15	17
	100	100

How Could Qualcast Make The Electric Cylinder Market Grow?

Several marketing options were theoretically open to Qualcast at this time.

In terms of product development Qualcast were unable to change Concorde in any meaningful way. Assuming it would have been affordable, Qualcast needed one, maybe two years in which to develop a new mower. In any case it would have been difficult to establish a new cylinder product, considering the public's attitude to these 'forgotten' machines.

Price is always a powerful weapon in a situation like this. However, a price war was not only unaffordable but also unnecessary if cylinder benefits could be communicated successfully to a largely ill-informed public.

Finally, product quality and performance was as good as it could be (reflected in very high purchaser satisfaction levels); so too was distribution.

Against this background Qualcast decided that advertising with promotional back-up was the only tool readily available to them which could be used first to halt and then to reverse this sales decline.

At the end of the 1979 season, Wight Collins Rutherford Scott were appointed to handle Qualcast advertising.

Qualcast Objectives in 1979

Qualcast needed to protect long-term volume and profitability. Specifically they wanted to:

1. develop Concorde sales within the Qualcast mix by developing a proposition which ultimately would not have to compete on price with rotary/hover mowers;

2. re-educate the consumer as to the advantages of cylinder mowers and develop a strong franchise for Qualcast and Concorde;
3. improve Qualcast's trade image by presenting the company as a dynamic force in the market with modern, high quality, effective products backed with heavy promotional and advertising support.

THE DEVELOPMENT OF AN ADVERTISING STRATEGY FOR QUALCAST CONCORDE

The task that faced advertising was a tough one. Advertising was to be in effect the *one* change in the overall marketing mix and from this one change Qualcast were hoping to halt the decline of a mower which, although competitively priced, belonged to an earlier generation of consumer attitudes and needs.

The first step was to be extensive consumer research, to paint for us a clear picture of the market against which to define relevant and achievable objectives and develop the correct communication strategy, and against which the effect could be evaluated.

What We Did

The programme of consumer research began with emphasis on qualitative research to achieve an understanding of the market and its complexities, consumer needs and interests; and of the nature of the hover franchise, especially Flymo's.

We also used qualitative research with subsequent quantification to explore the various consumer segments – for example, attitudes to one's garden, to gardening, to one's lawn.

We contacted people who owned hovers and cylinders to assess levels of satisfaction. And we experimented with lawnmower 'clinics'. These 'clinics' entailed the grouping together of people, at a suitable venue, to discuss first of all their knowledge and expectations of various models and brands. They were then given the opportunity to try out the lawnmowers so that we could get their reactions to them, monadically and comparatively, and could assess the influence of 'experience' on attitudes and purchase interest. This issue was also covered in placement tests.

What We Learned

The research confirmed out worst fears: the Hover/Flymo proposition had a firm grip of the consumer mind, spelling out lightness and total manoeuvrability (side to side, back and forth), thereby making grass cutting an extension of household cleaning – a sort of garden hoovering. It was versatile (it was believed to cope with all the awkward bits – under bushes, up to edges, over bumps, up and down banks). Together these spelt effortlessness, the perfect mower for a woman to use, and for the small garden.

In addition one other critically important factor emerged in this research: people were separating in their minds the grass cutting and grass collection/raking tasks.

What we also learned from our consumer research was that the Concorde E30, on trial, exceeded all expectations and was in fact thought to do the job better (it cuts closer than a hover). It was just as easy to use, it was versatile, and it proved in the end far less tiring because it collected the clippings as it mowed, so avoiding the need to rake up or the alternative of leaving untidy (weed-provoking) clippings on the lawn.

In fact, from an initial average two out of three interviewees who firmly stated their pre-trial preference for a hover, the vote switched, post-trial, to two out of three in favour of Concorde (i.e. half the hover franchise switched over)! (See Table 13.4.)

This meant that there was indeed a consumer franchise, which we would tap to Concorde's advantage if we could first of all break down some of the pro-hover myths and burst the Flymo bubble as an 'ease' machine. It also meant that 'trial' was critical to conversion, and since trial is largely impractical in this market, advertising would need to try and provide the trial experience vicariously.

The research identified for us certain target groups.

1. The committed cylinder group: people for whom finish is paramount, and for some of whom the Concorde represents the only 'right and proper' way of mowing one's lawn because of its close resemblance to the traditional hand mower.

    This franchise was basically ours.

2. The committed hover group: people basically interested in cutting the grass rather than mowing the lawn; for whom grass is really a bit of 'green concrete' and so for whom getting the job done (function) is more important than the end result.

    These were unlikely converts to Concorde.

3. The uncommitted middle group: people swayed by the powerful hover proposition of ease. People who enjoyed their gardens but had neither the time nor the inclination to devote too much attention to the upkeep of the lawn. Our dilemma: these people really wanted to believe the hover's ease proposition.

    This was the target we could try to 'educate' and hopefully persuade.

Meanwhile, independent mowing trials undertaken by the Production Engineering Research Association also supported Concorde's superiority in terms of closeness of cut and speed (if raking up was taken into consideration).

What We Had To Do

On the one hand, the research findings and the independent trials had given us the confidence that Concorde could support a very positive case made in its favour. On the other hand, however, we had a very strong hover franchise to break through, and this with a mower that had not altered in appearance. We would have to make a four-pronged attack:

1. Change the mower livery from its outdated blue colour to a well researched and preferred modern shade of green.
2. Undermine some of the hover myths.
3. Overcome the prejudices against the traditional (old-fashioned) cylinder which the Concorde E30 attracted to itself.

And within this context . . .

4. Assert with as much impact as possible, and as credibly and convincingly as possible, the positive features of the Qualcast Concorde E30.

Our initial inclination had been to follow a 'versatility' route in support of Concorde. However, as we reconsidered the earlier research findings, we realized that firstly, this area would be non-credible at this stage of the brand's reassertion; and, secondly, it was likely to prove irrelevant and non-productive. 'Versatility' was an aspect of mowing supremacy, whereas our likely targets were not interested in mowing as such – they wanted the job done quickly and easily and had converted the hover's versatility attribute into a synonym of EASE. Our 'enemy' was not a lawnmower but an *easemachine*.

We concluded, therefore, that we stood a far better chance of success by shifting the battleground into an area of undisputed Concorde superiority: the grass collection issue and its implications for *overall ease* (and for finish). This was the battle we could most readily win, and once won we could move on in later years to win the war. We had to remember that *nothing* had changed in the look (other than colour) or the performance of the Concorde E30.

Therefore, we had to select the issue that we were not only strongest on, but the issue which the actual mower itself could most visibly and convincingly support. With this as *focus*, the consumer would hear and listen to our case; we would then have made the first critical step towards an even fuller pro-Concorde case.

Year 1 Communication Strategy and its Implementation

— The hover is not as easy as you think.
— In fact, Concorde is easier (because you cannot separate grass cutting from removal of clippings from the lawn).
— Additionally, Concorde cuts closer and of course leaves a beautiful finish.

We believed that we had to convey these points with as much visual support as possible in a tone of voice that broke the inertia barriers and the prejudices of the market.

These considerations led us to:

1. *The choice of TV* as *prime* medium. It would have the right sort of impact and hold attention; it would provide 'see for yourself' evidence, i.e. vicarious mowing.
2. *A comparative stance* v. hovers (the bugbear) as the most direct way of dramatizing what we had to offer. The juxtaposition of hover results v. Concorde results (tidy, close, beautiful) had the immediacy as well as the commercial keenness that could tip the balance in our favour. In fact, it would go further in flagging down the hover prospect whose attention could be gained by their identifying with what one was saying/showing; Concorde needed to get into their mind's map.

   So the birth of '*A lot less bovver than a hover*'.
3. A commercial *90 seconds* in length in order to blast away our story, to develop the *whole* story with all the evidence needed, and to handle what was a very hard-nosed commercial proposition with the wit and style needed to make it acceptable.
4. *A creative/media solution* where we could 'afford' the critical 90-second time-length (alternating with a 60-second cut-down version) by restricting frequency to the critical days of the week when our audience was most likely to be interested in and listen to what we had to say, i.e. the build-up to Saturday buying and weekend mowing. Going to 90 seconds therefore did not necessitate any increase in original budget allocation, particularly in view of the fact that an advertising presence could be concentrated at the start of the season and so over a few weeks only.
5. *Press as a complementary medium* to develop certain arguments in more depth and detail, as well as to extend the arguments in time.

What do *you* do

Well, if you cut it with an airborne mower you'd better get out the rake.

Because if you leave grass cuttings on the lawn it's messy, and you'll almost certainly encourage weeds and wormcasts.

You'll encourage weeds because seeds are scattered all over the garden, and you'll encourage worms because there's nothing they like more than decomposing grass.

On the other hand if you cut the lawn with

after you've mown the lawn?

a Qualcast Concorde you can get out a deckchair.
You've already collected the cuttings in the grassbox.

The lawn looks good because it is cut lower with a beautiful striped finish.

And you feel good because the electric Concorde is so easy to use – even in long, wet grass.

So, isn't it time you came down to earth?

QUALCAST
Concorde
It's a lot less bovver than a hover.

WHAT OUR APPROACH ACHIEVED

Pre-testing (qualitative and quantitative) showed that even just one screening of the full Concorde story was well on the way to:

(a)   undermining the hover myth;
(b)   making Concorde a candidate for consideration.

We were getting people to link for the first time the two basic tasks of mowing and raking, and thereby we could score over the hover. We were succeeding in diverting attention *from* the obvious hover advantages of lightness, access under bushes and left to right movement, *towards* the disadvantage of clippings on the grass - their unsightliness, their encouragement of weeds.

We were succeeding in getting people to think a bit about the selection of a mower on practical grounds rather than purely irrational ones. On-air measures - Television Advertising Bureau (Surveys) Limited ratings - also confirmed that our approach was achieving very high levels of involvement in the commercial itself as well as in Concorde - with brand goodwill sustained even after the end of the television campaign.

COMPETITIVE REACTION

Flymo and Black and Decker challenged our claims on a total of five counts. We were upheld on all.

We had our factual evidence - research going as far back as 1921 - and knew that we were on safe ground. Clippings can cause weeds; they do not disappear into the ground or turn into mulch given normal mowing frequencies: you'd need to mow several times a fortnight for these to be true.

The Turf Research Centre was able to supply all the supportive evidence that the Independent Television Companies Association and Advertising Standards Authority required. And turf laid out in the WCRS offices for officials from both bodies to mow for their own conviction regarding 'ease', proved our case once more for us.

So Into Year 2

The 'Much less bovver . . .' campaign had been conceived as part of a long term strategy. However, before automatically extending it into 1981, further consumer research was carried out to satisfy ourselves that it was still appropriate for the brand, and to assess if we could broaden the spectrum of claims to include 'overgrown lawns' and banks and, albeit implicitly, more emphasis on ease.

We could.

The 1980 campaign had achieved huge impact. Qualcast Concorde had, after all, been the first major advertiser with a directly comparative stance on television. And this had taken our prime competitor (Flymo) by surprise.

We discovered, however, that one needed to restate the case and re-activate the market each year. But we had had sufficient earlier impact to be able to trigger consumer memory and so move on one step further in our overall communication. Sixty seconds could now do the job for us. And yet we could include additional selling points too.

Flymo retaliated in 1981 with a comparative stance as well, fighting in the press. Their claim was the speed (and implicit ease and effortlessness) advantage of the hover over the traditional cylinder: no need to worry about collecting the clippings as they mulch into the ground.

The Advertising Standards Authority were to uphold 13 out of 14 citations that the Flymo claims were in fact misleading.

THE MEDIA STRATEGY

As we have intimated, the media and creative solutions were closely knit.

Traditional levels of coverage and frequency had to be re-examined in year one to cope with the creative need for 90 seconds of dialogue. Our belief – to be subsequently proved accurate – was that if we could hold our target audience's attention for a minute and a half, we would only require the commercial to be seen one and a half times for the message to be fully established.

To heighten the impact still further, a refined time-buying strategy was developed which restricted advertising to the critical days of Friday (pre-shopping day), and Sunday (weekend mowing).

We also negotiated for year one a flexible start date to the television campaign, so we would not risk spending money on air *before* weather conditions were right to encourage the grass to grow.

Adult colour press was used in year one as a complementary medium to develop key arguments in more depth, and to extend coverage during and after the television bursts. In year two this extension policy was added to by using forty-eight sheet posters to gain maximum visibility *throughout* the mowing season.

Table 13.5 outlines the deployment of media monies.

TABLE 13.5:   CONCORDE MEDIA PLAN

	1980 £'000	1981 £'000
National TV and adult colour press	650	1038*

* plus 48 sheet posters.

WHAT WAS ACHIEVED

In 1980 Qualcast's investment in advertising was met by an equal investment by Flymo who virtually tripled their 1979 spend from £224 000 to £631 000 resulting in total advertising expenditure growing from £539 000 to £2 037 000. This meant that Flymo and Qualcast Concorde were jointly accounting for three-fifths of all lawnmower advertising.

The overall effect of this activity was to increase the total market by 18 per cent and the 'light mains electric' sector by 21 per cent.

Qualcast's forceful stating of the 'cylinder mower' case via Concorde had the effect of growing this sector by a staggering 45 per cent with Concorde increasing its brand share from the previous year's 80 per cent to 85 per cent; a 53 per cent increase in Concorde sales.

These massive gains were made without any major increase in retail distribution (already high) and with a small average price increase of 4 per cent, which was in line with the market as a whole.

TABLE 13.6:   LAWNMOWER ADVERTISING SPEND

	1979		1980		1981	
	£'000	%	£'000	%	£'000	%
Qualcast Concorde	–	–	650	32	1038	32
Flymo	224	42	631	31	837	26
Other Qualcast products	–	–	162	8	394	12
Black and Decker	–	–	100	5	140	4
Others	315	58	494	25	794	24
	539		2037		3203	
Index	100		378		595	

Source: TV and Press Expenditure

Encouraging research results showing high awareness of Concorde's product attributes and a good value-for-money rating gave Qualcast the confidence to raise their average model price in 1981 by 13 per cent and Concorde's on-shelf price by 25 per cent.

Raising the price of Concorde was critical to Qualcast's overall business objectives – not just for reasons of short-term profit but in order to afford long-term investment in machinery and product development. Another important consideration was the likely price war effect on the market of keeping prices down – with the inevitable result of none of the manufacturers being able to afford, long term, any product improvement or new product development.

This bold pricing strategy was supported by an increased advertising budget (£1 038 000) which was also necessary in order to maintain Qualcast's share of voice in what had become a very competitive advertising environment.

Competitors responded to Qualcast's initiative by keeping their on-shelf prices low and in some cases actually reducing them.

The Result of Qualcast's Bold Policy

For the second year running the total market grew – this year by 12 per cent in volume terms.

Qualcast effectively held on to their overall share (slipping just one point from 43 per cent in 1980 to 42 per cent in 1981) but the dramatic cylinder market growth seen in 1979 was not repeated (only 3.5 per cent growth). Obviously, subsequent cylinder gains were going to be much more difficult to make.

Concorde, having dramatically raised its price compared with the rest of the market, not only held on to its increased 1980 volume but grew by an additional 9 per cent, increasing its market share to a record 89 per cent (see Tables 13.7 and 13.8).

TABLE 13.7:   CONCORDE SHARE OF THE LIGHT MAINS
ELECTRIC CYLINDER MARKET

1978	1979	1980	1981
%	%	%	%
69	80	85	89

TABLE 13.8:   MARKET VALUE AND AVERAGE SELLING PRICE

	1979	1980	1981
Total market			
Value (£m)	65	80	90
Volume ('000 units)	1216	1439	1614
Average price paid in-store	£53.5	£55.6	£55.8
Percentage increase year on year			
Market	–	+4%	static
Qualcast			
—All mowers	–	+4%	+13%
—Concorde only	–	+4%	+25%

The hover/rotary sector in total clawed back some of its earlier market share (1979 – 67 per cent, 1980 – 60 per cent, 1981 – 65 per cent) mainly as a result of aggressive pricing policy and the introduction of new Flymo and Black and Decker models.

In profit terms Birmid Qualcast Home and Garden Equipment Division made steady gains in 1980 and 1981. As Table 13.9 shows, turnover throughout this period rose significantly and more importantly profit increased even more dramatically, reflecting a marked overall improvement in margin.

TABLE 13.9:   BIRMID QUALCAST PROFITABILITY

	1979	1980	1981
B.Q. Home & Garden Equipment Division *			
Turnover £m	34.9	41.8	46.8
Percentage increase year on year		+20%	+12%
Margin percentage	6.3	7.9	9.2
Profit £m	2.2	3.3	4.3
Percentage increase year on year		+50%	+30%

*Roughly one tenth of this turnover comes from export which is slightly less profitable.

Finally and most importantly, the 25 per cent increase in Concorde's on-shelf price in 1981 generated roughly 390 000 units × £10 average price rise per machine = £3.9 million. This additional revenue, in itself, paid for the advertising budget more than three times over.

CONCLUSIONS

The objective of this paper has been to demonstrate that advertising has not been an on-cost for Qualcast but an essential element in the marketing mix which resulted in a healthier and more profitable company.

Research enabled us to identify the key elements of the problem which formed the basis of a hard-hitting communication strategy.

A bold creative and media solution enabled the Concorde case to be reconsidered by a public which was largely prejudiced and uninterested.

The results of the campaign were unequivocal in sales and profit terms enabling Qualcast to invest in product development and build upon a meaningful and strong Concorde brand franchise.

Note. Sales figures quoted are Qualcast estimates based on quantified independent consumer research.

14
Kellogg's Rice Krispies

The Effect of a New Creative Execution

BUSINESS BACKGROUND

Rice Krispies has been a major brand in the breakfast cereal market since it was first launched in the UK in 1929 – long enough to have been a part of most shoppers' own childhood. Its crisp puffs of toasted rice have a unique appeal to children: in a description made famous by advertising, they go 'Snap, Crackle, Pop' in milk.

The product itself is very light, so its average retail price per kilogram is about 50 per cent higher than market average, making it one of the more expensive brands. Sales volume has remained fairly constant around 10 million kilograms a year (Nielsen) for the last decade. Consequently, the brand's share of the growing cereal market declined slowly through most of the 1970s. Its share of ready-to-eat (RTE) cereal advertising declined more steeply, as its advertising levels in real terms were progressively reduced.

By 1977, volume share of market was down to 5.7 per cent according to Nielsen (though its sterling share of 8 per cent still made Rice Krispies the third largest brand by value). Rising costs of raw materials and the pressure on margins from the retail trade were making it increasingly difficult for the brand to fund the high advertising-to-sales ratio that historically it had needed to maintain consumer demand for this premium product. Furthermore, the falling birth-rate meant that its primary consumers – children – would be getting fewer.

So the advertising strategy was reviewed and a new creative execution was developed for 1978.

MARKETING AND ADVERTISING OBJECTIVES

The marketing aim was to win sales growth, in line with market growth at first in order to arrest the fall in share, and subsequently ahead of market in order to regain some, at least, of the share that had been lost. But with a shrinking child population – children eat over half the tonnage sold – this aim would be achieved only by increasing the numbers of families who buy Rice Krispies, and, in particular, by winning a share of their cereal purchases at the expense of other brands also largely eaten by children, such as Sugar Puffs and other pre-sweetened cereals, and Weetabix.

This meant, in fact, reversing the trend of previous years. Rice Krispies had been losing franchise because:

1. It was rather expensive, and needed to offer something extra to justify the cost of buying it regularly.
2. It was light and insubstantial, and so was thought to have little nourishment value in it, at a time when more mothers were setting store by substantiality and food value in their children's breakfast cereal.
3. Its image had become more of a hedonistic 'fun' cereal – suitable as an occasional treat for children – and less that of an everyday all-family staple.

The effect had been to make Rice Krispies seem to many of its consumers a less important brand than it really was. So they had demoted it from being one of their usual brands to being a secondary, occasional purchase.

Advertising was given the task of reversing these trends, of making Rice Krispies more important and more highly valued, and of putting it back into the role of an enjoyable staple breakfast food.

ADVERTISING STRATEGY

Central to the strategy we developed to meet these aims was the *uniqueness* of Rice Krispies, not just in its 'Snap, Crackle, Pop', but also in the power of this phrase to remind adults of when they too, as children, listened to Rice Krispies crackling and popping in a bowl of milk. More than any other cereal, it says childhood. It is *the* childhood cereal.

We wanted to evoke in parents their own memories of eating Rice Krispies when little, to remind them of the magic of the cereal that makes a noise – because, to its eaters, this magic has a very real value.

So we decided to present, in television commercials and in print advertisements, an appealing and credible portrayal of childhood. Firstly, to catch mothers' attention and interest, because what children *really* do and think always interests them. Secondly to evoke their own childhoods (so we would show only children, and no adults, in the advertisements, and try to present a world as seen through a child's eyes).

A third reason was that a truthful and sensitive representation of childhood would be evidence that Kellogg knew and cared about children and implicitly, therefore, about feeding them properly. (This was a high risk route, because the slightest dissonance or unreality caused by the child actors could, as many advertisements with children have done, easily trigger disbelief and dislike among the mothers watching, with wholly negative effect.)

Lastly, we wanted to remind people that whilst the magic of Rice Krispies is so much a part of childhood, the appeal of the brand is not child*ish*, but much wider than that; that it is not simply an occasional treat for the kids, but a sensible and worthwhile breakfast food that all the family can enjoy.

Out of this strategy developed a campaign that appeared to stand this last intention on its head. A series of television and magazine advertisements featured Edward, Rachel and the rest of their 'gang', and their attempts to start a national protest campaign to make adults *stop* eating Rice Krispies and to reserve it for children only: drafting speeches for the media, sending delegates to raise support in other towns, writing to the Prime Minister! (And thus, of course, calling attention to the fact that many adults do eat Rice Krispies.)

The new campaign began in the spring of 1978, using the same media mix of television and women's magazines as in previous years, and at no greater rate of real expenditure (Table 14.1). An industrial dispute at the plant in summer 1979 brought advertising to a halt for the rest of the year, but the campaign is now continuing in its third year in 1980.

TABLE 14.1:   ADVERTISING LEVEL FOR RICE KRISPIES

		Annual television OTS[a] (Housewives)	Media expenditure at constant 1978 prices (MEAL) (£'000s)
	1976	17	1140
	1977	14	660
'Edward'	1978	13	600
campaign	1979 (Jan.–July)	9	350

[a] Average number of opportunities-to-see the television advertising per viewer per year.

EVALUATING THE EFFECT

Creative research during the development of the campaign suggested that the advertisements were achieving their aims. AGB's TCA audits of consumer purchasing revealed a sharp rise in the number of homes buying Rice Krispies each month, coinciding with the new campaign's start. Further analysis of buying patterns, from consumer panel data, showed that we were gaining in brand switching from Weetabix, instant porridge and the other competitive child cereals. Nielsen reported a $7\frac{1}{2}$ per cent sales volume growth in 1978, compared to a 3 per cent rise for the market in total. And apart from the period in 1979 when the brand was not available, sales have stayed buoyant.

The market indications are, then, that the campaign is on strategy and that it is working. More importantly, there is firm evidence that the new advertising increased the value that consumers put on the brand and thus raised demand for it, with a substantial and quantifiable effect on sales revenue.

Given the brand's price premium, relative price is naturally a major factor affecting demand. So much so, in fact, that the size of the price effect in month by month sales variations tends to swamp and obscure the effects of other variables. The logical step was to see if we could isolate, and remove, the price effect, and then look for an advertising effect. To do this, we examined TCA monthly data* for 1975–77 (the three years prior to the new 'Edward' campaign) for evidence of correlation between the relative price of Rice Krispies and demand for the brand.

The method we used was based on the economist's conventional 'demand curve', in which quantity purchased is related diagrammatically to price. In practice we have found it appropriate to take the *relative* quantity purchased (as represented by a brand's percentage share of market volume) and relate that to its *relative* price (expressed as a ratio of the average price in the market).

---

* Monthly audits, and the recording of actual prices paid, make TCA data more suitable than Nielsen for this technique. However, a cross-check using Nielsen data produced confirmatory findings.

Stills from Rice Krispies television advertisement: **'What's wrong Rachel?'**

'Are you still worrying about the grown-ups eating our Rice Krispies?'

'Are you thinking that they'll never stop eating our snap, crackle and pop?'

'I know Rachel, but we have to keep on trying.'

'Come on Rachel, it'll be all right.'

During periods of market stability, the observed measures of brand share and relative price tend to conform to the conventional demand curve pattern when they are plotted on a graph. That is, a relative price rise will tend to reduce share of sales (demand), whereas a fall in the relative price will tend to be accompanied by a rise in brand share.

New marketing action, when it is successful, can be expected to produce points on the graph that do not conform to the previously observed demand curve. So the technique provides a powerful means of monitoring, over relatively short periods of time, the effect of changes in marketing actions.

In the Rice Krispies analysis, we looked at the relationship between the brand's share of all RTE volume sales and its relative price (indexed to the all-RTE price per kilogram). The results (Figure 14.1) showed a modest correlation between price and share of the three

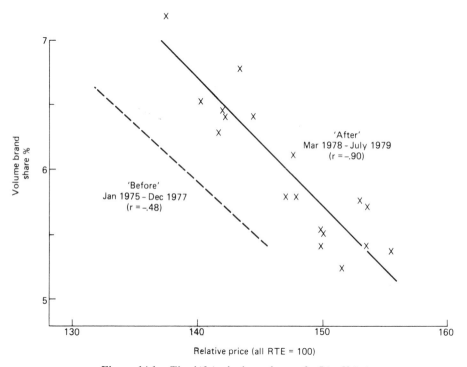

Figure 14.1   *The shift in the demand curve for Rice Krispies*

years 1975–77. Evidently other factors, in addition to price, were affecting demand. But the slope of the line* showed that Rice Krispies was fairly price sensitive, with a price elasticity of about − 2. That is to say, a 5 per cent reduction in the price, from 140 on the price index scale to 133, could theoretically be expected to result in a rise in brand share from 5.9 to 6.5, a 10 per cent increase in sales volume. Or, to simplify, a 1 per cent fall in price would lead

---

*The economist's demand curve normally relates *proportionate changes* in sales to *proportionate changes* in price and is thus a straight line in the *logarithms* of the variables. But the increased accuracy of fitting such a curve across a fairly narrow range of price differences is not significant, and a straight line in natural values is a lot easier to use in practice.

to a 2 per cent rise in sales volume. However, it must be said again that the correlation (−.48) between relative price and sales for the period 1975–77 was not strong, and accounted for only one-quarter of observed sales variations.

From the start of the new campaign, however, the picture changed. The 1978–79 data showed a clear shift to the right in the demand line, and a closer correlation between price and market share.

It is worth noting that this was not a change in price sensitivity – the slope of the line is the same as before – but rather a rise in the perceived *value* of Rice Krispies accompanied by a rise in the proportion of month-by-month sales variation that was due to price.

This rise in brand value, which took place immediately after the start of the new 'Edward' campaign, continued at least until the market was disrupted in summer 1979. (It has taken time for the market to get back to normality since then. But first indications for Rice Krispies look good.) The difference between actual market shares achieved and those predicted by the previous years' price/share relationship was substantial, amounting to an additional 14 per cent in sales volume between March 1978 and July 1979, or an extra £2¼ million in sales revenue (Figure 14.2).

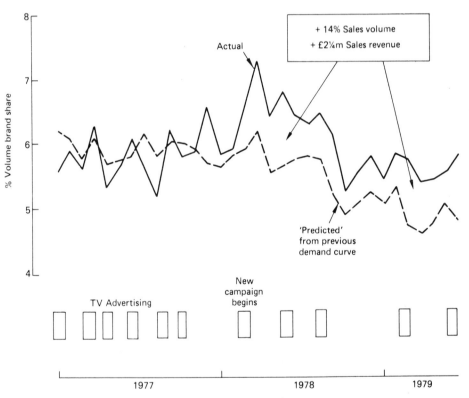

Figure 14.2 *The sales increase of Rice Krispies*

How Much was the New Advertising Campaign Worth?

Something, it was clear, added value to the brand in the spring of 1978. The evidence that it was the change in advertising that was the cause is circumstantial, in that no other factor – neither distribution, sales force activity, on-pack promotion, nor competitors' action – could be judged to have changed anywhere near sufficiently to have brought about such a lasting shift in brand value. The only realistically plausible explanation which could be found was that the new advertising campaign did it.

Any creative stimulus that brings in over £2 million in extra sales in under 18 months is obviously valuable. But could a cash value, we wondered, be put on it? An approximate answer emerged from an analysis of the relationship between sales share and advertising share in the RTE cereal market.

To look at this, we used the 'Dynamic Difference' model,* which relates two factors:

1. The difference between this year's share of advertising (representing current marketing effort) and *last* year's brand share of market (representing the consumer franchise base before this year's advertising stimulus began).
2. The change in brand share between last year and this (representing the effect of the marketing effort).

The data are summarized in Table 14.2, and plotted graphically in Figure 14.3.

TABLE 14.2:   MARKET AND ADVERTISING SHARES FOR RICE KRISPIES

	A Volume brand share %	B Advertising expenditure share %	'Dynamic Difference' (B minus previous year's A)	Brand share change
1970	7.0			
1971	7.4	14.3	+7.3	+0.4
1972	7.1	12.3	+4.9	−0.3
1973	7.0	11.2	+4.1	−0.1
1974	6.8	13.2	+6.2	−0.2
1975	6.2	10.2	+3.4	−0.6
1976	6.1	12.7	+6.5	−0.1
1977	5.7	8.5	+2.4	−0.4
1978	6.0	7.9	+2.2	+0.3

The results of this analysis showed a reasonably consistent relationship for 1971–77, followed by an exceptionally high market share achievement in 1978, when the brand gained 0.3 points. Such a gain, according to the regression equation for 1971–77, would have needed a Dynamic Difference of +8.5 points of advertising share in excess of brand share. In fact, the Dynamic Difference in 1978 was +2.2, so the effect of the campaign change was broadly comparable to the expected effect of an advertising expenditure increase of roughly 6.3 per cent of RTE cereals' advertising in 1978. According to MEAL, the market spent £7.6 million on advertising that year. So the extra sales effect on the new 'Edward' campaign was 'worth' the equivalent of about an additional £500 000 (6.3 per cent of £7.6m) spent on advertising in that year.

* Originated many years ago by M. J. Moroney of Unilever.

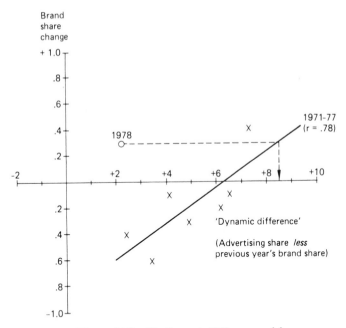

Figure 14.3   *The Dynamic Difference model*

The limitations of the data make this, at best, only a rough approximation. Nevertheless, they do suggest that the new strategy and execution just about doubled the effectiveness of the advertising.

CONCLUSIONS

We concluded that the new advertising had succeeded in its aims of making Rice Krispies a more important and more highly valued brand in consumers' eyes, and of rebuilding its role as a staple breakfast cereal.

On the basis of the evidence, we believe that:

1. The new campaign brought about a sustained increase in the value that consumers put on the brand.
2. This added value increased demand for the brand by about 14 per cent and brought in an additional £2¼ million in sales revenue inside 18 months.
3. This effect was very roughly equivalent to that of an extra £0.5 million a year spent on advertising.

THE METHOD OF EVALUATION

Growing experience of the 'demand curve' technique for assessing advertising's effects has convinced us that it is a very useful and practical tool. By separating out the price effect, it allows the effects of other variables to show up more clearly. By its simplicity, it makes exploratory analysis easier to undertake. By forcing the analyst to spell out his assumptions, it leads to better *understanding* of how brands and markets work. But, over and above all this, the technique has two major practical applications.

Firstly, it makes it possible to measure advertising and other effects not only on sales volume but also on the price a brand can command. Advertising may be aiming to raise volume or to raise value (or indeed both). Both effects, therefore, need to be assessable together, which is what the demand curve method does.

Secondly, once a stable demand curve has been detected, it becomes a simple matter of plotting each month's new data on the graph in order to *monitor* the continuing progress of the brand. On-trend readings show stability. Off-trend readings quickly reveal that something is changing, and provide a basis for diagnosing the cause.

15

The Renaissance of Manger's Sugar Soap

INTRODUCTION

This paper relates how a nationally distributed brand which had not been advertised for forty years was re-positioned in concept, re-introduced to the retail trade and advertised in a Granada television test market, producing a five-fold increase in annual sales. The cost of the media expenditure was recovered by the time the advertising ended.

A lightweight reprise of the campaign in the same area a year later added a one-third increase in sales over the year-ago peaks during an initial eight-month period.

At the same time, the campign was extended into the London television region in the first stages of a national roll-out. Over the initial eight months sales increased over three and half times.

This is not just the story of rejuvenating a brand, but of rebuilding a company. Advertising support for the brand has been an instrument for obtaining extra sales for the entire range of products marketed by the company, and for increased profits, and was the crucial factor in the financial restructuring of the company through a management buy-out.

BUSINESS BACKGROUND

In May 1980, Michael J. Dent was hired by Grimshawe Holdings Limited to manage one of their subsidiary companies, J. Manger & Son Ltd. Dent was the general manager of Dunlop Chemical Products Division, and had extensive retail marketing experience in the hardware/DIY sector.

J. Manger & Son Ltd, established 1849, originally owned salt mines. However, in the 1920s the company became involved in the marketing of a number of household proprietary products. One of these, Manger's Sugar Soap, survived to the present day. In recent years the business had come to serve the DIY market with a great variety of products – with special emphasis on decorators' sundries – the overwhelming majority of which were factored, or supplied by other Grimshawe companies.

Although total forecast turnover for 1980 was only around £2 million, profit on sales and return on capital were lower than most companies operating in the DIY field.

Dent's initial marketing appraisal was that Manger's business was mainly price-based: a small national sales force sold some 400 different products to retailers at wholesale terms.

The company had lost its way; sales of factored products were increasing, while sales of own-manufactured products decreased. Gradually, the multiples were beginning to regard the company as a kind of national wholesaler rather than a manufacturer, and therefore a declining force in the DIY market.

Only one product, Sugar Soap, was primarily distributed by wholesalers. Rarely was the range stocked in depth and the Manger's branding was not visible in the store. Nevertheless, it was a traditional name well-known to the retail trade and salesmen were received cordially; the company had access to the DIY market.

Dent concluded that the business lacked a mainline branded product *which the consumer wanted*. Such a product, with a good distribution base, growing loyalty and acceptability in the trade, could become a flagship which could carry other Manger's products into distribution in its wake.

He had a 'gut feeling' about Sugar Soap.

THE HISTORY OF SUGAR SOAP

In the 1940s Manger's Sugar Soap was a household name. Before the advent of television, self-service multiples, detergents and specialist cleansers, the brand enjoyed wide grocery distribution as an all-purpose heavy duty household cleaning product.

In modern marketing terms, there was considerable irresolution about the brand positioning. Old packets state that it was 'specially made for cleaning paint, floors, ovens and baths'.

By 1980 Sugar Soap was well into the old age pensioner stage of its product life cycle. It was first launched in 1923. The last advertising was in the 1940s and the last formula change around 1950. Grocery outlets were lost in 1959 as the new TV-advertised brands swept the household cleaning market, and distribution was now confined to hardware and DIY outlets.

The information on sales over the years was patchy, but dramatic (Table 15.1).

TABLE 15.1:   SUGAR SOAP SALES HISTORY OVER 50
YEARS: AVERAGE VOLUME (16) SOLD

Years	Index
1930–34	100
1935–39	116
1940–44	138
1945–49	570
1950–54	760
1955–59	637
1960–64	No data
1965–69	No data
1970–74	95
1975–79	83
1980	78

During the past decade Sugar Soap had sold less volume than in the 1930s, and only a small fraction of the sales it had enjoyed throughout the 1950s peak.

A switch from the rectangular packet to a brighter and more modern cylindrical 500 g tub in 1975 had failed to arrest the decline. Sugar Soap was now described as a paintwork cleaner with a wide range of other uses recommended back of pack: to clean bathrooms, kitchens and floors, to remove oil from driveways, act as a water-softener, as a toilet bowl cleaner; for soaking greasy overalls, stripping paint, unblocking drains, and softening paint brushes.

What was surprising about this history was not that Manger's Sugar Soap sales had slumped so drastically, but that the brand was still around. After all those years of marketing neglect people were still buying the product, and in the face of very strong generic competition.

It was cheap, but it was inconvenient to use, as it had to be mixed with water.

Manger's Sugar Soap appeared to be one of those venerable products which linger on a surprising number of shelves in the dustier types of retail outlet despite extremely low rates of offtake.

It had survived in a corner of the hardware/DIY sector, probably as a result of the company's re-orientation in that direction, but it had completely missed out on the great post-war DIY boom.

IDENTIFYING THE PRODUCT CONCEPT

Why had Manger's Sugar Soap survived so long in adverse circumstance? What was the secret of its appeal? Who was still buying Sugar Soap ... and why? The answers to these questions would provide the framework of an advertising strategy.

But the company had lost contact with its consumers years ago, and also with the retailers of Sugar Soap, as the product was sold largely through wholesalers. Moreover, not only did financial pressures limit the scope of research which might be undertaken, but their exigency compressed the time in which such projects might be undertaken.

One conjecture was that it was the decorating trade user who was still supporting Sugar Soap. However, Sugar Soap had little distribution in decorators' merchants, where the trade normally buys, and the small 500 g pack seemed inappropriate for volume usage.

On the other hand, purchases were unlikely to be attributable to the conventional DIY user. The heaviest users of paint are men aged 20–34, and it was apparent, from common sense and a bit of random questioning, that the product was virtually unknown to anyone under the age of 40. So, a third theory was that the brand continued to be bought by a dwindling number of older people as a cheap cleaning agent in one or more of its traditional uses.

Given the low penetration of the product and the limited funds available, the problem could not be approached meaningfully on a quantitative level. It was consequently, and perhaps unusually, approached qualitatively, through Market Research Ltd.

Research

There were two stages to this research, both extremely precise in target group selection. The first was a series of ten unstructured individual interviews with professional jobbing decorators who actually used Sugar Soap in their work.

A hypothesis was also fed into this research: namely, that perhaps Sugar Soap not only cleaned but also lightly abraded the paintwork to key the surface for better paint adhesion, thereby performing two operations in one. This was merely an inspired guess. The way the formulation worked had been forgotten, and Manger's did not then possess a significant research laboratory capability.

The research found that, on the whole, professional decorators used Sugar Soap as an efficient grease and grime shifter. And it was, they said, 'the only thing that will remove nicotine stains'. They affirmed that good preparation was an essential prerequisite for good painting, and it was a generally shared belief that if Manger's Sugar Soap were used at the preparation stage, a better paint finish would be achieved than if any other cleaning product were used.

The professional decorators admitted many other uses to which they themselves had put Sugar Soap, but these were all seen to be secondary. They appeared to have an emotional affection for Sugar Soap as an honest and traditional product. In effect, decorators 'swore by it'.

But it was *not* seen to 'key' the surface; on the contrary, it did not seem to be abrasive at all.

Given all of these plus points, there was a good chance the DIY enthusiast, who tends to look for and respect the tricks of the trade, could be persuaded to prefer the product in the same way that painters and decorators did. If so, there was enormous potential for Sugar Soap.

But this was begging the whole question of whether Sugar Soap should be relaunched as a specialist paintwork cleaner. Could it not, in these cost-conscious days, find a favourable reception with the housewife as a good, solid, dependable, old-fashioned and very cheap general purpose cleaning product, with many uses?

That generic positioning, of course, implied essentially a housewife audience, and a tremendous range of very powerful competitors, and, very probably, a requirement for additional sectors of retail distribution as well. Nevertheless, the all-purpose, cheap, magical housewives' friend was a very beguiling positioning concept.

To aid in this positioning judgement a second qualitative research study was commissioned. The product was placed with twenty male heads of household who were actually about to do some decorating, and also with twenty housewives from different households.

This research suggested that, with regard to the household cleaning function, versatility was seen as a very strong benefit, but one which had to be advanced with care in order not to defy credibility, as the more bizarre usages created a considerable degree of dissonance. This positioning would require functional re-packaging and probably the addition of a perfume.

An excuse or rationale for the lack of convenience in using Sugar Soap would also have to be found. Other competitive products were perceived as markedly superior in that respect.

But, the image of reliability derived from Sugar Soap's age and heritage was exploitable, particularly among the older respondents.

With regard to positioning it as a paintwork cleaner, its purchase would have to be justified as against already extant specialist products, many of which have applications beyond their specialist role. To do this would involve an educational campaign, persuading do-it-yourselfers of the need to prepare their surfaces correctly in order to get the best possible final results. It was felt that an emphasis on trade recommendation would go a long way towards achieving this.

However, one still did not know *why* Sugar Soap was felt by decorators to work better and why consumers endorsed this finding.

Manger's had lost the answer to this question in the mists of time. An old showcard which was not discovered until well after the relaunch, actually contained the claim that Sugar Soap keyed the surface of the paintwork. This was wrong. That hypothesis had been rejected by the qualitative research: Sugar Soap does not 'key' paint because it is not abrasive.

But the phrase 'chemically clean' on the same showcard is intriguing, and a clue to the answer uncovered by further researches. Conventional detergent cleansing agents, which are probably most commonly used by the average consumer for this job, contain silicates. Unless rinsing is extremely thorough, these invisible silicates remain on the surface and subsequently impair the adhesion of the paint. This is why the professional, expressing himself in his own terms, would say in the interview situation, 'It goes on smoother' or 'It gives a better finish'. There is even a recognizable symptom of faulty paintwork which has been executed over a silicate surface. In decorator's jargon that is the so-called 'orange peel' or 'fish-eye' effect, which can lead to subsequent flaking.

This very strong competitive product story in this particular application tipped the scales of judgement in favour of the positioning of Sugar Soap unequivocally as an excellent paintwork cleaner with subsidiary uses in the house.

THE MARKET

Size of the Market

A great many products can be used to wash down walls prior to decorating, so it was difficult to get a fix on the market. In broad terms, Mintel reported that amongst all social groups 43 per cent of men aged 25 to 44 had painted in the last six months. Among these males alone these would be around 6 million opportunities for purchase annually, and that was not counting women, who account for a very substantial proportion of the purchasing of decorating products. Nor did it include all of the other potential uses for Sugar Soap, once it had found its way into the home.

At any rate, given the current low rate of sale of Sugar Soap there seemed to be plenty of opportunity for increase.

Market Growth

Manger's compete within the £2000 million DIY market, which until 1979 enjoyed a boom which was more pronounced than consumer spending in general. However, in 1980 the market declined abruptly in real terms by 10 per cent and suffered a further 6 per cent decline in 1981.

Home decorating products comprise about half of this total market; their sterling growth had failed to keep pace with inflation since 1979. The £8 million all-purpose cleaner market, which tends to be distributed through other sectors of trade, appeared to be static.

Thus, 1981 was not an auspicious time to relaunch a DIY product. DIY sales were sluggish in 1981 and early indicators from the retail trade suggested that 1982 would achieve little, if any, growth.

Competition

In the specific area of a specialist paintwork cleaner prior to decorating, there are only two competitive brands. Polywash, retailing a 450 g pack at around 58p plus VAT, would offer somewhat better value than Sugar Soap at its new price. Vee Vic, offering only 350 g at the same price as Sugar Soap's 500 g pack, was quite poor value.

Vee Vic is an old-fashioned product, like Sugar Soap, marketed by a small company which would not appear to have the resources or initiative to contest a Sugar Soap relaunch very strongly. Polywash is quite another matter, being, of course, one of the items in the very strong and heavily advertised Polycell range. However, it was felt that as this company had very firmly committed itself to range advertising, it would be unlikely to respond very effectively to a Sugar Soap intrusion in this particular segment of the range.

In fact, as happened later, both of these brands mustered only a token competitive response to the Manger's Sugar Soap relaunch.

THE RELAUNCH OF SUGAR SOAP

In terms of communication, it was clearly necessary to identify the product proposition, provide clear usage details, remove the accretion of unnecessary and distracting information and use the pack as a communicating and selling medium. An in-pack leaflet was added to convey the manifold subsidiary uses of the product, once it found its way into the home.

The retail price of the standard 500 g tub was increased by 10p to 72p (plus VAT). But a new 1250 g plastic kettle was added to the range as a trade pack to satisfy shop owner's need for a more durable container. Gram for gram, it actually offered a lower price than previously.

The new packs were sold nationally from early March 1981. A television advertising test market was undertaken in Granada in April–May of that year. Television advertising was extended to the London area a year later, April–May 1982, together with a reprise of the same TV advertising at one-third the original weight in Granada.

Marketing and Advertising Objectives

The objectives listed here for the initial Granada test apply equally to the subsequent London area roll-out and the Granada reprise, both of which occurred a year later.

MARKETING OBJECTIVES

To increase sales of Sugar Soap in the Granada television region sufficiently to pay for the media cost of the television campaign in the short term, plus long-term benefits.

To increase distribution of Sugar Soap in the Granada television region, and particularly the quality of that distribution, by gaining multiple accounts.

To achieve good display of the new packaging, including the new 1250 g trade pack, and of associated point-of-scale material.

On a *national* level to achieve a sales increase over current levels and new distribution on the strength of the new packaging and the commitment to television advertising evidenced by the Granada test.

1. How do you clean nicotine stains off a pub ceiling?

2. Manger's Sugar Soap

3. The same with a greasy kitchen. A professional will use Sugar Soap even if your paintwork looks clean.

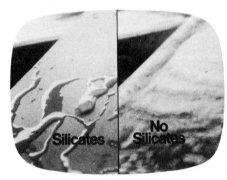

4. Because some ordinary cleaners foam up too much. Others deposit silicates, which shed paint like a used car in a rainstorm. Low-foam Sugar Soap has no silicates.

5. It leaves a chemically clean surface that paint will cling to...

6. like a barmaid to a sailor on payday
CHORUS: Shug-shug-shug-shug-Sugar Soap!

ADVERTISING OBJECTIVES

To increase distribution coverage and quality by persuading retailers to stock.

To persuade DIY decorators to buy Sugar Soap as an essential requisite for cleaning down surfaces prior to decorating.

Creative Strategy and Execution

Prime target group: Male DIY decorators
Secondary target group: Female DIY decorators

BASIC CONSUMER BENEFITS

Sugar Soap cleans even the grimiest surface better and provides a better surface for painting, thus assuring a better finished result.

SUPPORTING EVIDENCE

Unlike most other preparations commonly used for this purpose, Sugar Soap does not contain silicates. Silicates are difficult to remove through normal rinsing, and if they remain on the surface will impair the adhesion of the paint, giving a poorer result. Sugar Soap also foams less than other preparations, making rinsing easier.

CREATIVE PLATFORM

This was drawn directly from the qualitative research.

> Remember Sugar Soap? It's the tried and true product preferred by two generations of professional decorators for the proper preparation of all surfaces before painting. They use it to shift nicotine stains and grease; it is an excellent heavy duty cleaner.
> It's better than other products out of the wife's cleaning cupboard because it's low-foaming, and does not contain silicates. Silicates impair paint adhesion.
> So, if you want a really professional paint job, Sugar Soap is the only product to use.

CREATIVE EXECUTION

To convey all of this product information, as well as the feeling of the brand personality, a 30-second commercial length was required.

The script stressed empathy with the target consumer in characterization, setting, language, and tone of voice. The essential message was summed up in the phrase 'The Professional Decorator's Secret' which was featured on the pack and a range of advertising-related display material.

Media Strategy and Plan

MEDIA CHOICE

Television was the obvious choice because of:

1. Creative considerations: impact, demonstration, tone of voice.
2. Audience coverage.
3. An area test could be easily organized.

4. Attractive new advertiser/seasonal discounts kept capital cost low.
5. Clout with the retail trade. It is the brand leader medium, known to generate retail off-take. There is no better sell-in tool, and it would offer new account possibilities. Even outside the test area, the fact that Manger's were on television would signal the seriousness of their intentions to the retail trade.

CHOICE OF TEST AREA

Three television areas offered the very economic 'limited expenditure contract' to new advertisers. Of these, Granada was not unsuitable in terms of Manger's general pattern of distribution and offered the smallest capital commitment for a test area of reasonable size.

BUDGET

Because of the imperative that the campaign be self-liquidating, the budget was set at £20 000. Under the limited expenditure contract this bought a campaign equivalent to a £500 000 spend nationally.

MEDIA TARGET GROUP

Males

RATE OF STRIKE

Three hundred and fifteen male television ratings were achieved over the five-week period 6 April to 10 May, 1981.

ROLL-OUT

A year later the campaign was extended to London, with an £88 000 budget during the period 1 April to 16 May. This delivered 305 male TVRs. From April 1 to 10 the campaign was reprised in Granada with a £12 000 budget, delivering 102 male TVRs.

COMPETITIVE ACTIVITY

As the creative strategy put it, anything 'in the wife's cleaning cupboard' competes with Sugar Soap, but none of these brands undertook any advertising on the particular 'paintwork cleaner' platform during the period under discussion.

Vee Vic did not advertise. Polycell advertised massively, spending £1 385 000 on its decorating products on TV and the national press in 1981 and £40 600 in the first quarter of 1982, according to MEAL. However, none of these advertisements mentioned Polywash.

After the early success of Sugar Soap, the only significant marketing response from either brand was an action they took in common: both changed the name of their product to Sugar Soap. Presumably they discovered the name had become an unprotected generic term; the Oxford Dictionary describes it, with double inaccuracy, as an 'abrasive compound for cleaning or removing paint'!

MEASUREMENT OF RESULTS

Measurements of results of the Manger's Sugar Soap relaunch are available from two sources: ex-factory sales for Sugar Soap in the advertising and non-advertising areas, and a specific retail audit of Sugar Soap conducted at the time of the first Granada TV test.

The advertising/marketing approach is holistic: the brand was sold into the trade on the promise of advertising, and the advertising could not have been effective without the increased distribution that effort achieved.

Nevertheless, because the television advertising was regional, it is possible to make a discrete assessment of that element.

TABLE 15.2:   SUGAR SOAP: EX–FACTORY SALES £ MSP

| | % change over same period previous year | | |
| | Granada | Rest of UK | London |
	%	%	%
Mar. 81 – Jan. 82 (11 mths)	493	35	
Feb. 82 – Sep. 82 (8 mths)	32	6	354

Sugar Soap advertising appeared for the first time on Granada Television in April and May 1981, following a one-month sell-in in March. Ex-factory shipments were segregrated for Granada and, for the 11-month period before the next advertising activity began sales were almost five times higher than in the same period in the previous year. (Table 15.2).

In the rest of the UK, where there was no advertising, sales rose by 35 per cent. Thus, it could be concluded that the television advertising multiplied by a factor of 14 the level of sales gained on the strength of the new packaging only.

Precisely a year later, in April and May 1982, the campaign was extended to London at the original media strike rate. In April, the Granada TV advertising was reprised, at one-third the original strike rate. Both media bursts were preceded by a two-month sell-in, in February and March. During the eight-month period February to September, ex-factory deliveries to the London TV area increased more than three and half times over the same period a year ago. In Granada there was a one-third increase over the peak level achieved in the same months the previous year. In the non-advertising areas, sales increased by 6 per cent.

TABLE 15.3:   SUGAR SOAP: CHANGES IN MSP

| | Index: Price per g | | |
	500 g Tub	1250 g kettle	Total*
Old price	100	–	100
March 1981	116	97	114
February 1982	120	119	120

*Adjusted for 9:1 tub to kettle sales ratio – as achieved since introduction of kettle.

At the time of the first Granada sell-in MSP of the standard 500 g Sugar Soap tub was increased by 16 per cent (Table 15.3). However, the new 1250 g kettle was introduced at a price which, gram for gram, was lower than the 500 g pack had offered previously. In the event the ratio of sales between tub and kettle has been about 9:1, so the overall price increase at MSP was about 14 per cent.

The price increase explains about 40 per cent of the extra revenue achieved in the non-advertised areas and the remainder has been put down to the re-packaging and the increased stimulation of the sales force.

At the time of the second advertising sell-in a year later, the MSP of both packs was increased by around 20 per cent. This explains all of the increase in the non-advertised areas since that date.

In all cases the recommended retail selling price increased by the same percentage and was generally passed on by retailers, so increased sales volume was achieved in the face of higher consumer prices.

Like many DIY products Sugar Soap sales are influenced by seasonal consumer habits, with natural peaks in the spring and autumn, as shown in Figure 15.1.

This chart, taking the *average* monthly sales achieved during 1980 as 100, and plotting each month of that year against that average, shows firstly the usual fluctuation in the pre-advertising year, 1980.

The first Granada TV test in 1981 shows the massive effect of the sell-in push in March – more than 20 times the sales achieved in that area in the previous year.

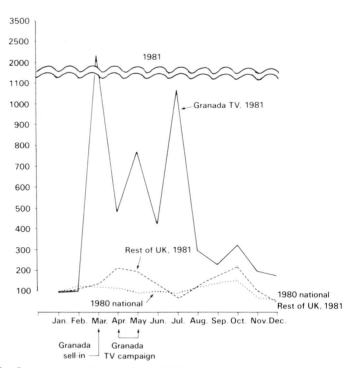

Figure 15.1 *Sugar soap, ex-factory sales £ MSP by month, 1981 over 1980. Index: 1980 average monthly sales = 100*

Sales continued to peak during and well after the advertising as retailers re-ordered, and remained well above year-ago levels throughout the rest of the year.

Sales in the rest of the UK, where there was no advertising, also benefited during the spring, rising to double year-ago levels, but returned to lower levels thereafter. The overall increase therefore, would appear to have been affected more by sell-in activity gaining better store presence, rather than stimulated by consumer demand.

Just prior to the 1982 advertising sell-in Sugar Soap was still selling at two or three times year-ago levels in Granada. The two-month sell-in in February–March, building on this

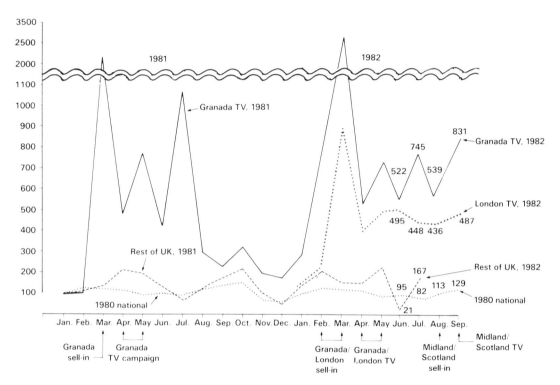

Figure 15.2   *Sugar Soap, ex-factory sales £MSP by month, 1981 and 1982 over 1980. Index: 1980 average monthly sales = 100*

strength, actually exceeded the highly successful result of the year before. (See Figure 15.2.) Following the April advertising – at one-third the original strike rate – the same general pattern began to emerge, with a fall-off followed by another smaller peak as re-orders came in. The increase in sales in the first six months, February–July, compared to the same period a year ago, was almost nine times higher than in the non-advertised areas. (Thereafter the campaign was extended to the Midlands and Scotland, so the comparison can no longer be made on the same base.)

The London sell-in and advertising at the original strike rate reflected the same pattern, registering more than 18 times the increase in sales observed in the non-advertised areas over the first six months, February–July.

Retail Audit

The company took retail audit information only to measure the initial Granada TV test. This provided ample verification that the vastly increased ex-factory sales in the Granada area were indeed selling through to the consumer in much larger volume than previously, and very rapidly.

The Granada sell-in started early in March 1981. The TV advertising extended from 6 April to 10 May. This research reported on the situation prevailing in the retail trade (paint and wallpaper shops, hardware/ironmongers, and DIY shops – including both multiples and independents) prior to 1 April (therefore including four weeks of sell-in activity) and just after 10 May, when the advertising ended.

Distribution in the Granada area had been independently estimated at 50 per cent of worthwhile outlets in a survey conducted by the sales force at the time of the sell-in. Largely it was confined to small independent shops; distribution in multiple outlets was negligible.

In the test market Sugar Soap achieved 69 per cent distribution overall and 81 per cent in the very important and hitherto largely neglected multiple sector. The then brand leader, Polywash, was stocked by only 27 per cent and 55 per cent, respectively, of these outlets. Vee Vic was hardly in evidence.

Good pack display was achieved as well, owing in large part to the presence of dump bins on the floor. Visible presence in the shop was four times that of Polywash.

At the conclusion of the sell-in operation, prior to the start of the advertising, the new packs of Sugar Soap were already selling through. New and old packs together were selling at the rate of 4.3 units per week overall, 7.3 in multiples. The prior rate of sale of the old pack is not known, but judging from ex-factory figures for the area at that time, could not have been more than 1.5 to 2.0 packs per week. So the greater in-store presence of the new pack presentation had probably doubled or trebled the previous rate of sale prior to the start of the advertising.

During the period of the advertising the number of units sold weekly almost trebled over that higher base to 12.2 units per week overall, and 16.0 units weekly in multiples. The marketing effort as a totality, therefore, is estimated to have increased retail off-take almost tenfold during the sell-in/advertising period and this also corresponds well with the increase in Granada ex-factory sales at that time (see Figure 15.1).

Of the 12.2 units of Sugar Soap sold weekly more than one quarter were the new 1250 g 'trade pack', with 225 per cent greater volume. In sheer volume Sugar Soap increased its average rate of retail sale by 343 per cent, and in sterling terms at RSP by 322 per cent during the five-week advertising period.

Retail shop off-take was doubtless assisted by a good presence in the shops of display material carrying an advertising-related message. Thirty per cent of all outlets, and 61 per cent of multiple outlets had Sugar Soap point-of-sale material of some kind on view. Forty-five per cent of multiples featured a dump-bin dipslay. Competitive in-store activity was negligible.

Retailers were in no doubt as to the contribution of the Sugar Soap advertising. The survey showed 83 per cent were aware of the advertising, 72 per cent had seen the commercial themselves, and, most gratifyingly from the advertiser's viewpoint, 66 per cent claimed that customers were asking for Sugar Soap by name. These impressive figures were much higher still in the more alert multiple sector of the trade, and according to the retail audit organization, are well above usual norms.

PAYOUT PERIOD

If the production of the television commercial itself is considered as an asset rather than an element of expenditure – indeed it is so carried on the company's books – then the payback period of the media expenditure was remarkably short.

By returning to the ex-factory sales, the period of time over which the media investment is recouped may be calculated by comparing the extra gross contribution gained from the additional turnover achieved in the advertised areas compared with the same period of the previous year.

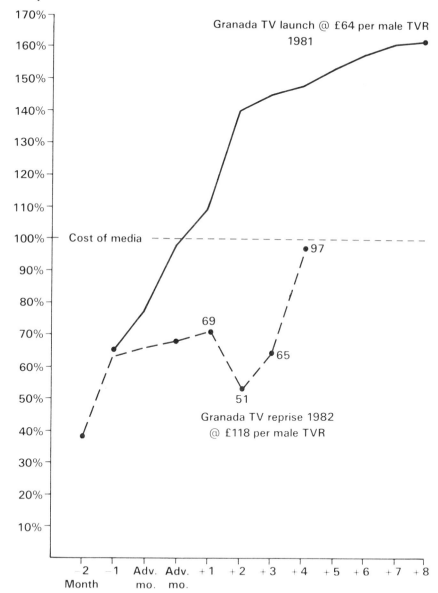

Figure 15.3 *Payout period, percentage of media cost repaid by gross contribution on additional turnover compared with the same month a year ago*

Naturally, the efficiency of the media buying greatly affects the rate of payout.

As shown in Figure 15.3, in the first Granada TV test, because of the highly attractive test discounts achieved, and the massive pre-advertising sell-in, the cost of the media spend had been totally earned by the time the final media bills came due for payment.

In the Granada reprise a year later, the TVR cost was 84 per cent higher; yet the investment had been virtually recovered four months after the advertising stopped.

The London TVR cost was four and one-half times that of the original Granada launch; 85 per cent had been recovered four months after the advertising ended (see Figure 15.4).

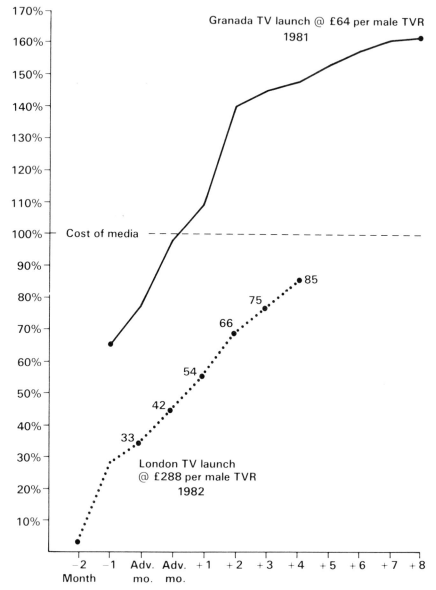

Figure 15.4   *Payout period, percentage of media cost repaid by gross contribution on additional turnover compared with the same month a year ago*

CONCLUSION

Success of the Campaign

Measured against any objective – the sales of the brand, the establishment of a mainline brand to two other products in its wake, the improvement of the company's position in the market-place – the relaunch of Sugar Soap was spectacularly successful.

It was a holistic marketing exercise, where the contribution of the advertising process was integral at every stage; nevertheless, the action of broadcasting the television commercial produced an immediate sales increase of well over 300 per cent whether measured in unit, volume, or sterling terms by the Granada test retail audit and a five-fold increase in ex-factory sales over an 11-month period by comparing advertising and non-advertising areas.

The early results of the lightweight reprise in the Granada area a year later and the simultaneous extension to London also augur well for the brand.

There's a final twist in the tale. With the success of the Granada test under his belt, Mike Dent obviously wanted to roll-out national advertising as soon as possible. However, the Grimshawe Group were unable to allocate the resources required. So Dent offered to buy out the company, and in December 1981 he did so. His timing was fortuitous. Within six months, Grimshawe Holdings had gone into liquidation.

In organizing the management buy-out Dent's main objective was not just to buy the business, but also to raise sufficient capital to fund the national television roll-out. Within a few months, this had begun in London. The Midlands and Scotland were added in the autumn of 1982. Sales forecasting is now based on the returns expected from the further deployment of the television advertising campaign, on the basis of these experiences.

The Way the Advertising Worked

The advertising process contributed crucially in two ways:

1. By identifying the central advertisable brand proposition: learn the trade decorator's secret of a professional painting job. Emotionally, the do-it-yourselfer admires the professional's skill and feels things are less likely to go wrong if he emulates the tradesman.
2. By communicating this proposition with great authority: while the reference to removal of nicotine stains and the 'no silicate' story gave a rational underpinning to a persuasive argument, the compelling element of the television presentation was undoubtedly the skilful evocation of the integrity and honesty of the product. As respondents said in the small group research: 'It's stood the test of time', and 'It probably costs no more than it has to'. The commercial was simple, straightforward, familiar and authentic – less an advertisement than a friendly bit of inside chat.

16

The Repositioning of Lucozade

BACKGROUND

While new product development work among marketeers often produces more excitement and effort, the successful repositioning of a well established brand is arguably a tougher job. For the company, financially it may be far more rewarding.

Lucozade is a glucose carbonated drink first made nearly 50 years ago. It is now marketed by Beecham Foods in the familiar dimpled 25 oz bottle with yellow cellophane wrap. The product is a highly concentrated source of energy, quickly assimilated into the bloodstream, it is easily digested, and its flavour, carbonation and relative sweetness make it easy to take in sickness.

This brand is a key source of profit to Beecham Foods and fluctuations in Lucozade volume and profit can radically affect the fortunes of the company.

THE PROBLEM

The period from 1974 to mid-1978 saw consistent volume decline. By mid-1978 it was clear that this was part of a long-term trend (Table 16.1). Leo Burnett and the Beecham brand group undertook a detailed analysis of all the possible causes of the situation. A brief review of the conclusions for each issue is made here.

TABLE 16.1: THE PROBLEM

Volume sales	Million doz.	% vs. last year
1974/5	3511	− 1.9
1975/6	3477	− 1.0
1976/7	3065	−11.8

Following four retail audit periods against Year Ago	
May/June	−17%
July/Aug	−16%
Sept/Oct	−22%
Nov/Dec	−15%

Illness

The brand history was steeped in illness/convalescence and so a close examination was made of the last ten years, on a monthly basis, of the relationship of volume sales to the levels of illness, as supplied by the Department of Health and Social Security.

The result of this analysis showed that there were fewer flu epidemics and a trend to lower illness levels generally – a healthier population. Peaks of illness and epidemics provided only 'cream' on the top of the volume sales trend. Levels of illness did not affect the fundamental shape and size of the trend.

Changing Consumer Attitudes

The housewife had been through four to five years of trauma in the high street: raging inflation and a shrinking purse. A new, more cautious housewife emerged from this period with a changing set of values which included an increasing degree of cynicism towards para-medical products. The effect of this trend alone on Lucozade was no more severe than for other products in similar fields. However, when taken in conjunction with the next factor of price, it was producing an effect.

Price

A careful examination was made comparing the reaction of volume sales to price movements over a ten year period. Until 1976 the rate of increase in Lucozade price had remained below the rise in the Retail Price Index. Since the beginning of 1976, Lucozade price increases had moved ahead of the Retail Price Index (Table 16.2). Lucozade was coming under severe scrutiny by the housewife in her new consciousness of price/value relationships.

TABLE 16.2:   LUCOZADE RECOMMENDED RETAIL PRICING
HISTORY (DEFLATED BY THE RPI TO 1970 PRICES)

Year	Prices in pence[a]
69/70	16.1
70/71	16.0
71/72	15.3
72/73	15.5
73/74	13.4
74/75	12.7
75/76	12.3
76/77	12.4
77/78	12.9
78/79 (forecast)	13.0

[a] Excluding bottle deposit.

Retail Distribution

Twenty per cent of Lucozade volume is sold through chemists and 80 per cent through grocers. However, Lucozade's grocery trading profile was not following the same pattern as other major food and drink brands. One would normally hope to see at least 40 per cent of volume coming from the dynamic and rapidly growing multiple sector. In Lucozade's case this was only 20 per cent, with the remaining grocery volume coming from symbol groups and independents.

Although clearly not the major cause for any volume decline, this was identified as a concerning situation.

Sales Force

Sales force attention is traditionally concentrated on areas of high volume and excitement and for the Beecham Foods sales force this was provided by an extensive range of canned and bottled soft drinks. Lucozade, on the other hand, although much more profitable to the company than soft drinks, sold very much lower volumes and generated very little excitement. The consequence of this was a lack of real sales force attention.

Advertising

There were two parts to this analysis: spend levels and copy.

The analysis of advertising spend showed all the hallmarks of a series of short-term actions being taken in order to achieve fiscal profit targets. In the short term, price had eased upwards, profit had eased upwards, advertising spend had declined – and the brand volume had declined.

The company had maintained short-term profit by pushing pricing while jeopardizing the future growth of the brand. Since 1973, real advertising weight had been reduced by nearly half (Table 16.3).

TABLE 16.3:   ADVERTISING WEIGHT AND VOLUME SALES (EX–FACTORY).
INDEX[a]: 1970 = 100

	Advertising	Volume sales
1973/4	129	123
1974/5	121	121
1975/6	96	120 (flu)
1976/7	70	105
1977/8	77	116 (flu)
1978/9	52	110

[a] Expressed as equivalent TVRs.

The copy analysis was equally revealing. For 12 years there had been a remarkable consistency in advertising strategy and execution. It showed slice-of-life situations promoting Lucozade as a unique source of liquid energy that helps the family when they are recovering from illness. In every execution, the emotional way of showing the family was through children.

The result of this was that while few brands in the marketplace could claim to have such a spontaneously strong and clear image, the brand was increasingly seen as being for sickness only, for kids only, for occasional use.

THE SOLUTION

It was clear, therefore, that the problem was centred on the brand being driven into a tighter and tighter funnel. To build volume for the brand it was likely that a fresh positioning strategy would be necessary.

Concepts were drawn up to cover a spectrum of options ranging from the existing convalescence positioning to unashamed in-health consumption (Figure 16.1).

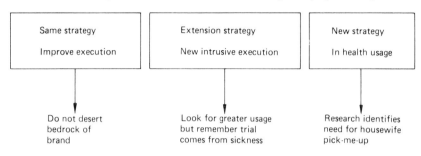

Figure 16.1

The results of a Usage and Attitude Study were analysed at this time, which helped to define the sample for the research which we were using to examine the strategy options.

More importantly, this Usage and Attitude Study revealed that only about 20 per cent of the volume of the brand was actually being used for straightforward convalescence and of the total volume only about 30 per cent was being used by children. A substantial volume of the product was being used in health and by adults (Table 16.4).

TABLE 16.4:   PROPORTION OF CONSUMPTION AND PURPOSE

User	% Housewives	% Volume	Purpose
Heavy	5	50	Refreshing drink
Medium	9	32	Pick-me-up. Minor sickness.
Light	46	18	In sickness

The strategy research showed that heavy and medium purchasers, who represented the larger proportion of volume sales, approved the dramatic imagery move to in-health projection, while the light users understandably remained loyal to the sickness usage.

In addition this research and further qualitative work identified a clear need for a housewife pick-me-up during the day. While many products were already used for this purpose – tea, coffee, fruit juice, squash, Mars Bar, alcohol, etc. – there were problems associated with each of the options and it was felt that none would give, with such convenience and authority, the refreshing energy boost that was associated with Lucozade.

Summary of the Need for a Repositioning

1. Lucozade is strongly positioned for child sickness.
2. Child sickness is a highly limiting position in itself.
3. Child sickness is declining.
4. Less child sickness means less adult usage.

5. 100 per cent child convalescence copy does not stimulate adult usage.
6. Growth will come primarily from finding ways to stimulate new uses within the family.
7. New family uses must be approached cautiously in order not to destroy the current franchise.
8. Mother pick-me-up is the best opportunity to grow the business while maintaining the strength of the existing franchise.

ADVERTISING STRATEGY

It was determined therefore to reposition the brand to the consumer as a unique source of energy in health as well as in sickness. The importance of sickness remained as it provided tactical sales, would still be the reason for gaining new trial and would provide an authoritative rationale for any in-health message. Additionally, a sickness positioning being the bedrock of the brand keeps out competition.

But the thrust of the communication was now to be an in-health message.

It was recognized that a fine balance was required for communication success: no change was to be made to the product and at this stage, none to the packaging either. The only change would be advertising positioning and style. It was to be a tonal change for the brand, promoting an extension of usage. To push the brand too close to soft drinks would destroy the subtle imagery of Lucozade for ever and yet a distinctive change from its previous positioning must be clearly evident to the consumer.

The new *advertising objective* was simply to turn the brand from an occasional purchase into a more regular purchase. This was the key to building volume and persuading the growing end of the grocery trade to give Lucozade the support a major brand should have.

The *competitive positioning* of Lucozade would be that it is a unique source of energy in health as well as in sickness.

The *targeting* of the new advertising was crucial in that initially it was chosen to influence the softer options. The advertising would be targeted at the current heavy and medium purchasers.

Either they already used the brand as the advertising would demonstrate, in which case it provided justification for them for still further usage. Or they were purchasing it for their children while not drinking it themselves. In this case, the advertising would persuade them to use the product themselves whilst it was in the home. Either way, the advertising was targeted to housewives for self-consumption.

The proposition for such a brand as Lucozade must stem from something tangible within the product and something that is understood and relevant to the housewife. We had already established the need for a housewife pick-me-up during the day and this qualitative research had also clearly shown that glucose and energy were seen as synonymous. The message, therefore, was that Lucozade helped the body regain its normal energy level.

New Creative Strategy

Advertising Objective: To turn Lucozade from an occasional purchase into a more regular purchase.

Product Positioning: Lucozade is a unique source of energy in health as well as sickness.

Target Audience:	Active women between the ages of 18 and 35 who care about the health and well-being of themselves and their children.
Proposition:	Lucozade helps the body regain its normal energy level.
Justification:	Refreshing Lucozade is glucose energy in the most natural form the body can use.
Tone:	Contemporary, active, helpful, dependable, optimistic.

CREATIVE DEVELOPMENT

Early on in the rough executional development of the new strategy there emerged an 'energy rate' idea which was felt to be so flexible and strong that it was agreed to execute this idea in various ways for communication research.

The basic idea was that we all have an energy rate: when we are active this rate oscillates vigorously; when we are tired, it is flat and depressed. This can be shown visually by an oscillating coloured line.

Four treatments of this idea were created and animatics were made and put into communication research.

The route we chose was made into the commercial shown on p. 207. The reasons we opted for this route were firstly, that the energy line was integrated into the action; it was in this context that it was best liked and understood. Secondly, it showed everyday situations to which the housewife could relate and it encouraged her to use the product frequently.

BUDGETS, MEDIA STRATEGY AND PLAN

It was accepted that one of the major causes of volume decline of the brand was the decline in advertising weight. The decision was therefore taken to halt the decline in advertising to sales ratio during the first 12 months after repositioning and then to reassess the situation. This by no means represented a return to the previously high levels of advertising but certainly represented reversal of a declining trend.

There had been a history of careful examination of media mix and deployment of funds over time. The results of this had shown that Lucozade is highly sensitive to the weight of TV advertising. Alternative media have not produced such an effect. In addition, past work had shown that continuous advertising at low strike rates was more profitable than any other deployment of funds.

While these issues were fully understood, it was recognized that the fresh positioning of the brand required the housewife to see Lucozade in a new light and therefore media planning had to play its part in creating a fresh boost for the brand.

Media Objectives

1. Create maximum awareness of new Lucozade usage opportunities as quickly as possible.
2. Maintain levels of awareness across the whole period.

Achievement of these objectives required a heavyweight burst pattern of TV at the start of the repositioning. The TV weight dropped to under half the initial burst weight later on in the plan, but was maintained over a longer period.

A women's press campaign began six months after the launch. This carried the traditional convalescence message to reinforce the roots of the brand, but in a media environment away from where we were concentrating the in-health advertising.

During the second half of the year posters were used to provide extra frequency of impact for the TV in-health message.

As the trade viewpoint was identified as a problem, a sales force and retail trade package was put together to tie-in with the new advertising:

   On-pack promotion
   Special 12 minute film for key account buyers
   Special sales force material explaining the rationale for the change

Isolating the Advertising Influence

Although judgementally little else happened after the relaunch to change sales other than a fresh advertising approach, unquestionably other factors do affect the market. The problem is how to disentangle the influence of advertising from all the other factors. In order to make this assessment, the decision was made to leave the old convalescence advertising in the Tyne Tees area and use Beecham's Area Marketing Test Evaluation System (AMTES) to gauge what success the new advertising produced over what may have happened in the marketplace.

RESULTS

The task of changing people's perspective about a brand whose benefits and usage pattern were so well recognized cannot be achieved overnight. It was known from the outset that advertising repositioning was only the beginning of this task: if it appeared to have some tangible success, then other elements to accelerate the change would be brought to bear - pack sizes, labelling, PR, promotions, etc.

Advertising Research

The finished commercials, prior to airing on television, were researched by Beecham Foods in a quantified manner producing good results in terms of:

—communicating energy replacement in health,
—understanding the wavy line,
—liking the commercial,
—projected imagery.

Consumer Sales

The acid test of the strategy is its effect on sales in the marketplace after the launch of the new advertising. In sharp contrast to the previous severe volume decline of the brand, volume sales increased by 13 per cent in the first year.

Lucozade Ups and Downs.

MAN: How often do you start out feeling full of get-up-and-go and then...

after you've been working hard, you start to slow down.

That's the time to sit down and have a glass of Lucozade. Lucozade's not just refreshing...

it provides glucose energy in the most natural form the body can use.

So, before you get up and get going again, have some Lucozade.

SINGERS: Lucozade refreshes you through the ups and downs of the day.

Isolating the Advertising Influence

It is unwise to attribute the sales increase entirely to the fresh advertising approach without further ado. Many things may influence sales.

The two principal scientific techniques that address this problem are market experimentation and econometric analysis. AMTES combines these two approaches in a computer model which utilizes the strength of both. The potential effects of many factors are removed by setting up an appropriately designed area test, an application of the experimental method of the natural sciences. The influences of the remaining factors that cannot be controlled in this way are measured and allowed for by AMTES in its calculation of the effect attributable to advertising. These measurements are derived from econometric analysis relating these factors to sales movements prior to the commencement of the area test.

The AMTES conclusion was that an 11 per cent volume sales increase was directly attributable to the change in advertising in the six months of the test. This should be compared with a volume sales increase of 21 per cent overall for the period of time. Clearly, nearly half of the sales increase observed was due to factors other than the change in advertising.

RELIABILITY OF THE AMTES RESULT

Because AMTES draws upon econometric analysis to arrive at its conclusions, it is subject to the caveats attendant upon the use of any statistical technique. Principally, the sales increase attributed to advertising is an estimate rather than an exact measurement. Other figures are possible, although of lower probability than the quoted estimate. AMTES provides a detailed analysis of the uncertainty attached to its calculations, which enables the user to assess the confidence that may be placed in them.

In this case, the analysis of the uncertainty associated with the best estimate of 11 per cent sales increase showed that the probability of a sales increase was 90 per cent. Put another way, there was a 90 per cent chance that the true sales change lay between the extremes of a 24 per cent sales increase and a 3 per cent sales decrease. Consequently, there was considerable confidence in the efficacy of the new advertising and it was introduced into Tyne Tees as well without further delay.

HOW AMTES WORKS

The objective of the econometric component of AMTES is to provide as good an estimate as possible of sales levels expected *if the area test had not been carried out*. Comparison of estimated with actual sales levels serves as the measure of the sales effect attributable to the test. In order to arrive at an estimate of expected sales levels, data for a period of time prior to the start of the test are analysed so as to explain sales movements in terms of market variables expected to influence sales. Actual values of these market variables during the test can then be used in the econometric model to produce the required sales estimates. The statistical quality of this model provides the basis on which the associated analysis of uncertainty is erected.

Operationally, fluctuations in the ratio of sales in the test area to those in the control area during the pretest period (March/April 1973 to May/June 1978 in this case) are related to similar ratios for the market variables. Subject to data availability, many market variables can be submitted to the AMTES programme, but not all will necessarily explain sales movements, e.g. some may not have changed much over the duration of the pretest period. AMTES uses a multiple linear regression procedure which examines all of the submitted market variables singly and in all combinations so as to choose automatically just that combination which best explains the observed sales ratio fluctuations, subject to the statistical quality of the chosen model being satisfactory.

For this AMTES analysis, all of the submitted variables were chosen for inclusion in the selected model. These were:

1. Lucozade sterling distribution.
2. Lucozade average retail price.
3. Lucozade advertising weight (in TVRs).
4. Sickness levels (new claims to sickness benefit).
5. Dummy variable to account for the change in the Nielsen retail audit universe in 1975.

These variables contributed nearly half of the observed sales increase, the remainder being attributed to the change in advertising platform (note that the effects of advertising *weight* are not included in the advertising effect of an 11 per cent sales increase).

Clearly, the fairly common practice of evaluating area tests in terms simply of sales changes on a year ago is totally inadequate and is likely to be highly misleading.

Usage and Attitude

Following the repositioning advertising, a regular Usage and Attitude Study went into the field. While no dramatic results were expected at an early stage, a number of movements in a positive direction were recorded:

(a) A significant increase in claiming to buy Lucozade 'nowadays'.
(b) A significant increase in strong likelihood of 'ever buyers' to repurchase.
(c) A significant increase in claims to purchase Lucozade for 'refreshment' reasons among frequent purchasers.
(d) A significant increase in the recall of Lucozade television advertising.

CONCLUSIONS

Old product development requires skilful balancing. The old consumer franchise is vital, the new consumer franchise is the future life blood of the brand. This case history demonstrates how advertising can play the key role in revitalizing an established brand of great importance which had been in severe volume decline. This is not just a case of one campaign being better than the previous one but the development of more productive, better quality, more relevant advertising, building sales to provide the funds for renewed investment in the brand, which in turn will stimulate future growth.

17

The Effect of Advertising on Sanatogen Multivitamins

INTRODUCTION

This chapter reviews the past sales performance of the Sanatogen Vitamin brand and the effect that advertising has had on its recent sales increases.

BACKGROUND

Sanatogen was originally a nerve tonic which Fisons Limited acquired in the thirties.

In 1963 the company launched a range of multivitamin products under the Sanatogen name with an aggressive advertising programme. Within two years Sanatogen Multivitamins had achieved market leadership.

The brand grew steadily until 1974 when factory sales, both in sterling and unit terms, slumped drastically (Table 17.1).

TABLE 17.1:   EX-FACTORY SALES, 1970 TO 1975

Indices	1970	1971	1972	1973	1974	1975
Sterling ('000)	100	103	117	153	124	127
Units (packs 000)	100	101	113	114	90	81

Consumer purchase data from Nielsen generally showed trends parallel to the ex-factory data. Differences were due to the fact that Nielsen does not audit Boots. Nielsen also indicated that the market outside Boots was sliding even more precipitously than was Sanatogen (Table 17.2).

TABLE 17.2:   NIELSEN UNITS, 1970 TO 1975

Indices	1970	1971	1972	1973	1974	1975
Market	100	96	100	100	90	85
Sanatogen	100	111	124	125	113	109

THE DIAGNOSIS

McCormick's were appointed advertising agents for Sanatogen and all the products of the Pharmaceutical Division of Fisons in 1975.

After extensive study of the available data and conducting consumer research, the following facts emerged:

1. Sanatogen as a brand name was seen as old fashioned and dated. It was respected for its traditional values, but a majority of people thought of it as a tonic – or, even more often, a tonic wine – not a vitamin range.
2. Usership of vitamins in general was low and declining and they were of low interest value amongst non-users.
3. Users saw vitamins as a quasi-medicinal product to correct a sub-par feeling, not as a means of safeguarding good health.
4. The market depended on Sanatogen for its leadership and promotion.
5. The vitamin manufacturers (including Sanatogen) believed vitamins were winter orientated, while those consumers who used vitamins took them all year round.

The overall marketing objectives were then set:

1. Arrest the brand's sales decline and rebuild its consumer franchise.
2. Expand the total market for vitamins while maintaining and growing Sanatogen's leadership of it.

BRAND OBJECTIVE ONE

The Media

This had previously been national press. It was changed to women's press, which provided:

1. A way to focus advertising spending on the people who research had identified not only as prime purchasers but also as major users.
2. Colour, to liven up the brand's grey, dated image.
3. A sympathetic reading environment.

The spend pattern was also modified to even out the previous bias towards the winter months, and therefore reflect consumer purchasing habits, as well as provide a more consistent spread of advertising messages.

The Message

Historically, Sanatogen had used a typically proprietary medicine advertising theme, promising to provide tired, middle-aged people with longer, healthier, more active lives. This appeared at odds with the attitudes of vitamin users and non-users alike, and, we believed, was contributing to the geriatric image of the product.

A new creative strategy was devised to:

1. Establish the use of vitamins as an aid to healthy living for normal people.

2. Present credible reasons for taking vitamins.
3. Present Sanatogen as an up-to-date product, totally attuned to today's lifestyle.
4. Establish the use of Sanatogen vitamins as an everyday habit as natural as brushing your teeth.

The creative technique used was to identify people whose photographs seemed to convey a feeling of health, well-being and quiet happiness to a cross-section of women.

These photographs formed 'The Sanatogen Smile' campaign. Body copy presented a reasoned, non-strident, very credible case for the daily use of vitamins as a kind of health insurance policy.

The Results

The recovery of the brand was quite rapid, and within 20 months it had returned to its 1970 level of unit sales (Table 17.3).

The decline of the total market had been arrested, whilst Sanatogen began to grow again (Table 17.4).

TABLE 17.3:   EX-FACTORY SALES, 1970 TO 1977

						'Sanatogen Smile'	
Indices	1970	1972	1973	1974	1975	1976	1977
Sterling (£'000)	100	117	153	124	127	158	197
Units (packs 000)	100	113	114	90	81	88	100

TABLE 17.4:   NIELSEN UNITS, 1970 TO 1977

						'Sanatogen Smile'	
Indices	1970	1972	1973	1974	1975	1976	1977
Market	100	100	100	90	85	78	78
Sanatogen	100	124	125	113	109	111	120

BRAND OBJECTIVE TWO

With the brand's ex-factory unit sales back to its previous position, the way was now clear to pursue Objective Two – to build the market and increase Sanatogen's sales and develop its market position with it. A price increase during 1977 provided the additional funds to do this.

The Media

Television offered the brand:

(a) A medium never used before by any adult multivitamin product, and
(b) The ability to mount an area test and monitor its effectiveness in producing sales.

Stills from Sanatogen Multivitamins television advertisement.

All through life, your body changes.

But sometimes it changes more quickly.

That's when there may be a chance of vitamin deficiency. And that's when Sanatogen Vitamins can help.

They contain essential vitamins and minerals, to help ensure good health.

 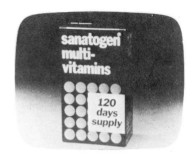

So, whether you're growing up, pregnant, or at retirement age, Sanatogen vitamins help you stay on top of the changes in your life.

Sanatogen Vitamins.
One a day, every day.

A test was implemented in London and Southern over the eight-week, September/October Nielsen period in 1978, at a national equivalent of £250 000.

The Message

Creatively, it would have been ideal to extend 'The Sanatogen Smile' story to television, but the strict regulations set by the IBA did not permit this. The IBA states that only three categories of people could be in need of vitamin supplementation: growing children, pregnant/lactating mothers, and the elderly. This apparent problem was turned into an opportunity. A script based on these categories was prepared, approved and produced with the only restriction that it could not be shown before 9 pm.

The Results

Nielsen sterling data were used to monitor the test (unit data by area were not available) (Table 17.5).

TABLE 17.5:   NIELSEN UNITS, 1977 VS. 1978

Area	Consumer sales Sept/Oct 1978 vs. 1977	Brand shares % 1977	1978
TV test area (London & Southern)			
Total market	+38%	100	100
Sanatogen	+70%	35	43
Control area (remainder UK)			
Total market	+16%	100	100
Sanatogen	+16%	37	37

This indication that television, overlaid on the Sanatogen Smile campaign in women's press, could produce up to a fifty per cent increase in consumer purchases of Sanatogen (and pull the market up with it) was immensely encouraging, since any increase of this magnitude, if sustained for only four months, would generate enough incremental gross profit to recover the cost of the incremental advertising.

To confirm the indications, test activity was extended to a larger area for the four-month period January to April 1979. Spending was again at a national equivalent of £250 000.

Nielsen sterling data were again used as a measurement device (Table 17.6).

TABLE 17.6:   NIELSEN UNITS, 1978 VS. 1979

Area	Consumer sales Jan/April 1979 vs. 1978	Brand shares % 1978	1979
TV test area (London, Southern, ATV & Harlech)			
Total market	+31%	100	100
Sanatogen	+66%	33	42
Control area (remainder UK)			
Total market	+15%	100	100
Sanatogen	+13%	38	37

With incremental sales in excess of 50 per cent, we confirmed that, for a four-month period, the commerical viability of television and women's press was proven. Extra funds were therefore requested and provided by Fisons to permit the use of TV advertising nationally, in late 1979.

At the end of 1979, the Sanatogen Multivitamin position was as shown in Tables 17.7 to 17.9.

TABLE 17.7:   EX-FACTORY SALES, 1970 TO 1979

			'Sanatogen Smile'		Television and 'Sanatogen Smile'	
Indices	1970	1974	1976	1977	1978	1979
Sterling (£'000)	100	124	158	197	286	429
Units (packs 000)	100	90	88	100	141	201

TABLE 17.8:   CONSUMER PURCHASES (NIELSEN UNITS)

Indices	1970	1974	1977	1978	1979
Total market	100	90	78	96	100
Sanatogen	100	113	120	150	186

TABLE 17.9:   BRAND SHARE (NIELSEN STERLING)

Brand	1970	1974	1977	1978	1979
Sanatogen	29	34	36	38	42
Haliborange	28	24	19	20	18
Superplenamins	9	9	7	5	5
Vykmin	8	10	11	11	11
All others	26	23	27	26	24
Total	100	100	100	100	100

Nielsen does not audit Boots and therefore cannot measure sales of that company's own brands of vitamins, which have always led the market in penetration (but probably not in value). However, the Sanatogen advertising campaign has helped Sanatogen narrow Boots' lead significantly, as TGI indicates (Table 17.10).

TABLE 17.10:   TGI UNITS

Brand usage	1976	1977	1978	1979
Boots	27.5	30.1	27.2	26.8
Sanatogen	16.6	18.1	20.0	21.6

ADVERTISING SPEND

Whilst the advertising spend has grown substantially, the A/S ratio has declined significantly (Table 17.11).

TABLE 17.11:   ADVERTISING SPEND

£'000	1972	1974	1977	1978	1979
Index	100	131	175	280	313
A/S Ratio	29	36	30	33	25

CONSUMER USERSHIP

In addition to improving Sanatogen's sales, share and profitability, the advertising campaign (Sanatogen spends over 60 per cent of all advertising on vitamins) appears to be making significant changes in consumer usage of vitamins.

As noted previously, 1974–75 vitamin usership was in decline, Sanatogen's penetration was slowly being eroded, and its profile was skewed to the older consumer than the market as a whole.

TGI data now show:

(i) a reversal in total usership and an increase in Sanatogen's penetration (Table 17.12), and
(ii) its age profile becoming younger (Table 17.13).

TABLE 17.12:   TGI DATA

Usership/Penetration (%)	1971	1975	1977	1978	1979
Total usership	21.9	18.6	16.4	20.3	20.7
Sanatogen penetration	3.5	3.3	3.0	4.1	4.5

TABLE 17.13:   TGI DATA

Age profiles	1971		1975		1977		1978		1979	
	T	S	T	2S	T	S	T	S	T	S
15–34	31.5	23.8	33.8	27.8	34.1	30.7	35.7	31.0	38.4	35.8
35–44	16.9	17.7	17.2	18.0	16.7	14.9	16.5	17.5	15.5	16.3
45+	51.6	58.4	48.9	54.3	49.2	54.5	47.7	51.5	46.3	47.9

Key: T = total market; S = Sanatogen. All figures are percentages.

CONCLUSION

The evidence presented shows how the effective use of advertising has improved the sales performance of Sanatogen Multivitamins over the two two-year periods set (see Figures 17.1 and 17.2).

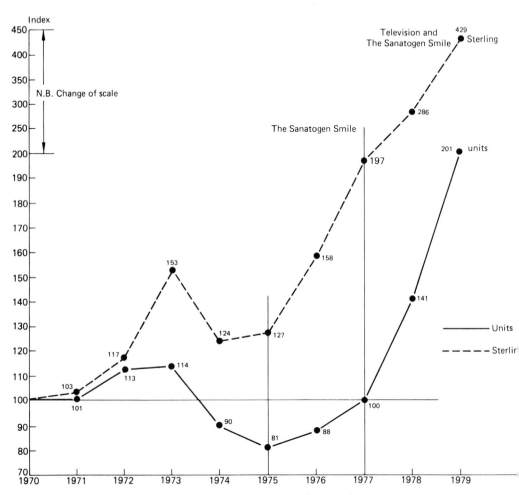

Figure 17.1   *Sanatogen ex-factory sales*

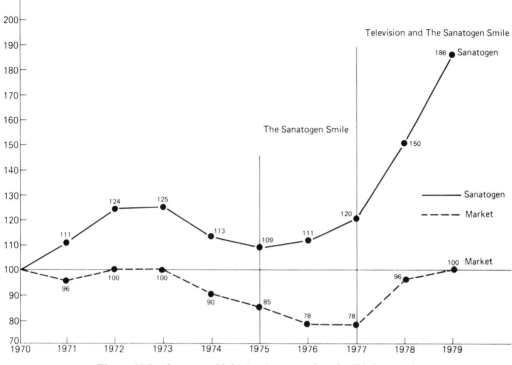

Figure 17.2 *Sanatogen Multivitamins vs. total market (Nielsen units)*

18

Swan Vesta Matches

BUSINESS BACKGROUND

In 1975, the situation facing Bryant & May in the UK match market was a less than encouraging one. The market had been steadily declining for 15 years, in which time it had lost a quarter of its volume. Bryant & May was the leading manufacturer with about half of the £43m market. Its volume, however, had declined faster than the market despite an annual expenditure on advertising of £250 000. Bryant & May was losing share to cheaper, imported matches which sold in multiwraps and undercut its trade price by as much as 20 per cent.

The following case history illustrates how the company arrested this decline by identifying the markets in which it was operating more accurately and by promoting more effectively against its existing strengths.

Matches compete in the lights market against various forms of mechanical lighter. 'Lights' are match marketing terminology for acts of ignition and in 1975 the lights market constituted 224 billion lights – of which 40 per cent were matches. This match share had fallen in volume terms by 27 per cent since 1960, in spite of an increase in *total* lights – an expansion which was more than absorbed by lighter sales, and, in particular, by sales of disposable lighters.

The lights market comprises lights used for smoking (70 per cent of all lights) and those used for domestic purposes.

In the smoking market, the company's main competitors – lighters – had been heavily advertised over the previous decade not only as a means of obtaining a light, but also as an object which signalled social distinction. Matches were increasingly seen as the poor man's alternative.

MARKETING AND ADVERTISING OBJECTIVES

The company identified as its main objective the need to reverse the trend whereby matches were losing share of the lights market. This would be accomplished by creating a consumer brand franchise for match brands in order to develop sales volume profitably.

The first step was clearly to establish the perceived strengths and weaknesses of the product in the consumer's mind.

Qualitative attitude research showed matches to have considerable latent appeal. They were seen as a natural, readily available commodity; a traditional part of our way of life; a

220

completely reliable source of a light. Lighters were seen as expensive, easy to lose, and, most importantly to smokers, liable to break down or run out of fuel or flint.

Distinctions between brands of matches were minimal. Only Swan Vesta was seriously seen as a branded product worth asking for by name.

An NOP survey into the usage of matches for smoking showed that nearly one third of smokers (31 per cent) alternated between matches and lighters, seeing each as more appropriate on different occasions. Qualitative research expanded upon this information, showing that it would be harder to persuade the 44 per cent of smokers who used only a lighter to use matches than it would to persuade those who already used both to use more matches.

On the basis of this information Bryant & May constructed its strategy on the smoking market. It was decided to put the main thrust of the promotional support behind the one national brand – Swan. The qualities latent in the brand were the essential qualities which made the case for matches against lighters. Swan matches were reliable because they were a traditional quality match, well made and well packed. This was the focus of the attack on lighters: 'The unreliable light'.

But this was not a claim which offered much promise at a rational level, as it was battling against a lot of carefully constructed unconscious associations for lighters, built up by advertising over a considerable period.

Lighters were 'socially superior'.

SWAN CAMPAIGN 1976-1979: CREATIVE STRATEGIES AND EXECUTIONS

On being appointed in mid-1975, the agency, with the company's help, formulated a creative strategy for Swan which homed in on the chief virtue of matches – their reliability – and claimed it both for Swan and for the Swan user. The strategy adhered to over this four year campaign from 1976 to 1979 is reproduced below:

Advertising Strategy

The problem the advertising should address: Matches are seen as socially inferior to lighters. Smokers need to be reassured that Swan is acceptable in any company.

The people the advertising should reach: All smokers who use matches.

What the advertising should aim to achieve: To position Swan as the match that one can use anywhere.

What the advertising should say: Swan is a really reliable match, so you can depend on Swan not to let you down.

Tone of voice in advertisement: Will complement the brand image by being masculine, contented and relaxed.

The advertising for Swan took on the lighter one-upmanship instilled through past advertising for lighters by depicting social occasions of offering a light for smoking, where the lighter lost its superficial glamour by failing to produce a light, and where the Swan user took over the situation.

The advertising was constructed to bring out the qualities discovered from research to be associated both with the Swan user – the 'strong, silent type' – and with the product itself, i.e. *reliability*.

Cowboy.

Prisoner of War.

Bunker.

Husband.

K6.

"It's nice to know there's something you can rely on—Swan."

Stills from Swan Vesta television advertisements 1976–78.

The theme of the campaign, showing the product in its social role, and briefly demonstrating the comparison with other lights, demanded television.

In addition, the medium was needed for its ability to deliver modernity and urgency – necessary for what is essentially a low-interest product with an old-fashioned, downmarket image. The credibility of a highly visible TV campaign was required.

Five situations were used to create 30 second commercials with the common theme: *'It's nice to know there's something you can rely on – Swan'*.

In each case, the 'Swan man' user is dependable and mature and in complete control of the situation in which he finds himself. He uses Swan with quiet confidence when more flashy individuals with mechanical lighters fail to produce a light.

MEDIA STRATEGY AND PLANS

The prime marketing objective of the Swan Vesta campaign was to stem the flow of light sales from matches to lighters, and, more specifically, to halt the decline in Swan Vesta sales. This would be accomplished through improving feeling towards the brand amongst the target audience by building positive attitudes in the dimensions of reliability, quality and suitability for use anywhere.

A regular pattern of advertising was, therefore, felt to be the most important consideration. Awareness of Swan Vesta as shown by NOP data (see Table 18.1) was already very high, and the secondary objective was maintaining this high level.

The media strategy and planning was biased towards male smokers, who made up a high proportion of the 'sometimes use matches' smokers. The committed Swan man was traditionally very loyal so the main purpose of the commercials was to reassure occasional users that Swan was worth buying more often.

Research and judgement backed the feeling that young smokers under 25 years were very fickle in their lighting habits and that people tended to mature into Swan usage. Thus, in age terms the media planning bias was to mature, stable individuals under 45, as it was felt to be extremely difficult to change the associated smoking habits of older regular smokers.

Post analysis of the results of the first series of television bursts indicated the optimum pattern of advertising to be 400–450 TVRs over four weeks followed by an eight-week gap.

Television advertising commenced in April 1976 with a four-week national burst followed by further bursts in June/July and August/September 1976. This pattern of advertising was continued up until March 1979 as funds allowed.

Although the initial objective had been to advertise nationally at the optimum TVR level, insufficient funds made it necessary to drop regions from the schedule for some of the bursts. This was judged preferable to continuing to advertise nationally at a less effective weight.

CAMPAIGN EVALUATION

In the three financial years 1976–78, Bryant & May spent a total of £1 118 006 on regular Swan advertising. Clearly, at this level of commitment it is essential to be assured that the expenditure is productive.

A statistical project to evaluate the effects of Swan advertising on actual sales – rather

TABLE 18.1:   SPONTANEOUS AWARENESS/PROMPTED AWARENESS OF SWAN VESTA

	Jul 75	Oct 75	Jan 76	Mar 76	Oct 76	Mar 77	Mar 78	Oct 78	Oct 78[a]
Total	75/96	69/96	65/94	73/96	72/93	72/92	75/95	77/98	80/100
Scotland	86/98	75/97	69/96	77/97	72/96	70/89	76/92	83/97	82/100
North	75/95	67/95	65/96	74/97	74/92	78/95	79/96	76/98	82/100
Mid/W.W/E. Ang	76/97	69/96	65/93	72/97	75/95	70/92	75/95	78/97	82/100
London	75/97	68/96	63/91	68/92	64/93	67/90	68/94	76/99	79/99
S/S. West	65/96	70/95	64/94	73/95	71/92	71/92	76/96	74/98	79/99

NOP Match Survey – all adults.
[a] All smokers.

than merely on image and awareness – was embarked upon. The project examined the differences made by varying weights of advertising by area on an annual financial year basis for the three years 1976, 1977 and 1978, when a relatively stable pattern of regular Swan advertising was adhered to.

Due to budget cuts it was not possible to run national advertising over this three-year period. The result was regional variations in the weight of advertising. It was aimed to hold at least one area as a control with a regular pattern of advertising; this area was Yorkshire. The areas with the next highest weights of advertising were, in descending order: London, Tyne Tees, Lancashire and Midlands (Table 18.2).

TABLE 18.2:   TV RATING POINTS FOR SWAN VESTA

Adult TVR	1976	1977	1978	Total
London	1077	1215	1554	3846
Southern	1016	0	769	1785
Harlech	979	0	0	979
Midland	1031	1009	432	2472
Lancs	1090	1088	511	2689
Yorks	1074	3042	1503	5619
Tyne Tees	1074	1745	427	3246
Scotland	1017	1219	0	2236

Over this three-year period all other marketing activity was constant, with no real peaks of promotional activity in any areas or at any special time. There were also no major competitive launches in the smoking match area. The launch of Winners occurred in 1979.

The evaluation of regional advertising effects on Swan sales at different exposure weights was then calculated. The areas were listed in order of the total TV rating points achieved over this three-year period and compared with the Nielsen regional Swan volume sales increase over the same period (Table 18.3).

TABLE 18.3:   EFFECT OF TV ADVERTISING ON SWAN VESTA SALES VOLUME, 1976–78

	Adult TVR	Volume index
Yorks	5619	117
London	3846	113
Tyne Tees	3246	112
Lancs	2689	110
Midland	2472	111
Scotland	2236	98
Southern	1785	108
Harlech	979	101

Volume index = Nielsen Match Swan volume, 1978 indexed on 1976.
N.B. Anglia is not shown owing to non-availability of Nielsen data for the early part of the period 1976–78.

The result was an extremely positive correlation between the amount of sales increase and the advertising weight per area (Figure 18.1).

The only aberration was Scotland, which had a medium weight of advertising and Swan sales did not increase. This can be explained by the fact that Bluebell – 'the only Scottish match' – was advertised and strongly promoted during this period.

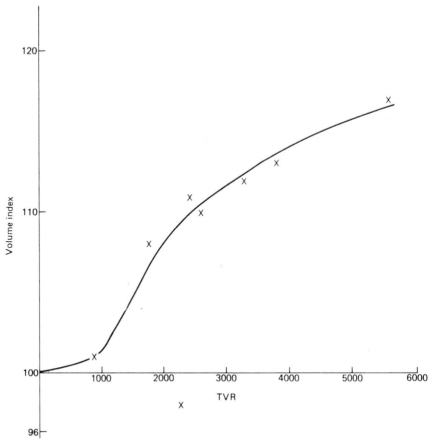

Figure 18.1   *Relationship between change in Swan Vesta volume and weight of TV advertising, 1976 to 1978*

Yorkshire, the area with the highest TVR total – 5619 – achieved a sales increase of 17 per cent while Harlech, with the lowest level at 979 TVRs, experienced only a 1 per cent gain. Each area, apart from Scotland, was correlated well in descending order.

It is not only these increases in the sales of Swan Vesta which demonstrate the effectiveness of the campaign 1976-78. Over this period, against a history of decline, matches consistently increased their share of smoking lights at the expense of all other lights (Table 18.4).

TABLE 18.4:   THE SMOKING LIGHTS MARKET, 1975–78

	Smoking lights 000m	Matches 000m	Matches index	% share	Lighters 000m	Lighters index	% share	Disposable lighters 000m	% share
1975	156.2	62.8	100	40.2	93.4	100	59.8		
1976	154.1	63.6	101	41.2	86.0	92	55.8	4.5	2.9
1977	149.2	65.7	105	44.0	77.0	82	51.6	6.5	4.4
1978	147.8	66.3	106	44.9	72.3	77	48.9	9.2	6.2

Source: Bryant & May.

CONCLUSION

The data presented above are strong evidence for a relationship between advertising and sales response and for the effectiveness of the Swan Vesta campaign 1976-78 as the cornerstone of the marketing policy for the brand.

Marketing rarely has the opportunity of working in perfect conditions; it is not a science. It is in essence the art of managing limited resources in an imperfect, real world. The reason for claiming that the strategy adopted since 1976 is a proven success is that Bryant & May has addressed its real problems – a shrinking market and a declining share of smoking lights – and has reversed both these trends. Its marketing strategy is established and on course, and the foundations are secured for further development.

19

How Advertising on Milk Bottles Increased Consumption of Kellogg's Corn Flakes

INTRODUCTION

The leading brand of breakfast cereal, Kellogg's Corn Flakes, has a 20 per cent share of the ready-to-eat (RTE) cereal market. It has been advertised mainly and consistently on television, a medium that has proved its worth in this market. The effectiveness of the Kellogg's Corn Flakes television campaign that began in 1978-79 – and continues still in 1982 – in adding value to the brand, was demonstrated in a paper awarded a commendation in the 1980 Advertising Effectiveness Awards Scheme. The TV advertising case history is not, therefore, repeated here.

Rather, the purpose of this paper is to prove the effectiveness of advertising for Kellogg's Corn Flakes in a new and minor medium: printed milk bottles. This novel medium started up in 1981, and Kellogg's Corn Flakes was the second brand to use it, spending just £58 000.

For comparison, expenditure on television airtime for Kellogg's Corn Flakes in 1981 was £2.5 million. Yet, for all that the relative levels of expenditure were so vastly different, Kellogg's and J. Walter Thompson were as intent on verifying the effectiveness of their milk bottle advertising as on continuing to monitor the success of the television campaign.

The evaluation technique used was a classically simple one: a test sample compared with a control, with a before and after comparison. What distinguished this particular analysis was, first, that using continuous panel data made it possible to detect the changes in behaviour through time which were crucial to determining how the advertising had altered consumption; and second, that being able to separate those homes exposed to the advertising from the unexposed, made it possible to measure the effect of a £58 000 campaign which ran in the shadow of a contemporaneous market expenditure of several £ millions on television.

That we were able to pick out an effect at all was unusual; that we were able to measure it with the degree of accuracy achieved is remarkable.

THE MEDIUM

Milk bottles printed with an advertising message were initially distributed through Unigate dairies who deliver daily to three million homes, i.e. to 15 per cent of homes in the country.

Penetration is substantially higher in the London and Southern TV regions, where Unigate dairies deliver to one home in three. The distribution does not reach Scotland or the northern counties of England.

A milk bottle has an average 'life' of 28 trips. Allowing for collection and cleaning between trips, three-quarters of the deliveries of one print run will have been achieved within three months, with a small and declining number of bottles continuing to circulate for up to three months more.

Thus a print run of one million bottles will reach three million doorsteps on average nine times each, at least six of these deliveries being within the first three months. Larger households who drink above-average quantities of milk will receive the printed bottles correspondingly more often.

The advertisement for Kellogg's Corn Flakes was printed on one million Unigate bottles, which began to go into circulation in mid-August 1981 and were at their maximum distribution level between mid-September and December of that year.

ADVERTISING STRATEGY

The television advertising had twin objectives: to remind consumers of the brand's inherent enjoyability (its crisp, refreshing taste and 'sunshine breakfast' qualities) and to draw their attention to the presence of vitamins and iron in it, as evidence of its nutritional value.

The milk bottle advertisement was assigned a more specific task. The obvious link between the product and milk gave us the opportunity to try directly to stimulate extra *consumption* of a bowl of the cereal by calling up memories of the highly pleasurable sensation of crunching crisp flakes in cool milk. If the stimulus led to the pouring out of a bowlful there and then, whatever the time of day, then this would be as close to real direct response advertising as it is possible to get.

Of course, this strategy was only made possible by the fact that four homes in ten have Kellogg's Corn Flakes in the larder at any one point in time, and that most homes have at least one Kellogg cereal product in stock. We recognized, though, that there might well be a generic effect, that is, that we might stimulate consumption of other cereals as well as Kellogg's Corn Flakes.

For that reason, the milk bottle advertisement - in effect, a mini poster - was strongly branded. It had to be kept very simple, yet it had to communicate brand values as well as say 'eat some now'. In the end, we reduced it to four essential elements:

— the brand name
— the distinctive branding motif of the cockerel
— the strong colours that also identify Kellogg's Corn Flakes advertising and pack
— the words: 'the sunshine taste - anytime of day!'

MEASURING THE EFFECTS

To examine what happened to *consumption* (i.e. numbers of helpings eaten) would have required a special ad hoc research study at a cost quite out of proportion to the media expenditure. Accordingly, it was decided to look at consumer *purchasing* behaviour, using AGB's Television Consumer Audit panel in the London and Southern regions.

Analysis was based on a sample of 1442 homes who were on the panel throughout the 32 weeks to December 1981. The data were divided into two 16-week periods, the first covering the four months immediately before the milk bottle advertising began (26 April to 15 August), the second covering the four months in which the one million bottles were in full distribution (16 August to 5 December).

The sample was similarly divided into two groups: a 'test' group of 530 homes (37 per cent of the sample) to whom milk was delivered by a Unigate dairy, and who were therefore able to see the milk bottle advertisements; and the 'control' group of 912 homes (63 per cent) whose milk was delivered by a non-Unigate dairy or who did not have milk delivered.

The differences between the demographic profiles of these two samples are small, except that the Unigate homes were rather more likely to be of ABC1 socio-economic class and to be households with children and therefore more mouths to feed. Consequently, their rate of purchase of ready-to-eat cereals was slightly higher than that of the non-Unigate homes.

In the analysis that follows, we look at 'before' and 'after' patterns of purchasing behaviour in the Unigate homes, compared with the control sample, to determine the effects of the milk bottle campaign on the cereal buying and, by inference, on the cereal consumption of those homes exposed to the advertising.

MARKET CIRCUMSTANCES

Three factors have to be borne in mind in assessing the findings. Firstly, there is a seasonal factor. The ready-to-eat cereal market declines slightly between summer and autumn (Table 19.1).

TABLE 19.1:   SEASONAL VARIATION IN SALES

Ready-to-eat consumer purchases (million kg)	Period 1 26 Apr.–15 Aug.	Period 2 16 Aug.–5 Dec.	Change
GB	67.1	66.2	–0.9
London and South	26.6	25.7	–0.9

Source: AGB's Television Consumer Audit.

In addition, there is a seasonal swing from those brands eaten almost exclusively in cold milk (like Corn Flakes) to those more suited to consumption in hot milk (such as Weetabix). Secondly, Kellogg's Corn Flakes has a below-average share of market in London and

TABLE 19.2:   BRAND SHARES (VOLUME)

	Period 1 26 Apr.–15 Aug. %	Period 2 16 Aug.–5 Dec. %	Change
GB – Kellogg's Corn Flakes	21.7	20.6	–1.1
– Own Label Corn Flakes	7.9	7.7	–0.2
– Weetabix	12.4	13.4	+1.0
Lon/Sth – Kellogg's Corn Flakes	15.8	14.7	–1.1
– Own Label Corn Flakes	9.8	9.5	–0.3
– Weetabix	9.2	10.6	+1.4

Source: AGB's Television Consumer Audit.

South, as Table 19.2 shows. This is in part due to the greater prevalence of supermarkets' own label corn flakes in the south-east of the country.

And thirdly, there was a good deal of other advertising activity for cereals going on, apart from the subsidiary milk bottle campaign under review. The ready-to-eat market in total spent over £5 million on television during the time our milk bottles were in circulation.

WHAT HAPPENED?

Behind the advertising strategy lay the hypothesis that we would stimulate additional cereal consumption, mainly of Kellogg's Corn Flakes but possibly also of other brands, which would show up as an increased rate of purchase, largely but not exclusively of Kellogg's Corn Flakes. In other words, we expected to see an increase in the *frequency* and *volume* of purchase rather than in the *numbers* of purchasers, and a greater volume of sales for Kellogg's Corn Flakes than would otherwise have been the case.

This was precisely what we observed in the panel data (Table 19.3): penetration followed the seasonal trend, but there was a rise in frequency of purchase of Kellogg's Corn Flakes in Unigate homes plus a substantial contra-seasonal increase in volume purchased. Rate of purchase (kilograms per buyer) went up 10 per cent, whereas it fell by 5 per cent in the control sample.

TABLE 19.3:   PURCHASING

	Non-Unigate homes (Control: N = 912)			Unigate homes (Test: N = 530)		
	Period 1	Period 2	Change	Period 1	Period 2	Change
Penetration (% homes buying)						
Any RTE	83.9	84.4	+0.5	87.1	87.1	—
Kellogg's Corn Flakes	37.5	33.4	−4.1	32.6	29.0	−3.6
Purchase frequency (purchase weeks per buyer)						
All RTE	6.4	6.3	−0.1	6.2	6.0	−0.2
Kellogg's Corn Flakes	3.2	3.0	−0.2	2.9	3.1	+0.2
Volume purchased (kilograms per buyer)						
All RTE	4.05	3.86	−5%	3.97	4.01	+1%
Kellogg's Corn Flakes	1.60	1.51	−5%	1.35	1.49	+10%

Source: AGB's Television Consumer Audit.

These figures also show an increase in sales of all ready-to-eat cereals. So there did seem to be a generic effect. But had we increased *consumption* of other cereals, or was it just that other cereals were picking up some of the repurchase after increased consumption of Kellogg's Corn Flakes?

It is the latter explanation that is supported by the evidence. The increased rate of purchase was limited solely to those homes who bought Kellogg's Corn Flakes. Where it was not stocked, the advertising had no effect (Table 19.4).

The inescapable implication is that the milk bottle advertisement did stimulate additional consumption, but only in homes which bought Kellogg's Corn Flakes (who can be

TABLE 19.4:   RATE OF PURCHASE

Volume purchased (kg/home – 16 weeks)	Non-Unigate homes			Unigate homes		
	Period 1	Period 2	Change	Period 1	Period 2	Change
Homes buying Kellogg's Corn Flakes						
Kellogg's Corn Flakes	1.60	1.51	− 5%	1.35	1.49	+ 10%
Other	3.23	3.14	− 3%	3.45	3.65	+ 6%
Total RTE	4.82	4.66	− 3%	4.80	5.14	+ 7%
Homes buying other RTE, not Kellogg's Corn Flakes						
Kellogg's Corn Flakes	–	–	–	–	–	–
Other	3.42	3.35	− 2%	3.47	3.45	− 1%
Total RTE	3.42	3.35	− 2%	3.47	3.45	− 1%

Source: AGB's Television Consumer Audit.

seen, incidentally, to be heavier consumers of cereal) and therefore that it was Corn Flakes that was being eaten in the extra bowlfuls.

As we had expected, though, not all this extra consumption was being converted into repurchase of the same brand. When shoppers bought again to restock their larders, they chose from their normal repertoire of brands. Kellogg's Corn Flakes got the lion's share, being picked for 42 per cent of the repurchases made by Corn Flakes buyers to replace the additional amount of cereal eaten (Table 19.5). The rest was shared between the other brands on the market, tending to go slightly more than pro rata to those brands on a rising sales trend due either to seasonal movement or to advertising effects (such as Kellogg's Special K which had recently started a new advertising campaign).

TABLE 19.5:   ESTIMATED SHARES OF
INCREASED PURCHASES IN KELLOGG'S
CORN FLAKES HOMES

Brand	%
Kellogg's Corn Flakes	42
Kellogg's Special K	7
Weetabix	7
Own Label Corn Flakes	5
All other brands	39
Total	100

Source: AGB'S Television Consumer Audit.

WAS IT COST EFFECTIVE?

The milk bottle advertising had clearly increased consumption and repurchase of Kellogg's Corn Flakes. It had also had something of a generic effect on purchases by Corn Flakes buyers. A manufacturer like Kellogg's with a large share of market can afford a generic effect that benefits other brands (many of them his own) as well, but the real question still was: had the advertising profitably helped sales of Kellogg's Corn Flakes specifically?

The data showed that Kellogg's Corn Flakes was the principal beneficiary: its sales to Unigate homes were no less than 17 per cent higher than they would have been without the milk bottle advertising (Table 19.6).

That the *brand* effect was much greater than the generic effect was easily demonstrated by the performance of Own Label Corn Flakes, which might have been expected to benefit more than other cereals from the advertising. But they did not. The generic effect was of a very secondary order compared to the brand effect.

TABLE 19.6:   SALES VOLUME CHANGE, PERIOD 1 – PERIOD 2
(Index, P1 = 100)

	Expected in P2 (Control)	Observed in P2 (Test)	Increase %
Kellogg's Corn Flakes	84	98	+17
Own Label Corn Flakes	93	97	+4
Other RTE	99	102	+3
Total RTE	96	101	+5

Assuming that purchase behaviour through the three million homes (15 per cent) served by Unigate dairies followed the pattern observed in the test panel, then the effect of the milk bottle campaign was to add 2.5 per cent to national sales volume of Kellogg's Corn Flakes during the four months August–December $(0.17 \times 0.15 = 0.026)$.

Even without allowing for the greater in-home availability of the brand outside the London and Southern regions, which would have increased the efficiency of the milk bottle advertisement, it was apparent that an expenditure of £58 000 had boosted Kellogg's Corn Flakes sales revenue by over £400 000 in four months: an excellent rate of return on investment.

CONCLUSIONS

We concluded that the milk bottle campaign had been entirely effective as a tactical supplement to the main television campaign for the following reasons.

1. It stimulated increased consumption of Kellogg's Corn Flakes.
2. It led to increased frequency and volume of repurchase to replace the extra volume of consumption.
3. The brand effect was substantially greater than the generic effect in share of replacement purchases.
4. It increased sales of Kellogg's Corn Flakes by 17 per cent in homes served by Unigate dairies, equivalent to a 2.5 per cent volume increase nationally, in four months.
5. The estimated £400 000 extra sales revenue that resulted was a satisfactory return on investment.

As to the medium, we were satisfied that it was working. Admittedly, we had the advantages of its novelty and the close connection between milk and Corn Flakes to help us. But there is particular value in a medium that gets so close to the point of consumption. The advertisement measured no more than 3 inches square. And it worked.

POSTSCRIPT (1982)

Kellogg's Corn Flakes was again advertised on milk bottles in the summer of 1982. The print run this year was increased to three million bottles, circulating to Unigate-served households in London and south-eastern England between May and September.

Purchasing was again measured through AGB's Television Consumer Audit panel, with a sample of 1545 homes in the London, South and Anglia regions, of which 539 (35 per cent) had their milk delivered by Unigate.

Purchasing in the test period (the 20 weeks ending 11 September 1982) was compared with the same households' purchases in the 20 weeks ending 15 August 1981, that is, before any of the milk bottle advertising began.

Results of this analysis, completed just before this book went to print, confirmed the findings of the 1981 analysis. We found, as before, that:

— Penetration of Kellogg's Corn Flakes was not affected by the milk bottle advertising.
— The brand's frequency of purchase rose in Unigate homes, but not in non-Unigate homes.
— The brand's volume of purchase (kg per buyer) also rose in Unigate homes, but not in non-Unigate homes.

Also as before, the evidence strongly supported the hypothesis that the advertising had a direct response effect by stimulating extra *consumption* of Kellogg's Corn Flakes. Where the brand was not stocked, the advertising had no effect. The increased volume of purchase was limited to those homes which bought Kellogg's Corn Flakes.

TABLE 19.7:   RATE OF PURCHASE, 1982

	Non-Unigate homes (Control: N = 1006)			Unigate homes (Test: N = 539)		
	Summer 1981	Summer 1982	Change %	Summer 1981	Summer 1982	Change %
Homes buying Kellogg's Corn Flakes						
Kellogg's Corn Flakes	1.78	1.67	−6	1.59	1.72	+8
Other	4.28	4.50	+5	4.24	4.40	+4
Total RTE	6.06	6.17	+2	5.83	6.12	+5
Homes buying other RTE not Kellogg's Corn Flakes						
Kellogg's Corn Flakes	—	—	—	—	—	—
Other	4.46	4.67	+5	4.23	4.28	+1
Total RTE	4.46	4.67	+5	4.23	4.28	+1

Table 19.7 also shows that it was Kellogg's Corn Flakes that again got most of the additional purchases made to replace the extra quantity of cereal eaten. The *brand* effect was strong, as Table 19.8 demonstrates.

However, comparison with Table 19.6 suggests that the brand effect in 1982 was less than in 1981, and the generic effect (e.g. on Own Label Corn Flakes) somewhat greater. What's more, the additional sales return did not appear to have gained extra benefit from the print run's increase to 3 million. It seemed that a saturation level had been reached.

TABLE 19.8:   SALES VOLUME CHANGE, SUMMER 1981–SUMMER 1982
(Index, Summer 1981 = 100)

	Expected in Summer 1982 (Control)	Observed in Summer 1982 (Test)	Change %
Kellogg's Corn Flakes	86	97	+12
Own Label Corn Flakes	106	113	+6
Other RTE	107	102	−5
Total RTE	104	103	−1

FURTHER CONCLUSIONS

As a result of the extra experience gained in 1982, we believe that:

1. The further evidence strongly supports the previous conclusions that the milk bottle advertising has stimulated extra *consumption* of Kellogg's Corn Flakes, leading to increased frequency and volume of *purchase* to replace the extra helpings eaten.
2. The *brand* effect has been substantially greater than the generic effect.
3. However, as the novelty value has worn off, the total effect of the medium, and the brand effect, have both reduced.
4. The effectiveness of increasing the print run, which raises the frequency of exposure of the advertisement and not the coverage of the medium, is subject to diminishing returns.

20
Daily Mail Classified

INTRODUCTION

This case history looks at the successful campaign for increasing the *Daily Mail's* share of the Classified Advertising market. The campaign took place in two phases, the first in September 1981 and the second in 1982 in the traditionally buoyant 'classified' period of January and February.

Radio was the prime medium used, with support from tube cards. These are the small cards (23 inches by 11 inches) that one sees in the train, when travelling on the underground. It was not possible specifically to measure the effectiveness of the tube cards; consequently they will not play a part in this case study.

The campaign was a success, with increased market share, and a significant return on expenditure. It should be noted that the whole campaign cost under £45 000, including the production of all the material and the radio commercials.

MARKET BACKGROUND

Between 1979 and 1981, classified advertising revenue declined in real terms by 20 per cent (Source: Advertising Association).

Since 1980, many national newspapers have seen their classified advertising volume decline considerably:

Daily Express	43% down when 1st quarter 1980 is compared with 1st quarter 1982.
Sun	68% down when 1st quarter 1980 is compared with 1st quarter 1982.
Daily Mirror	65% down when 1st quarter 1980 is compared with 1st quarter 1982.
Daily Telegraph	20% down when 1st quarter 1980 is compared with 1st quarter 1982.
Daily Mail	20% down when 1st quarter 1980 is compared with 1st quarter 1982.

THE COMPETITION

As well as competition from the national press many non-traditional and less expensive media have developed. This is particularly true of the London area, from which the *Daily Mail* draws the majority of its Classified revenue.

Telesales operations have grown quickly since the initial launch of Computacar in 1977.

The telesales market divides into two main categories, Property and Motoring, with two companies offering a non-specialist service.

Motoring	*Property*	*General*
Computacar	Dial-a-Home	Teledata
Car Data	Home-Line	Leisure Line
Bike Tel	Flat Tel	

All these companies demand a one-off payment to get the information on to their computers.

There is some evidence that this 'until sold' proposition is perceived as being a strong competitive advantage over newspapers.

It must be stated that one of the stiffest areas of competition is the local press. It is however, impossible to quantify this competition in share terms, but it will always remain the sleeping giant of classified advertising.

COMPETITIVE ACTIVITY

At the time of our campaign there was not a great deal of competitive activity. There was no advertising by the classified departments of national dailies and only a token presence by some of the telesales operations. The telesales operations use radio and television as their prime media with support from press, tube cards and underground station posters.

Recruitment Classified

With the continued recession, recruitment itself has been in decline. Over the past three years, the volume of recruitment advertising has fallen by 66 per cent, according to industry sources.

Seasonality

The classified market is particularly sensitive to seasonal demands. Traditionally, the worst months are August and December, as people become involved in holidays and Christmas. The most active periods are from the end of January to the end of March, and mid-September to mid-November. (See Figure 20.1).

MARKETING OBJECTIVES

(1)   To increase market share, and maximize revenue for the *Daily Mail's* Classified pages.
(2)   To launch two new categories for classified advertising.
(3)   To give additional momentum to the classified sales force.

ADVERTISING OBJECTIVES

(1)   To increase awareness of the Classified section amongst potential commercial advertisers and advertising agencies.

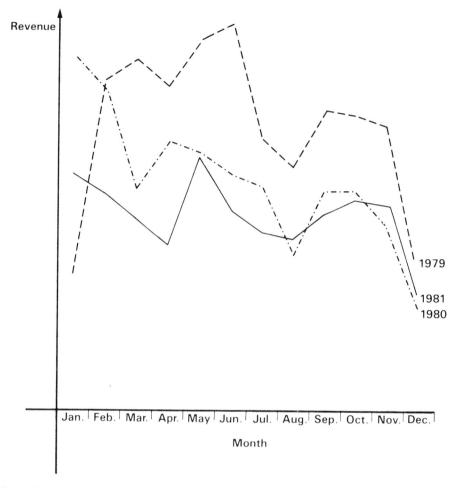

Figure 20.1 *Daily Mail classified revenue*

(2)   To increase volume and revenue from existing advertisers both commercial and private, and agencies.

(3)   To improve awareness amongst *Daily Mail* readers of the Classified pages.

(4)   To ensure an acceptable rate of return was achieved for each £ spent.

THE TWO NEW CATEGORIES

The *Mail* felt that there was an obvious gap in the marketplace that needed to be filled. The *Financial Times* and the *Telegraph* were offering the senior financially based positions, while the trade press catered for all levels of financial appointment. There was no one offering a specific service for the middle ground positions, and as a result the 'World of Finance' was launched.

The other new category 'International Appointments' arose purely from demand. Previously, engineering and overseas appointments had been put together for layout purposes.

The Engineering advertisements began to dominate the sector and to an extent the International Appointments were lost. To overcome this problem and meet with the increased demand the International Appointments category was launched.

MEDIA STRATEGY AND PLAN

The budget was set at £40 000 which included production. This was equal to a national equivalent of approximately £140 000 for both phases of the campaign. The target audience was defined as all ABC1 adults. The most important group within this very broad target was all commercial users of classified advertising, both advertisers and respondents.

Media Selection

The limited budget naturally narrowed our choice of media. Radio seemed to be the obvious medium to use, as it fulfilled the following criteria.

The creative requirement necessitated using up-to-the-minute information from the Classified sections of the newspaper. Consequently, we would only have a few hours to produce a commercial. Radio offered that ease and flexibility of production.

Production costs also had to be taken into account on this small budget, and radio is far cheaper than any other medium. With these constraints radio was found to be the most cost efficient way of reaching our target audience.

It was decided to launch the campaign in two areas. These were: London – which is traditionally the main source of classified revenue; and Manchester, a large conurbation with its own quantifiable sales operation.

The final reason for selecting radio was that it was felt there would be very little wastage with respect to the target audience.

Phase 1

After negotiations with Capital Radio, it was established that 48 spots (30-second) could be purchased over a period of four weeks, from 7 September 1981 to 2 October 1981. This would give an estimated coverage of 44 per cent and an average opportunity to hear of 5.7.

Phase 2

This second phase used Capital again, and Piccadilly Radio in Manchester, for a four-week period from 18 January 1982 to 18 February 1982. The following spots were purchased:

	Number of spots	Estimated coverage %	Average opportunities to hear
Capital	60	48	6.0
Piccadilly	42	35	6.6

The campaign was structured so that the spots would go out in the 'morning drive time'. (Between 6 a.m. and 10 a.m. when radio listening peaks, with people listening when they wake up and while travelling to work.) Two days each week were used; we varied the two days of the week, thus creating an illusion of a far heavier campaign than was actually running.

CREATIVE STRATEGY AND EXECUTION

Key proposition
Look in *Daily Mail* Classified today, there is something to interest you.

In order to maximize immediate response, it was decided to make the commercials reflect what was appearing in that day's Classified columns. Consequently, the commercials were recorded the day before the paper was printed. With the inevitable time constraints, it was essential that the scripts were kept as simple as possible.

The only other creative requirement was that the commercials should maintain the stylish, 'sophisticated' image that the *Daily Mail* has consistently projected.

30-SECOND RADIO SCRIPTS

Sound Effects	Dialogue
RUSTLING OF PAPER THROUGHOUT.	Today's *Daily Mail Classified.* Here we are, International Appointments: Let's have a look ... Whittaker offers nursing opportunities in the Kingdom of Saudi Arabia. Benefits include free air fares, accommodation and ... medical attention. You could really treat yourself in a job like that. Crumbs. Biscuit manufacturers in Lagos require a packaging engineer to modify and install wrapping machinery. Hm. It's a long way to go, but when it comes to the crunch you would make a packet. *V/O:* You'll find it all in today's *Daily Mail Classified.*
Sound Effects	Dialogue
RUSTLING OF PAPER THROUGHOUT.	Ah. *Daily Mail Classified.* Here we are. Opportunities in the North. Cimfab looking for a sales executive with building and architectural experience to promote a new wall-covering. Nice job if you can stick it.

This should generate some interest. Salesmen to sell savings and pensions plans with Barclay Life Assurance.

Ah ... Johnson Progress require a technical sales engineer experienced in liquid/solid separation systems employing filter processes. That should separate the men from the boys.

V/O:

You'll find it all in today's *Daily Mail Classified*.

CAMPAIGN EVALUATION

The success of the campaign was based on the following facts:

1. Despite a steady decline in classified advertising revenue throughout 1981, over the period of the two campaigns no fewer than 637 new accounts were opened (see Tables 20.1 and 20.2).

2. In terms of revenue and volume against forecast, a significant increase was noted when compared with a similar period last year. It should be noted that all forecasts were set at a realistic and profitable level.

TABLE 20.1:   NEW BUSINESS BY CATEGORY

	1981*	1st Campaign	2nd Campaign
Recruitment (excluding Opportunities in the North)	76	81	128
Opportunities in the North	33	32	58
Property	39	36	33
Antiques	8	17	59
Holidays	46	19	198
Odds	4	0	8
Total new accounts	206	185	484

*Equivalent five weeks in 1981 as above.

TABLE 20.2:   OPPORTUNITIES IN THE NORTH
(In recruitment section of Northern edition)

	No. of new accounts
February 3rd 1981	7
February 2nd 1982	16
February 17th 1981	6
February 16th 1982	15

The new business figures were extremely encouraging. It was particularly pleasing to see the excellent response from the 'opportunities in the North' commercials, which more than **doubled the number of accounts opened during the same period last year** (Table 20.2). This is even more remarkable when one considers the unemployment situation and the generally depressed economic climate of the North.

TABLE 20.3:   REVENUE (INDEXED FOR REASONS OF CONFIDENTIALITY)

	Forecast	Actual	Actual/ forecast %
18 Jan. 1981–20 Feb. 1981	100	79	−21
18 Jan. 1982–20 Feb. 1982	100	126	+26

Table 20.3 shows a revenue increase over the previous year of 22 per cent; rate increases accounted for only 16 per cent of this increase.

TABLE 20.4:   VOLUME

	Forecast Scc*	Actual Scc*	Change %
18 Jan. 1981–20 Feb. 1981	25 066	20 749	−17.3
18 Jan. 1982–20 Feb. 1982	17 915	24 746	+38.1

*scc = single column centimetres.

Volume achieved was 19 per cent higher than last year in a fairly static market (see Table 20.4).

Not forgetting one of our most important objectives, we increased our market share in volume terms (Table 20.5).

TABLE 20.5:   MARKET SHARE

	Jan. 1981 %	Sept. 1981 %	Jan. 1982 %	Feb–May 1982 %
Daily Mail	16.9	19.4	24.4	21.2
Daily Express	16.3	17.6	18.3	17.7
Daily Telegraph	66.8	63.0	57.3	61.1

Source: Industry Monitor

CONCLUSION

The campaign achieved all the original objectives:

1. Market share increased.
2. Revenue increased.
3. The style and image of the advertising clearly motivated the various target markets. As a result, this gave a morale boost to the sales staff which was an imperative aspect for the success of the campaign.

This result goes to show that an extremely successful advertising campaign can be achieved without an enormous outlay. The fact that the outlay can be more than justified by increased revenue and volume should give the smaller advertiser greater confidence for future investment.

Index